Bastard
Prince

Bastard Prince

Henry VIII's Lost Son

Beverley A. Murphy

SUTTON PUBLISHING

This book was first published in 2001 by
Sutton Publishing Limited · Phoenix Mill
Thrupp · Stroud · Gloucestershire · GL5 2BU

This paperback edition first published in 2003

British Library Cataloguing in Publication Data
A catalogue record for this book is available from the British
Library

ISBN 0 7509 3709 2

Typeset in 10/13pt Georgia.
Typesetting and origination by
Sutton Publishing Limited.
Printed and bound in Great Britain by
J.H. Haynes & Co. Ltd, Sparkford.

Contents

	Acknowledgements	vi
	Preface	vii
1	Mother of the King's Son	1
2	Heir Apparent	36
3	Sheriff Hutton	66
4	Lord Lieutenant of Ireland	105
5	Young Courtier	149
6	Landed Magnate	181
7	Legacy	214
EPILOGUE	Henry the Ninth	245
	Family Trees	259
	Notes	263
	Bibliography	275
	Index	283

Acknowledgements

I would like to thank Professor David Loades for encouraging my conviction that Richmond's life merited further investigation. I am indebted to the British Academy, who funded much of the initial research. In compiling this study I have benefited from the expertise of many friends and colleagues, whose input has enriched the finished work. I am particularly grateful to Dr Alan Dyer, Dr Simon Harris, Dr S.J. Gunn and Dr Hazel Pierce for their contributions. Thanks are also due to all those archives and libraries whose staff and collections have provided invaluable assistance in my search for a true picture of the duke.

Finally, my debt is to those of my friends and family who have had to live with the ghost of a little known Tudor Prince. The many ways in which they have provided support and assistance are especially valued.

Preface

Our Only Bastard Son

The marital misfortunes of Henry VIII are one of the most notorious episodes in English history. Even those with little or no interest in the history of Tudor times can name the king who had six wives. His pursuit of a legitimate son and heir was not the sole factor in the events of the Reformation which shook England and became the scandal of Europe in the sixteenth century. Henry's desire to father a male child and secure the future of his dynasty cannot be overestimated. Yet it was to take him twenty-eight years and three wives, before Jane Seymour was finally able to present the King of England with his prince.

The events of the preceding years, with Katherine of Aragon as the wronged wife and Anne Boleyn as the other woman, would not seem out of place in a modern soap opera. As such the popular perception of events is often at odds with historical fact. Henry VIII is berated for his repudiation of Katherine on a whim, without any appreciation that the couple lived as man and wife for almost twenty years. Anne Boleyn's reputation as a whore is not dimmed by the centuries, despite the fact that she was apparently Henry's 'mistress' for five years before she actually had full sexual intercourse with him.

Any mention of the fact that for much of this time Henry VIII had a healthy, promising, albeit inconveniently illegitimate son, generally evokes one of two responses. Either there is the assumption that all monarchs had hordes of illicit offspring, which rendered bastard children insignificant in the broader fabric of political affairs. Or, more commonly, there is a profoundly sceptical enquiry as to the identity of the child.

This is not entirely unreasonable. The existence of the Duke of

Richmond was no secret to his contemporaries. However, he has fared rather less well in attracting the attention of historians. The main printed source for his life remains John Gough Nichols' *Inventories* published in 1855.[1] Richmond has occasionally benefited from the notoriety of other figures at the Tudor court, for example, featuring in the biographies of his childhood friend, Henry Howard, Earl of Surrey. On other occasions his envisaged role in Ireland has stirred some interest. However, even those with a well informed knowledge of Tudor history would be forgiven for thinking there were only three events of note in Richmond's life. His birth in 1519, his elevation to the peerage in 1525, followed by his death in 1536.

The true picture is rather more complex. In 1525 Henry VIII had been married for sixteen years, with only a nine-year-old daughter to his credit. When his illegitimate son was created Duke of Richmond and Somerset it prompted intense speculation that Henry VIII was intending to name him as his heir. In 1536 that speculation intensified when Anne Boleyn had been able to present the king with nothing more than two miscarriages and yet another daughter. In the meantime, Richmond's tenure as Lord Lieutenant of the North and his appointment as Lord Lieutenant of Ireland heralded new departures in Tudor local government. His contemporaries believed he would become King of Ireland. Those suggested as possible brides included Catherine de Medici, the future Queen of France. His unprecedented status as the duke of two counties made him the foremost peer of the realm. In almost every way Henry VIII treated him as his legitimate son and in almost every way that is the role Richmond fulfilled.

Since Richmond was only a child, some of the traditional areas of a biography are inevitably lost to us. There can be little examination of his ability as a soldier, nor is it feasible to build up a picture of a personal affinity in the same way that would be expected of an adult magnate. Yet there are compensations. We know far more of Richmond's childhood than we might have done had circumstances not required his dispatch to Sheriff

Hutton. His youth also allows for the reconstruction of his character in a vivid manner which is often difficult for his fellow nobles. At the same time, because Richmond's activities often encroached on the traditional preserves of the adult world, those areas where one would usually look for traces of an established lord, such as litigation, diplomacy and patronage, are by no means lacking.

Much of Richmond's importance stems from the fact that while he lived he was the king's only son. He did not survive to see his fortunes eclipsed by the birth of the legitimate Prince Edward, who was born on 11 October 1537. Indeed, when Richmond died on 23 July 1536, Jane Seymour was not even pregnant. Examples of Henry's affection for his only living son abound and during the King's marriage to Katherine of Aragon, Richmond was widely considered to be:

> very personable and of great expectation, insomuch that he was thought not only for ability of body but mind to be one of the rarest of his time, for which also he was much cherished by our King, as also because he had no issue male by his Queen, nor perchance expect any.[2]

There can be no doubt that Richmond was Henry's son. In his case, the distinctive red hair and wilful Tudor personality were merely secondary considerations. The king's chief minister, Thomas Wolsey, stood as his godfather at his christening and he was openly acknowledged and proudly accepted by Henry VIII.

There have been several other candidates offered as possible natural children of Henry VIII. Ethelreda or Audrey Harrington, the daughter of Joan Dobson or Dingley, is believed to be an illegitimate daughter of Henry VIII. She married John Harrington and died in 1555. Mary Berkley, the wife of the courtier Sir Thomas Perrot, is also supposed to be the mother of two of Henry VIII's illegitimate issue: Thomas Stukely, born in 1525, who married Anne Curtis and Sir John Perrot, who was born in 1527.

In the case of Sir John Perrot it is his physical attributes that have cast him as an illegitimate son of the king. Writing in 1867 his biographer claimed:

> If we compare his picture, his qualities, his gesture and voice with that of the King, whose memory yet remains among us, they will plead strongly that he was a surreptitious child of the blood royal.[3]

Sir John Perrot went on to have a colourful career under the Tudors. Made a Knight of the Bath at the coronation of King Edward VI, he was briefly imprisoned in the Fleet Prison in the reign of Mary, served Elizabeth in a number of posts, notably Lord Deputy of Ireland, only to die in 1592 in disgrace for attempting rebellion against Queen Elizabeth. However, he was never officially acknowledged as a son of Henry VIII.

The poet and musician Richard Edwards has also been cast as a natural son of the king. Apparently born in March 1525, the evidence for his paternity is the fact that he received an Oxford education which his family could have ill-afforded to provide. His biographer writing in 1992 is confident that:

> It would be difficult, if not impossible, to account for facts concerning Richard's life beginning with his education at Oxford in any other way than as the son of Henry VIII who provided for his education and set the stage for the rest of Richard's life.[4]

Richard Edwards' career was rather less dramatic. After receiving his Master of Arts from Oxford, he was ordained. After a brief spell as Theologian at Christ Church, Oxford, much of his career was spent as one of the gentlemen of the Chapel Royal. However, once again, Henry VIII never took the opportunity to recognise him as his son.

Henry VIII's most infamous alleged offspring are, of course, Mary Boleyn's children, Henry and Catherine Carey. At least here it is possible to be absolutely certain that Mary Boleyn was in fact Henry's mistress. Their affair began after her marriage to William Carey in February 1520. Speculation about the parentage of the children was first fuelled by attempts by Katherine of Aragon's supporters to slander the Boleyns with the suggestion that Henry Carey was in fact Henry VIII's bastard.[5] In 1535 John Hale, the vicar of Isleworth in Middlesex, said that he had been shown 'young Master Carey saying he was the King's son.' Such a tantalising prospect has been grist to the mill of historical debate ever since. New theories continue to be advanced in an attempt to prove conclusively that both were indeed Henry's children.[6]

In each of these cases it can be argued that the women concerned were already married, something which could not be said of Elizabeth Blount when she began her liaison with the king. However, if Henry VIII's morals would allow him to sleep with another man's wife, would his conscience truly prevent him from acknowledging the child? Given that Henry was not exactly overendowed with legitimate issue, it seems reasonable to assume that he needed all the children he could lay claim to. When a marriage betrothal was the accepted way to seal a diplomatic treaty even a natural daughter could be a useful tool. If the child were a son, any arguments against acknowledging him would surely have been outweighed, if not by Henry's pride in his achievement, then by his desperate need for other male relatives to help carry the burden of government.

Since Richmond was the only illegitimate son Henry VIII ever chose to acknowledge, it is tempting to conclude that he was the only illegitimate son he had. Writing in April 1538, regarding the arrangements for a proposed marriage between his eldest daughter Mary and Dom Luis of Portugal, Henry advised the Emperor, Charles V, that he was prepared to:

> assure unto him and her and their posterity as much yearly rent as the late Duke of Richmond, our only bastard son had of our gift within this our realm.[7]

In a sense it does not matter whether Richmond was the king's only bastard issue or not. What is most important is that he was the only one that Henry was prepared to acknowledge and employ on the wider political stage. The king's precise intentions for Richmond's long term prospects are, of course, a very different matter.

1

Mother of the King's Son

According to the King's Book of Payments, on 8 May 1513 Elizabeth Blount received 100s 'upon a warrant signed for her last year's wage ended at the annunciation of our Lady last past'.[1] This indicates that she made her début at the court of King Henry VIII on 25 March 1512, when she was about twelve years old. The manner of her payment, which was not included in the regular lists of wages paid at the half-year and the amount, which was half the 200s per annum paid to the queen's young maids of honour, suggests that she did not yet have a formal place in Katherine of Aragon's household. Yet, even then, observers must have glimpsed something in the lively, fair-haired girl of those 'rare ornaments of nature and education' that were to mark her out as 'the beauty of mistress piece of her time'.

Twelve was the minimum age that a girl could be accepted for a court position and competition for such places was fierce. Elizabeth was fortunate that her family conformed to the Tudor ideal of beauty, with fair skin, blue eyes and blonde hair. Equally praised for her skills in singing, dancing and 'all goodly pastimes' she was well suited to the glittering world of the court, with its masques, dances and endless occasions to impress. On the other hand, her ownership of a volume of Latin and English poetry by John Gower suggests this was no empty-headed moppet, but a girl with a lively mind to match her merry disposition, a quality which would no doubt have recommended her to an educated woman like Katherine of Aragon.

When a girl's best chance of advancement was to make an advantageous marriage, Elizabeth's parents must have hoped that she had made a good beginning. The prospect of a full-time position at court, mixing with some of the finest families in the realm, was the surest route to a beneficial match. However, they probably did not expect that one day their daughter would be the mother of the king's son.

The peaceful accession of King Henry VIII on 21 April 1509 had been greeted with unrestrained delight. 'All the world here is rejoicing in the possession of so great a Prince' wrote William Blount, Lord Mountjoy. Here indeed was a prince among men. At around six foot three inches tall, Henry was, quite literally, head and shoulders above many of his contemporaries. Even the ambassadors of other realms were lavish in their praise of the young king. His skin was pink and healthy, his auburn hair shone like gold, his whole body was 'admirably proportioned'. The epitome of vigour and youth, it was believed 'nature could not have done more for him'.

Decades away from the bejowled colossus depicted in his last years, the man Elizabeth Blount would remember from their courtship made a stunning first impression. The Venetian Ambassador, Sebastian Giustinian, could hardly contain his admiration:

> His Majesty is the handsomest potentate I ever set eyes on; above the usual height, with an extremely fine calf to his leg, his complexion fair and bright, with auburn hair combed straight and short in the French fashion, and a round face so very beautiful that it would become a pretty woman, his throat being rather long and thick.[2]

It was the best of new beginnings. The realm Henry had inherited was peaceful and prosperous. Unlike his father he had not been required to assert his claim to the crown on the battlefield. Nor was England to be burdened with the difficulties and dangers of a minority government. Best of all, despite being several weeks short of his eighteenth birthday when he ascended the throne, from the outset Henry VIII looked the king.

His impressive stature and handsome features inspired awe and admiration. Equally lauded for his athletic prowess with spear or sword, he was an accomplished rider, who hunted with such enthusiasm that he tired eight or ten horses in a day, not to mention those of his courtiers who did not share his formidable stamina. In an age when kings were still required to lead their forces in person, those who applauded his amazing feats in the jousts knew they might one day be called upon to follow this man into battle. At the very least, Henry's abilities were a means to encourage his forces to greater glory. Also praised for his learning and other talents, the new king may well have merited the accolades, which were heaped upon him. Yet beneath the admiration must have been a significant degree of relief.

Of the children born to Henry VII and Elizabeth of York only three survived to adulthood. Two of those were daughters: Margaret, born in 1489, had married James IV of Scotland in 1503 and Mary, born in 1496, was betrothed to Charles of Castile. Of the three recorded sons, the death of the youngest, Edmund, in 1500, before he reached his second birthday was a natural disappointment. The death of the heir apparent, Arthur, Prince of Wales, in 1502 at the age of fifteen had been a devastating blow. Everyone was acutely aware that Henry VIII had been the sole male heir to the Tudor throne since the age of eleven. It was only good fortune that Henry VII survived until his heir was a respectable seventeen years old.

Although the youth of the thirteen-year-old Edward V had not been the only factor in Richard III's unprecedented decision to usurp his nephew's throne in 1483, it was universally accepted that a country needed a strong ruler if it were to thrive. Furthermore, the Tudors' own claim to the throne was very recent. Henry VII's reign had been troubled by the plots of the Yorkist pretenders Lambert Simnel, masquerading as the Earl of Warwick and more seriously, Perkin Warbeck posing as Richard, Duke of York. In addition, the genuine offspring of the House of York, in particular the nephews of Edward IV and Richard III, had reason to feel they had a better claim than any Tudor.

Henry VII made stalwart efforts to ensure the security of the succession.[3] During the negotiations for Katherine of Aragon's marriage to Arthur, Prince of Wales, the continued existence of Edward, Earl of Warwick, raised sufficient concern to warrant his execution, even though he was safely captive in the Tower. The offspring of Edward IV's sister, Elizabeth de la Pole, were treated as a serious threat. When the question of who might succeed Henry VII arose in 1503, when Prince Henry was still a child of twelve, Sir Hugh Conway reported:

> It happened the same time me to be among many great personages, the which fell in communication of the king's grace, and of the world that should be after him if his grace happened to depart. Then, he said, that some of them spake of my lord of Buckingham, saying that he was a noble man and would be a royal ruler. Other there were that spake, he said, in like wise of your traitor, Edmund de la Pole, but none of them, he said, that spoke of my lord prince.[4]

The threat would not be extinguished easily. Henry VII secured the return from exile of Edmund de la Pole in 1506 and confined him in the Tower. However, his brother Richard remained at large and would be a thorn in Henry's side for some years to come.

In 1513, as Henry VIII prepared for war in France, Richard de la Pole persuaded the King of France, Louis XII, to recognise him as King Richard IV. Henry was sufficiently concerned by the danger that this represented to order the execution of Edmund before crossing the Channel. The Duke of Buckingham, whose own claim to the throne was derived from Edward III, profited little from this ominous example. Amid claims that he intended to usurp the throne, he was executed in his turn in 1521. Henry VIII was all too aware that the only way to secure the Tudor dynasty's grip on the crown was to produce a viable male heir.

That Henry VIII chose to make Katherine of Aragon his bride must be seen, at least in part, as a response to this pressing need. Although the couple had been betrothed since 1503, their union was by no means a foregone conclusion. The youngest daughter of Ferdinand and Isabella of Spain, Katherine had come to England in 1501 to marry Henry's elder brother Arthur, then Prince of Wales. After Arthur's sudden death in 1502 Henry VII had decided that his interests would be best served by preserving this alliance. After some negotiation it was agreed that Katherine should marry the twelve-year-old Prince Henry as soon as he had completed his fourteenth year on 28 June 1506. Yet as that time approached, Henry VII became increasingly uncertain that this was the best possible match for his only remaining son and heir.

In 1505 Prince Henry, at his father's instigation, made a formal protest against the contract made during his minority. In 1506 Henry might describe his betrothed as 'my most dear and well-beloved consort, the Princess, my wife', but his father was looking at other possibilities. Once Henry VIII became king in 1509, several questions, not least the important matter of Katherine's dowry and rival negotiations for a marriage to Eleanor, the daughter of Philip of Burgundy, were simply swept aside.⁵ After seven years of dispute and delay Henry VIII married Katherine of Aragon just six weeks after his accession.

At twenty-three Katherine was 'the most beautiful creature in the world', still blessed with the fresh complexion and long auburn hair that had entranced observers at her arrival in England. She was also of an age to bear children, something that could not be said of the eleven-year-old Eleanor. Henry's excuse that the marriage was his father's dying wish was conveniently difficult to disprove. Shortly afterwards he wrote to his new father-in-law, 'If I were still free I would choose her for wife above all others'. There can be little doubt that Henry was eager to marry Katherine and chose to exercise his new found authority to settle the matter.

Henry and Katherine were wed on 11 June 1509 at the Church of the Observant Franciscans at Greenwich. Despite the difficulties created by Henry VII, it was a most suitable match. Katherine was descended from one of the most respected royal houses in Europe and her pedigree would do much to bolster the credibility of the fledgling Tudor dynasty. Henry VIII was fired with the desire to reclaim the English crown's ancient rights in France; from the outset his attitude was clear. The policy of peace and security followed by his father would not be his, far better was the esteem and respect earned by success in campaigns and the glory and honour that came from dispensing the spoils of war. 'I ask peace of the king of France, who dare not look at me let alone make war!' he thundered. Katherine's support, or more to the point that of his new father-in-law, seemed to place all this within his grasp.

Katherine's piety was also a desirable attribute in a queen, encouraging God's blessings on the realm. When Henry was so determined to seek glory by waging war on his fellow Christians, always a complex moral issue despite appearances to the contrary, her devotional and charitable activities would help redress the balance. It is also clear that the couple themselves enjoyed a warm and mutually satisfactory relationship. 'The Queen must see this' or 'This will please the Queen', Henry would enthuse. In her turn Katherine bore Henry's boyish japes with affectionate indulgence. However, it was widely acknowledged that 'Princes do not marry for love. They take wives only to beget children'.

The importance of fecundity was evident in Katherine's chosen emblem. The pomegranate was not just a representation of her homeland, but also a symbol of fertility. Sir Thomas More had good reason to believe that she would be 'the mother of Kings as great as her ancestors': Katherine came from a family of five surviving children and her sister Juana produced a brood of six children. At first it seemed as if the queen would have little problem in fulfilling the nation's expectations. Only four and a half months after the wedding Henry was able to advise his father-in-law that 'the child in the womb was alive'. That this pregnancy ended with a stillborn daughter at seven months was a disappointment but not a disaster. Such things were not unusual. Katherine and Henry had at least proved their fertility and therefore it was only a matter of time before she conceived again. Indeed, when Katherine wrote to advise her father of the miscarriage, she was already pregnant again.

It is perhaps no coincidence that the first indication of any infidelity on the king's part occurs at this time. Sex during pregnancy was generally discouraged as being harmful to the health of the mother and the unborn child. While it is doubtful that every husband followed this recommendation, Henry had more reason than most to be careful of his wife's condition. However, despite the rumours, it is by no means certain how far, if at all, Henry strayed. In 1510, the Spanish ambassador, Don Luis Caroz reported that one of the young, married sisters of the Duke of Buckingham had attracted the attention of the king. According to the ambassador, Sir William Compton, a favoured companion of Henry, had been seen courting Lady Anne Hastings. Perhaps because Compton was no fit paramour for a duke's sister it was thought that he was acting on Henry's behalf.

The ambassador reported, with some glee, the dramatic scenes that ensued when another sister, Lady Elizabeth Ratcliffe, informed the duke of Compton's behaviour. Buckingham quarrelled with Compton and the king before storming from the court. Anne was carried off by her husband to the safety of a nunnery and Henry ordered an emotional Katherine to dismiss Elizabeth for her meddling. Henry was clearly angry, but none of this makes it clear whether Compton or the king was in fact the guilty party. Garrett Mattingly suggests that the ambassador was relying on gossip fed to him by one of Katherine's former ladies-in-waiting, Francesca de Carceres. If this was the case, neither of them was sufficiently close to the centre of things to know exactly what had been going on. Since Don Luis was primarily concerned with demonstrating how much Katherine was in need of his advice and counsel, he was probably all too willing to believe that the incident was more significant than it really was.

It is possible that Henry did engage in a degree of harmless flirtation with the Lady Anne in the tradition of courtly love. In 1513 her new year's gift from the king was a suspiciously extravagant thirty ounces of silver gilt. As the third most expensive present that year, it was 'an unusually high amount to be given to one of the queen's ladies by Henry'.[6] The elaborate game of courtly love, with its exchange of tokens and protestations of undying devotion, was a popular pastime at the Tudor court. Enthusiastically played by all of the queen's ladies and the king's courtiers, it was not in itself evidence of a serious attraction. Like any game it had rules, which were supposed to be observed. Those occasions when the heartfelt sighs overstepped the boundaries into genuine emotion were cause for anger and recrimination, as Henry Percy found to his cost when his romantic pursuit of Anne Boleyn exceeded accepted limits.

Although Katherine was exempt, since propriety required that the only man who romanced her was her husband, Henry was a keen player. Yet it is significant that none of Henry's known mistresses came from families above the rank of knighthood. It was one thing to pay homage to a duke's sister as an unreachable goddess, but quite another to seduce her. While Henry's conduct may have encouraged suspicion among the gossips, subsequent events indicate that Sir William Compton's attraction to Lady Anne Hastings was the genuine article. In 1527 Wolsey drew up a citation accusing Compton of adultery with Anne. Compton apparently took the sacrament in order to disprove his guilt. However, his will belies his protestations of innocence. Not only did he ask for daily service in praying for Anne's soul, but also the profits from certain of his lands in Leicestershire were earmarked for her use for the remainder of her life.[7]

On New Year's Day 1511 Katherine of Aragon was safely delivered of a son. At only her second attempt she had fulfilled her ultimate duty and provided England with a male heir. The child was 'the most joy and comfort that might be to her and to the realm of England'. The baby was apparently healthy and there was no reason to suppose that the little prince would not be joined shortly by a host of brothers and sisters. Yet only fifty-two days later the child was dead. The grief and shock of both his parents at this bitter blow was echoed by the whole nation. It can have been of little comfort to Katherine that unlike a miscarriage or a stillbirth, which was universally looked on as the fault of the mother, infant mortality was seen as God's judgment on both parents for their sins. To make matters worse, this time Katherine did not conceive again for another two years.

The idea that Henry might have spurned his wife for the pleasures of other women seems an empty revenge for a man who was so desperate to secure a legitimate heir. If he did there is no evidence of it. In contrast to many of his contemporaries Henry was a model of restraint and discretion. Fidelity was not a prerequisite for a king, who generally married for financial and political advantage rather than for love. Nevertheless, Henry is only known to have had a handful of mistresses and never more than one at a time. Given Katherine's indisposition during successive pregnancies, few would have rebuked him for occasionally seeking solace elsewhere. Exactly how Etiennette la Baume, a young lady from the court of the Archduchess Margaret of Savoy, extracted the promise of a dower of 100,000 crowns from the King of England can only be imagined. Yet until the queen was known to be with child Henry had every incentive to concentrate his attentions on his wife.

Since Katherine was still only twenty-five, her age should not have been a bar to conception. Jane Seymour was twenty-eight and Anne Boleyn already in her thirties when they conceived. Unfortunately, his grief over the loss of his infant son may have proved too great a distraction. Henry's relationships all suggest that he was a slave to his emotions. If his antipathy to Anne of Cleves was enough to ensure he could not 'do the deed', perhaps his shattered confidence after this devastating loss meant that, despite his best efforts, England still waited expectantly for the much-desired male heir.

It was in the wake of this latest disappointment that Elizabeth Blount made her formal début at the court of Henry VIII. That she secured an entrée into the queen's household as soon as she reached a suitable age was a testament to her more than average attributes. Although Henry had been King of England for just three years, his court was rapidly gaining a reputation as one of the most spectacular in Europe. It had long been established that it was the duty of a monarch to spend his money 'not only wisely, but also lavishly'. Even the parsimonious Henry VII had realised the benefit of extravagant display to make a political point. It might take the young Henry VIII years to earn the kind of reputation enjoyed by seasoned monarchs like Ferdinand of Aragon, but in the meantime he would boast a court to rival the best in Christendom.

Life was a round of music, dancing and entertainments, with elaborately staged tournaments, spectacular pageants and fashionable Italian masques. The revels were accompanied by some of the finest singers and musicians from England and abroad. The gold and silver on display, the many lavish clothes and the numerous sparkling jewels, were designed to impress. The beauty of the queen's ladies was especially remarked upon. In June 1512 the ladies of the court, resplendent in red and white silk, danced in an elaborate pageant, featuring a fountain fashioned from russet silk to mark the jousts at Greenwich. At Christmas that year the festivities were capped by the appearance of a fabulous mountain from which six ladies, dressed in crimson satin and adorned with gold and pearls, emerged to dance. In the midst of such splendour it is perhaps no surprise that Elizabeth's arrival caused no great impact. She was, after all, still very young and engaged in a very junior position. It is unlikely that she would have progressed this far unless it was intended that she would be granted a regular place in the queen's service as soon as a suitable post fell vacant.

Her success was probably primarily due to the influence of William Blount, the 4th Lord Mountjoy. Sometimes described as Mountjoy's sister or his niece, Elizabeth's exact relationship with him was rather more distant, their last common ancestor having died in 1358.[8] However, the two branches of the family had a long history of mutual support and assistance. In 1374 Elizabeth's ancestor, Sir John Blount, had conveyed a significant part of his inheritance to his half-brother, Walter Blount, the forbear of the Blounts, Lords Mountjoy. In 1456 Elizabeth's great-grandfather, Humphrey Blount, had fought alongside Walter Blount, later 1st Baron Mountjoy, against King Henry VI's forces at Ludlow. The present Lord Mountjoy was a trustee of Elizabeth's parents' marriage settlement and would be instrumental in ensuring that they were able to enjoy their rightful inheritance.

An established figure at the Tudor court, Mountjoy had served Henry VII before being appointed Master of the Mint by Henry VIII in 1509. Since he was also the husband of Agnes de Venegas, one of the few Spanish ladies-in-waiting who had remained in England with Katherine of Aragon, he was well placed to smooth Elizabeth's entry into the Queen's service. In any case, his appointment as Katherine of Aragon's chamberlain on 8 May 1512 must have been a significant factor in her continuing success. Since Mountjoy was now the chief officer of the queen's household it was perhaps no hardship to see that his attractive and accomplished young relative was granted the next vacancy. From Michaelmas 1512 Elizabeth joined the ranks of the queen's maids of honour, under the watchful eye of Mrs Stoner, 'the mother of the maids', at the full wages of 200s per annum.[9]

In many respects Elizabeth was ideal mistress material: sufficiently well born to actually meet Henry, sufficiently accomplished and interesting to catch his eye, yet of a status where her prospects would be enhanced, rather than her reputation diminished, by a liaison with the king. Her family, the Blounts of Kinlet, were a cadet branch of an established and extensive family. Originally from Staffordshire, they still enjoyed estates in Balterley and other places in the county which they had held since the fourteenth century. Elizabeth's great-great-grandfather, who died in 1442, was described as 'Sir John Blount of Balterley'. The family had acquired the Lordship of Kinlet in Shropshire through a piece of fortunate misfortune, when all four of the male heirs died without issue. In a grant dated 2 February 1450 Elizabeth's great-grandfather, was described as 'Humphrey Blount of Kinlet'.

The Blounts of Kinlet were county rather than court. They served their king as sheriffs, escheators and justices of the peace, occasionally representing Shropshire in parliament. However, the local nature of their offices did not make them immune from the tremors of wider concerns. Humphrey Blount earned his knighthood fighting to secure Edward IV's throne at the Battle of Tewkesbury in 1471. Yet none of Elizabeth's immediate relatives ever rose above the rank of knight. Prosperous rather than wealthy, Sir Humphrey Blount's will included a gold collar for his eldest son, Thomas, a gold cross for his second son, John, a gold chain to be sold to pay for masses for his soul and there were a few pieces of plate and several gowns, both furred and velvet, as well as a doublet of red damask. Yet while his two eldest sons both received gilt swords, the youngest son, William, had to make do, not with a sword at all, but a gilt wood knife. Similarly, his daughter Mary was allowed 120 marks towards her marriage. However, this significant sum was not available in ready cash, but represented money owed to him by the Bishop of Durham.[10]

When Elizabeth made her début at the court of Henry VIII, the head of the family was her grandfather, Sir Thomas Blount. A man of some local eminence, he had first served as Sheriff of Shropshire in 1479 when he was twenty-three years old. He had earned his knighthood fighting to defend Henry VII's title to the throne at the Battle of Stoke on 16 June 1487. Never much of a courtier, his appearances were confined to great ceremonial occasions, like the coronation of Elizabeth of York on 25 November 1487; his own interests remained firmly centred on the shires. In 1491 his lands in Shropshire were considered to be worth a respectable £108 10s and he would remain a significant force in county politics until his death in 1524.[11]

However, in the winter of 1501, the Blounts must have felt that all the opportunities of the court in London had arrived on their doorstep. The heir apparent, Arthur, Prince of Wales and his new bride, Katherine of Aragon established their household at Ludlow in Shropshire. Sir Thomas Blount's marriage to Anne

Croft, the eldest daughter of Sir Richard Croft, one of Arthur's principal officers, ensured the Blounts were welcome visitors. Regrettably, the chance was short-lived. On 2 April 1502 Prince Arthur died and Katherine was recalled to London. Yet many of Katherine of Aragon's enduring memories of her initial time in England would not have been of the London nobility, but of the gentry who flocked to salute her at Ludlow. The Blounts may well have utilised this connection to smooth Elizabeth's acceptance as a maid of honour in the queen's household.

Elizabeth was the second daughter of the eight surviving children of John and Katherine Blount.[12] She cannot have been born until at least 1499, the year after her parents consummated their marriage, and since she had to be at least twelve to take up a court post, she must have been born before March 1500. She probably spent much of her childhood in Shropshire or Staffordshire, yet any concept of Elizabeth as a simple, rural girl plucked from the shires would be misleading. In the years prior to her formal appointment as a maid of honour to Katherine of Aragon, she had had several opportunities to come to court.

As an esquire of the body to Henry VII, her father was one of those granted livery from the crown at his funeral in 1509. At the coronation of Henry VIII, he was among the assembly of the King's Spears. Modelled on the corps formed by Louis XI, the Spears were a group of about fifty gentlemen and sons of noblemen under the captaincy of the Earl of Essex. It was both a military and a ceremonial appointment. The regulations were martial in tone and exercise in arms was a primary function. The Spears were to play a significant part in the French war of 1513. However, in their distinctive crimson uniforms, they also took an active part in the colourful pageantry of Henry VIII's court. When Leonard Spinelly, delivered to the king the cap and sword presented by Pope Leo X in 1514, he was met at Blackheath by a host of dignitaries escorted by all the Spears. Since the regulations required 'their rooms and their board to be provided at the king's pleasure' and commanded them to lodge where the king decided,[13] John Blount's duties were ample reason and excuse to bring him to court.

While there is no evidence that his family always accompanied him, it is unlikely that he would have missed the chance to show off such a promising young daughter. At the very least, Elizabeth might secure entry into some noble household, much as her uncle, Robert Blount, was accepted into the service of the Earl of Shrewsbury. Although S.J. Gunn has termed membership of the King's Spears as 'belonging to only a very broad charmed circle'[14] it did bring John Blount into the same orbit as men of influence, like Charles Brandon, later Duke of Suffolk. Since the exact nature of Brandon's relationship with Elizabeth has been the cause of some speculation, it should be borne in mind that he would have been sufficiently acquainted with her family to have more than a passing familiarity with the pretty, blonde child.

Elizabeth also had other kin and allies who could help smooth her path at court. Her relationship through the Crofts, her paternal grandmother's family, with the Master of the Revels, Sir Edward Guilford, would have helped to ensure that she did not remain a wallflower for very long. Her great-uncle, Sir Edward Darrell of Littlecote in Wiltshire, later Katherine of Aragon's vice-chamberlain, was already well known to the queen, having been one of those appointed to escort her on her arrival in England in 1501. Elizabeth could also claim kinship with the Stanleys, the Earls of Derby, through her maternal grandmother, Isabel Stanley, and while her relationship to the Suttons, the Lords Dudley, was rather more distant, being rooted in her great-grandfather's wardship to John Sutton, Lord Dudley in 1443, such things mattered little if presuming on the acquaintance might produce a favourable result.

Yet all her connections would have come to nothing if she herself had not been able to create a good impression. Elizabeth Blount was clearly something out of the ordinary. When the Dean of Westbury, one of Anne Boleyn's supporters, was asked to compare Elizabeth to Anne in 1532, he thought Elizabeth was the most beautiful.[15] Even twenty years later the king's cousin,

Lord Leonard Grey, could still declare that he had 'had very good cheer' when visiting with her in Lincolnshire. At twelve she would have been expected to be well schooled in needlework and in all those aspects of learning which were a desirable part of any ambitious girl's repertoire. Elizabeth's primary purpose in being at court was to attract a suitable husband and the queen's household was an ideal place to cultivate those skills and accomplishments which would do so, and the slightly different talents expected of the ideal Tudor wife.

A contemporary reported that Katherine of Aragon 'set a high moral tone for her Household'. Although the queen's excessive piety belongs to a later date, no doubt a considerable part of Elizabeth's day would have been spent accompanying the queen in her devotions, hearing mass and divine offices. The young maid of honour would also have been required to attend the queen at meals and in the presence of visitors and foreign ambassadors. Katherine of Aragon prided herself on embroidering her husband's shirts herself, like any good wife, and the queen and her ladies would have spent many a companionable hour sewing together. Whatever proficiency Elizabeth had in Latin was perhaps a legacy from her time in Katherine's service. The queen herself may have encouraged her young attendant in her studies of the language, much as she did with her sister-in-law, Mary Tudor. Elizabeth would also have learnt by, arguably, the best example in the realm, the duties and responsibilities of a great noblewoman: not only to dispense care and succour through her charitable deeds, but to manage her own household and estates. This example must have stood Elizabeth in good stead in later life when she presided over her own interests.

In the meantime, while Elizabeth's duties required her to be both an asset and ornament to the court and her family saw her primary duty as making a good marriage, Elizabeth had plenty of opportunities to have a good time. Although Katherine did not choose to dance in public, in the privacy of her own apartments she would often dance with her ladies. Sometimes there would be music and singing, at other times there might be table games like cards or dice. Often the king and his attendants would join the queen and her ladies, on occasion putting on one of his elaborate disguises when everyone would pretend not to recognise the handsome stranger and his fellows until he was unmasked. Given that few men could match Henry's distinctive stature as he towered over his courtiers, these episodes may have been rather more amusing than the king intended to the queen's ladies, as they watched their mistress feign astonished surprise.

In the summer of 1513 this idyll was interrupted for a time when the pleasures of the court were put aside in favour of the splendour of martial deeds. So far, Henry's warlike exploits had been a disappointment. A previous military venture, under the command of Thomas Grey, Marquess of Dorset in 1512, had ended in disaster when the English armies at Fuentarrabia had waited in vain for the expected Spanish reinforcements. The English army disintegrated into disorder and disease 'which caused the blood so to boil in their bellies that there fell sick three thousand of the flux'. When, on the point of mutiny, they fled for home, Ferdinand added insult to injury by blaming them for the lost opportunity. The true fault lay with Ferdinand who had concentrated on his own personal objectives of obtaining Navarre at the expense of Henry's ambitions. However, eager to prove himself in battle, Henry decided to lead his forces in person.

All who could be spared followed their king to France. Even Elizabeth's grandfather, Sir Thomas Blount, now in his fifty-seventh year, went as a captain in the retinue of the Earl of Shrewsbury. For a time Elizabeth was almost bereft of male relatives at court, her father and her uncles all being included in the party which sailed across the Channel, although Lord Mountjoy did remain behind until September as one of those appointed to advise Queen Katherine in her role as regent.

The threat of the Scots ensured that it was not entirely a quiet time at court, although it is doubtful that Elizabeth enjoyed being 'horribly busy' in the making of standards, banners and badges against the hostilities (as Katherine proudly reported to her husband) quite as much as singing or dancing. The king's return in October was an occasion for both triumph and sadness. The victories at Flodden and Tournai were a marked success for the new reign, but, in the wake of the celebrations on 8 October 1513, it was reported that the queen had been delivered early of a son.[16] This was Katherine's third pregnancy in four years of marriage. This time everyone must have hoped that the odds were in favour of a successful outcome. However, it was not to be. When God had already blessed England with such good fortune in battle, it must have seemed especially cruel to withhold the much-desired heir. That Henry and Katherine remained childless was a personal tragedy for them; however, as long as the realm was without a male heir their private grief was also a matter of public concern.

Henry VIII's relationship with Elizabeth Blount is often thought to have begun as early as the winter of 1513 upon Henry's return from France, perhaps in the wake of Katherine's latest miscarriage. Writing to the king from France in 1514, Charles Brandon, recently created Duke of Suffolk, had a special message for Elizabeth and her young associate Elizabeth Carew, another of the maids of honour:

> and I beseech your Grace to [tell] Mistress Blount and Mistress Carew, the next time that I write unto them [or s]end them tokens, they shall either [wri]te to me or send me tokens again.[17]

The letter has caused some modern authors to speculate that Elizabeth may have been Suffolk's mistress before she was the king's. Suffolk was notoriously charming and handsome. He was also one of the few men whose marital history could rival the king's for scandal and complexity.[18] Elizabeth herself is not traditionally cast as shy and retiring, but nor is there any hint of the kind of notoriety earned by Mary Boleyn, who was once described as 'a very great wanton with a most infamous reputation'.[19] The exchange of tokens was a conventional part of the elaborate game of courtly love and this may have been nothing more than what it appears, a piece of harmless flirtation.

Elizabeth could be charming and gracious, but when it came to matters of the heart she clearly knew her own mind. When the king's cousin Lord Leonard Grey, a younger son of the Marquess of Dorset, first expressed his interest in marrying her in May 1532, he wrote to Thomas Cromwell asking the secretary to approach Elizabeth on his behalf. During an obviously enjoyable visit to Elizabeth's house at Kyme he dashed off a note, hoping that Cromwell would also persuade the king and the Duke of Norfolk to back his suit, even sending blank paper for their letters and £5 in gold for Cromwell's cooperation. He was very keen, assuring Cromwell that he would 'rather obtain that matter than to be made lord of as much goods and lands as any noble man hath within this realm', although, Elizabeth's substantial estates may also have had their own attraction. Cromwell was happy to oblige, but Elizabeth was not to be persuaded. In July 1532 Grey plaintively stressed the king's acquiescence to the match, even as he urged Cromwell to try harder to secure Elizabeth's agreement.[20]

Even though she succumbed to the king's attentions, it does not make her a loose woman. Putting aside the fact that Henry was rather difficult to refuse, Elizabeth may well have been attracted to him and she could also rest assured that their liaison would bring her some benefit. In the light of the way Suffolk had treated his wives, Elizabeth ought to have been more wary of risking her reputation by a casual sexual relationship with him, if she had any hopes of subsequently making a respectable marriage.

The assumption that Henry and Elizabeth were already romantically involved has been fuelled by Elizabeth's appearance in a masque during the Christmas celebrations in 1514. Dressed in blue velvet and cloth of gold, styled after the fashions of Savoy, she was one of four lords and four ladies who 'came into the Queen's chamber with great light of torches and danced a great season'. When at last the dancing was over these mysterious revellers took off their masks and Elizabeth Blount's partner was revealed as Henry VIII.

If Katherine was worried, it was not at the spectacle of her husband dancing with a slip of a girl. Recent months had seen strained relations at court as Henry grew increasingly frustrated at a Spanish alliance that had not brought him the gains he had expected. The Spanish ambassador complained mournfully that he felt like 'a bull at whom everyone throws darts'. Katherine's confessor, Fray Diego Fernandez, accused Henry of having treated the queen badly. Rumours circulated that Henry was planning to put aside his childless wife in order to marry a daughter of the Duke of Bourbon. Katherine no doubt bore the brunt of her husband's ire at her father, but their marriage was not in doubt. Not only had Henry considered avenging himself on Ferdinand by asserting Katherine's claim to her mother's kingdom of Castile, but also by the autumn of 1514 he had succeeded in making his twenty-eight-year-old wife pregnant for the fourth time.

Once Katherine was known to be with child Henry may well have felt at liberty to stray, but the object of his affections was probably not the fourteen-year-old Elizabeth Blount. A few nights after the entertainments in the queen's chamber at Christmas 1514, Henry took part in the Twelfth Night masque at Eltham. This time he had a different partner. Jane (or Jeanne) Poppingcourt was a Frenchwoman who had originally been employed by Henry VII as a companion to his daughters. By 1502 Jane was serving as one of Mary Tudor's maids of honour and by 1512 she was receiving 200s per annum as a member of the queen's household. Jane continued to feature in the court revels until she returned to France in 1516.

During this period Katherine was twice indisposed. The pregnancy in 1514 would certainly have been reason enough for Henry to look for a suitable diversion. Several years older than Elizabeth Blount, Jane Poppingcourt seems a more likely candidate. This was a woman who was the known mistress of the duc de Longueville and was censured by Louis XII for her promiscuous behaviour.[21] After the birth of a prince 'which lived not long after', in the early part of 1515 it was only a short time before Katherine fell pregnant again. Henry may have resumed his attentions to a willing and apparently discreet companion from May of that year. Certainly, when Jane finally took her leave of the court the king gave her a substantial parting gift of £100. In the circumstances, it seems highly likely that Henry's generosity stemmed from something more than mere royal largess.[22]

As Elizabeth turned fifteen, she increasingly featured in the pleasures and pastimes of the court. In May 1515 she was one of twenty-five young ladies mounted on white palfreys, with 'housings [harness] all of one fashion, most beautifully embroidered with gold' who accompanied the Queen to Shooters Hill near Greenwich as part of the traditional May Day celebrations. Dressed in an outfit 'slashed with gold lama with very costly trim' and attended by a number of footmen, Elizabeth must have felt almost like royalty herself as she gracefully entertained the visiting ambassadors. In July 1515 her father was granted a two-year advance on his wages as a Spear, amounting to over £146. Since it was not unusual for the males of the family to reap the benefit of a daughter's success (as Mary Boleyn would discover), this certainly seems to indicate that Henry had come to appreciate Elizabeth's undoubted talents and was feeling generous towards her family. Was this the opening salvo of a hopeful suitor?

Any consideration of the king's courtship of Elizabeth Blount is hampered by the fact that the only firm references to the progress of their affair are retrospective. After the event it was recorded that:

> The king in his fresh youth was in the chains of love with a fair damsel called Elizabeth Blount, daughter to Sir John Blount, knight, which damsel in singing, dancing, and in all goodly pastimes, exceeded all other, by the which goodly pastimes, she won the king's heart: and she again showed him such favour, that by him she bore a goodly man child, of beauty like to the father and mother.[23]

This in itself is the strongest argument that Henry did not yet look at Elizabeth with any serious intent. If episodes like Henry's supposed attraction to the Duke of Buckingham's sister Lady Anne Hastings could be seized on and blown out of all proportion, could a relationship of some four years' standing really escape all gossip and censure? A romantic dalliance, such as he may have enjoyed with Jane Poppingcourt, when the queen herself was pregnant was one thing; an enduring relationship, when a woman and her relatives might gain the ear of the king, was another thing entirely. Also, if this was the first indication of interest stirred, why is there no record in the years to follow to indicate where Henry's affections lay?

In fact, it is unlikely that Henry became involved with Elizabeth before 1518. Certainly the birth of Princess Mary, on 18 February 1516, gave Henry every incentive to remain faithful to his wife. The arrival of a healthy daughter did much to revive the king's hopes of an heir. After seven years of marriage, marred by miscarriage and infant mortality, Henry's confidence was restored. He rather optimistically declared to the Venetian ambassador 'The Queen and I are both young and if it is a girl this time, by God's grace the boys will follow'. If he wanted to capitalise on this fortuitous omen he needed to make Katherine pregnant again as soon as possible.

Although the following year saw the appointment of Elizabeth's great-uncle, Sir Edward Darrell, as the queen's vice-chamberlain, this probably had little bearing on his great-niece's relationship with the king. Even if he had wanted to use his position to encourage Henry's attentions in Elizabeth's direction, events in 1517 were not conducive to the onset of an affair. From July until December the capital was hit by an outbreak of the sweating sickness. An infectious and usually deadly disease, the outbreak abruptly curtailed the accustomed round of gaiety and society at court. At first Henry merely removed into the country, leaving orders that no one who had been in contact with the disease should approach him. By September he had grown sufficiently alarmed at the spreading plague to decamp from the body of the court, taking only the queen and a few attendants to a remote location. By December the worst of the outbreak was past but, even so, Christmas was kept very quietly that year in order to minimise any risk of infection.

If Henry needed anyone to console him in his time of peril it seems he looked to Katherine. Hopes that the queen might be with child in August 1517 proved unfounded, but Henry clearly persevered, for by April 1518 she was pregnant again. It is a sad irony that Katherine's happy condition was probably the impetus for her husband to seek solace in the arms of Elizabeth Blount. Henry had become increasingly solicitous of his wife's precious pregnancies, advising Wolsey that 'about this time is partly of her dangerous times, and because of that I would remove her as little as I may now'. Having reached a respectable eighteen years old, Elizabeth was now a far more viable candidate for one of those pleasant interludes Henry seems to have indulged in when Katherine was pregnant. Given that Fitzroy was six years old in June 1525, it is quite feasible that he was conceived at some point between April and November 1518.

All the evidence suggests this was not an affair of any duration, but a short-term liaison with an unexpectedly pleasant result. That Mary Boleyn was apparently the king's mistress for some time without such a tell-tale result is not necessarily a reflection on Henry's abilities. He was perfectly capable of making Katherine pregnant sooner or later, the real danger came in the latter months as she struggled to carry the child to term. If Mary had miscarried the king's child, Henry may not have been so convinced that her sister would present him with a son. Mary's two children, Henry (generally thought to have been born in 1524) and Catherine (usually supposed to have been born in 1526) are evidence that she was not barren. The fact that they were not followed by a brood of offspring, the 'every year a child' that was the lament of many hard pressed families, tends to suggest another solution. Indeed, if Mary had ever been anywhere near as sexually active as her reputation suggests, she must surely have successfully practised some form of contraception.

Although this was frowned upon by the Church, single people did seek to avoid unwanted pregnancy and even married couples might take steps to space their families as Mary seems to have done. Remedies to promote fertility, using certain times in a woman's cycle and certain sexual positions, were common. It took little imagination to realise that the inversion of these ideas might hinder conception. Though moralists argued against the 'sin of Onan' (who in Genesis cast his seed on the ground), the practice of coitus interruptus, was well known. Certainly, Catherine Howard was well aware that there were ways and means that 'a woman might meddle with a man and yet conceive no child unless she would her-self'. Since Mary was actually supposed to be a respectable married woman during her affair with Henry she may have been reluctant to present her new husband with a bastard, even if it was the king's.

It is doubtful that Elizabeth had managed to spend the last six years at court without broadening her education a little, but rather than being an indication of promiscuity, the fact that she bore the king a son actually strengthens the argument that she was not accustomed to sleeping around. If she had any other suitors there is no record of them. Such things are, of course, not easy to ascertain. Jane Seymour was twenty-seven and in all likelihood a spotless virgin when she married Henry VIII. Catherine Howard at nineteen had amassed considerably more experience. Yet given the lack of evidence to the contrary, perhaps Elizabeth Blount deserves to be given the benefit of the doubt.

It is, of course, impossible to determine exactly when Elizabeth fell pregnant. Even she may have remained in doubt of her condition for anything up to four months. Sixteenth-century diet and lifestyle meant that medical conditions such as amenorrhoea (abnormal absence of menstruation) were not uncommon. Therefore the absence of a period was not in itself a reliable guide to pregnancy. Most women would wait until they felt the baby stir in the womb before they could be sure they were actually with child, rather than suffering from some illness or disease.

On 3 October 1518 Elizabeth participated in the celebrations organised by Wolsey at York Place to mark the betrothal of the two-year-old Princess Mary to the Dauphin of France. On this occasion she was one of a large party of more than thirty performers, including the king, who donned their masquing hoods to entertain the assembled company. The ladies wore an elaborate uniform of green satin covered with cloth of gold and decorated with braids of damask gold and white gold. As usual, 'after they had danced they put off their visors and then they were all known'. Perhaps as a concession to the political importance of this event the couple did not dance together. Elizabeth's escort was Francis Bryan, one of several fashionable young gentlemen of the court, while the king danced with his sister.[24]

On such a sensitive diplomatic occasion it is unthinkable that Henry would have openly courted scandal and allowed Elizabeth to appear if she were visibly pregnant. Certainly the eagle-eyed court observers made no comment. This means that she is unlikely to have conceived before June 1518. Assuming that the pregnancy ran to full term this would have led to a birth in February 1519. Since Fitzroy was six in June 1525 he must have been born before June 1519, which would place conception, at the very latest, in October 1518. Given Henry's track record the odds are against a single brief encounter. The experience of Henry's wives also suggests that the birth was more likely to be premature than overdue. This was to be Elizabeth's last recorded appearance at court and it is entirely possible that she was already carrying the king's child.

Certainly, Elizabeth could not have remained long at court once her condition was generally known. Katherine's own pregnancy ended in disappointment on 9 November 1518 when she was delivered of a girl, who was either stillborn or died shortly after birth. In contrast, Elizabeth's baby, born at the Priory of St Lawrence at Blackmore, near Chelmsford in Essex, where Elizabeth probably spent the remainder of her pregnancy, was a living, healthy son.

The arrangements for Elizabeth's confinement were handled by the king's chief minister, Thomas Wolsey. Since his own mistress presented him with two illegitimate children, he was an ideal choice to handle such a matter with discretion.[25] Elizabeth was not quartered with the monks, but was allowed the use of a nearby manor-house, which served as a residence for the prior, Thomas Goodwyn. Perhaps because of her presence there, it has acquired a reputation under the name of 'Jericho' as the place where Henry VIII conducted his illicit relationships. However, the choice was probably designed to stem the flow of gossip that might have wound its way back to the court had Elizabeth been placed in a nunnery peopled by the daughters of noblemen. After all, to display with pride a healthy male child was one thing, but another failed pregnancy need not be advertised. Since Henry spent part of the summer of 1519 in Essex, this was perhaps another factor in the selection of the priory.

It was the custom for a woman to withdraw for about a month before her anticipated delivery, in order to prepare for her lying-in. During this time she would be attended only by women, not to re-emerge into male society until she was churched after the birth. Elizabeth probably had to spend rather longer than this in discreet retirement at Blackmore. However, it does seem her child arrived earlier than planned. Wolsey was out of London from 9 June 1519. On 18 June he was back with the court at Windsor. The following day he was expected at Hampton Court. Yet not until 29 June does he reappear at a Council meeting at Westminster.[26] Since 18 June was also the date chosen for Fitzroy's elevation to the peerage in 1525, it is tempting to conclude that the minister was unexpectedly waylaid by the child's birth.

The policy of discretion seems to have been successful. The infant's arrival caused no great stir. In the various diplomatic dispatches and personal correspondence of the period there is no reference to his birth. For this period in the summer of 1519 the Venetian Sebastian Giustinian actually wrote 'since my last, nothing new has taken place, save the desired arrival of . . . my successor'. Yet there can be no doubt that the baby was Henry's child. He was given the surname Fitzroy (a patronymic also adopted by Charles II for his illegitimate issue) and Thomas Wolsey stood as his senior godfather. Lifting the infant out of the font, he diplomatically named the child, Henry, after his royal sire. The identity of his other godfather, or indeed his godmother, is not known. Despite his interest in Fitzroy's later life, it was probably not Thomas Howard, 3rd Duke of Norfolk, for in 1519 he was still only Earl of Surrey. If Henry VIII had looked to a Howard to be godfather to his son, the Flodden Duke was the more prestigious choice. Given the indelicacy of asking one of the ladies of the court, the godmother was perhaps one of Elizabeth's relations.

Garrett Mattingly supposes that there was some formal celebration of Fitzroy's birth which Katherine was required to endure.[27] If there was, it was not recorded. However, during his time in Essex Henry would have had ample opportunity to show off his son. The king just might have been tactless enough to parade the child at the 'sumptous banquet' given by the queen in August 1519, at her manor of Havering-atte-Bower, in honour of the French hostages. Indeed, his rivalry with Francis I may even have required it. In June 1519 Henry VIII had been invited to stand as godfather to Francis's second son (whom he modestly called Henry) and it may have been some consolation that for the first time in eight years he now had a promising son of his own to show off. Alternatively, if the child was presented at the banquet held at the king's recently refurbished residence of Newhall, this would also accommodate the myth that Henry had been revamping the property for the use of his mistress.

It is generally thought that Elizabeth's relationship with the king came to an end once she was with child. Certainly she did not resume her duties at court. Even in 1520 when almost everyone, including her grandfather Sir Thomas Blount and her great-uncle Sir Edward Darrell, were in attendance at the spectacular summit with the King of France, known as the 'Field of Cloth of Gold', Elizabeth was not present. Speculation exists that, even prior to the début of Mary Boleyn, she had been replaced in the king's bed. Hubert S. Burke cites an Arabella Parker 'the wife of a city merchant' as being Elizabeth's successor. This seems doubtful and is not corroborated. Although there was a Mistress Parker in the revels of March 1522, this was probably Margery Parker, who had been part of Princess Mary's household since 1516.[28]

Was Elizabeth so hastily put aside? In June 1542 Elizabeth's second child, a daughter, also named Elizabeth, was twenty-two years old which means she could have been conceived as early as August 1519.[29] Was this child also the king's? In truth, the answer is probably not. Given Henry's desperate lack of useful issue, it seems untenable that any offspring of his, even if she were only a daughter, would have remained unacknowledged. It seems equally improbable that Henry would have let Elizabeth go if there was any chance that she might be carrying his child. Proof, perhaps, that Henry and Elizabeth did not resume their relationship after Fitzroy was born, but that Elizabeth was swiftly married off as soon as she was safely delivered of the king's son.

Elizabeth's first husband was Gilbert Tailbois, the son and heir of Sir George, Lord Tailbois of Kyme and his wife Elizabeth Gascoigne, the sister of Sir William Gascoigne of Gawthorpe. Their principal residence at Goltho in Lincolnshire had been in their possession since the fourteenth century. Gilbert's father, Sir George Tailbois, was knighted in 1497 and sat as knight of the shire in the parliament of 1509. His mother, Elizabeth, was a granddaughter of Henry, 3rd Earl of Northumberland, which gave the Tailbois' links with both the Dukes of Buckingham and Norfolk. In comparison to the Blounts they were a wealthy family. Sir Robert Tailbois' will in November 1494 liberally bestowed jewels and money, not just to the Church, or his immediate family, but to a large number of servants and retainers. His son George received 'six bowls of silver with a covering, and a basin and a ewer of silver, and two pots of silver and two salts gilt.' In addition to their significant interests in Lincolnshire, they also had lands in Yorkshire, Northumberland, Cambridgeshire, Suffolk and Somerset.

Although his father was still living, Gilbert Tailbois had been a ward of the crown since March 1517. Sir George Tailbois had fallen ill in 1499, while he was serving as Henry VII's lieutenant of the east and middle Marches. The sickness described as the 'land evil' apparently left him 'somewhat enfeebled of his perfect mind and remembrance'.30 If Sir George had indeed lost his mind, then his lands and possessions (as in a minority) would be taken into the hands of the crown. Sir George was apparently sufficiently alert to be alarmed at such a possibility and it was agreed that Henry VII would forbear from exercising this privilege in return for the sum of 800 marks in cash and bonds. He may have had periods of lucidity, for in 1508 he was treated as if he was of sound mind when he was included in a bond of surety with several of his neighbours and in 1513 he was listed among those to provide service in the French war. In 1516 an inquisition held at Lincoln to investigate his state of mind apparently found Sir George to be of 'sound mind and perfect memory.' Yet on 2 March 1517 a royal warrant granted Wolsey, Sir Robert Dymmock and others custody of his lands, on the grounds that he was a lunatic.

The first record of Elizabeth as a married woman does not appear until 18 June 1522, when the king granted her and her husband the valuable manor and town of Rugby in Warwickshire.31 The date strongly suggests that Henry's generosity had its roots in his gratitude that his infant son had lived to see his third birthday. There seems no reason to doubt that Henry VIII took an active interest in the welfare of his boy throughout his infancy. He was a loving father to all his children, unless circumstances dictated otherwise. While the importance allowed to Fitzroy by the king might ebb and flow with the political tide, Henry's affection towards his son never seems to have wavered. A degree of paternal pride in a child who grew to so acutely resemble his father is perhaps understandable. In the climate of 1519 here was tangible evidence, perhaps even a sign from God, that he could sire a living, healthy, male child.

Ironically, it was this very success that ensured Fitzroy's birth was not immediately greeted as a solution to the problem of the

succession. The hope engendered by Mary's birth in 1516 seems
to have been revived once again. Henry's thoughts immediately
turned to the prospect of a legitimate male heir. In August 1519
he assured Pope Leo X:

> If our longed-for heir should have been granted before the
> expedition sets out to do battle with the Infidel, we will
> lead our force in person.[32]

Henry's reasoning is clear. If God would grant him a son, not just
out of wedlock, but in adultery, how could such a blessing be
withheld in lawful marriage? Wolsey's attitude was probably
more realistic and he was probably already considering ways to
exploit the usefulness of this valuable new asset. Wolsey was to
be a prominent influence on Fitzroy's early childhood. Shortly
after his elevation, the child's Council would acknowledge
Wolsey's 'gracious favour towards him, in like manner as
evermore your grace (without any his desert) hath always been in
times past'. As his godfather he honoured the tradition of New
Year gifts, even before Fitzroy entered public life. In January
1525, for example, he presented him with a gold collar with a
hanging pearl worth £6 18s 8d.[33] A king's son, even an
illegitimate one, was potentially a valuable, political tool.

That so few details of Henry Fitzroy's infancy survive is not in
itself surprising. A king's bastard son was not supposed to be an
unusual occurrence. In these early years he was referred to as
'Lord Henry Fitzroy', an acknowledgement that his blood
relationship to the king conferred a certain innate rank. He was,
we are assured, 'well brought up, like a Prince's child'. While it is
possible the boy was initially raised alongside his half-sister,
Elizabeth Tailbois, and his brothers George (born in 1523) and
Robert (born in 1524) in their nursery in Lincolnshire, this was
some distance from the court and his doting father. A note in
the arrangements for his elevation hints at a more suitable
solution. At that time he was based at Wolsey's mansion of
Durham Place 'where at he kept his household'.

Given the peripatetic nature of noble Tudor households, which were continually on the move so that the residences might be cleansed and refreshed, this cannot have been his sole residence for the first six years of his life. However, the Cardinal could easily have arranged for suitable alternatives. The establishment of a natural son need not have been particularly large or notable. In the ordinances of 1493 a single nurse and four rockers were considered sufficient to attend a royal newborn in the nursery. Fitzroy could easily have been housed at any one of the numerous royal manors around London. Certainly, Henry VIII's other children, Mary, Elizabeth and Edward, all had their own households at one time or another and were found at a variety of royal palaces in a corresponding orbit to the court.

The reorganisation of Princess Mary's household in 1519 certainly suggests that Henry made some provision for his son. Margaret Pole, Countess of Salisbury, now replaced Margaret Bryan as Lady Mistress of Mary's household. At the same time at least two of Mary's rockers appear to have left her service. In a letter written in 1536, Margaret Bryan seems to confirm that she was responsible for all of Henry's children during their infancy:

> When my Lady Mary was born it pleased the king's grace [to make] me Lady Mistress, and made me a baroness, and so I have been a m[other to the] children his grace have [sic] had since.[34]

Unless her grammar is at fault this indicates another child between Mary and Elizabeth who was her charge in 1536. Since Edward was not yet born, that child must have been Henry Fitzroy. In addition, the correspondence of the child's first known tutor makes it clear that Fitzroy also received some rudimentary education, prior to his elevation to the peerage in 1525. John Palsgrave grumbled loudly that the child had been taught to recite his prayers in a 'barbarous' Latin accent and dismissed the man who had instructed him as 'no clerk'.[35]

How far Elizabeth was allowed to participate in her child's upbringing is less clear. John Palsgrave's eagerness to associate her with his difficulties in teaching the child 'whereof yourself was as guilty in any of them as I was' certainly seems to suggest that she had some input.[36] More flatteringly, he also believed that her intervention would carry some weight and invited her to come and see things for herself. She certainly had contact with her son. Two of her brothers, George and Henry Blount would find places in their nephew's household. An inventory of the child's goods taken in 1531 records her gift to him of 'a doublet of white satin' and 'two horses, colour bay, one ambling and the other trotting'. Her younger son, George Tailbois, would later receive a good deal of his half-brother's cast-off wardrobe.[37]

What is certain is that Elizabeth was no Alice Perrers[38] to interfere with the political policy of her king, nor did she enjoy the pseudo-wife status of Charles II's long-term mistress Barbara Villiers. Decisions about Fitzroy's future would not be hers to make. Her influence in matters of patronage was limited. The occasional grants that she received appear to have been sporadic gestures on Henry's part rather than an orchestrated policy of preferment. Prior to her marriage there is no record of any grants at all. She may have received personal gifts of jewels or money, but there were none of the marked instances of favour towards her family which charted Henry's relationship with Mary Boleyn, culminating in Sir Thomas Boleyn's creation as Viscount Rochford in 1525.[39]

The Blounts of Kinlet do not seem to have accrued any particular benefit from their daughter's intimate association with the king. That her grandfather Sir Thomas Blount was Sheriff of Shropshire in 1518 was perhaps not coincidence, but nor was it unusual. Her father John Blount fared little better. The grants in February 1519 of the keepership of Cleobury Park and joint stewardship (with Sir Thomas) of Bewdley and Cleobury Mortimer, in Shropshire, would not have been seen as remarkable. Far from securing entry to the peerage, he was not even knighted until 1529 and this probably had more to do with the politics of the

Reformation Parliament than any gratitude on Henry's part. Yet Henry could not have rewarded Mary Boleyn, who was already married, as he had Elizabeth, by providing an excellent match. Since Mary seems to have accrued little personal benefit from her liaison, Elizabeth had good reason to feel she had struck the better deal.

Gilbert Tailbois could be forgiven for thinking that his father's indisposition was his good fortune. When parliament opened in June 1529 Gilbert was called to take his place as Baron Tailbois of Kyme, even though his enfeebled father was still alive. However, the question of his landed inheritance was rather more complex. A popular theme in Henry VIII's courtship of Elizabeth Blount is the king's audacity in proclaiming his gratitude to his mistress by means of lands and rewards bestowed openly in an Act of Parliament. In fact the statute is couched diplomatically as the petition of Sir George and Gilbert, regarding their 'great love and affection' towards Elizabeth. Only careful reading and knowledge of the truth reveals the king's hand in the matter:

> by which marriage aswell the said Sir George Tailbois Knight, as the said Gilbert Tailbois have received not only great sums of money, but also many benefits to their right much comfort.[40]

The act allowed Elizabeth to hold Tailbois lands in Lincolnshire, Yorkshire and Somerset for the term of her life. The package included lands to the value of £200 and a further annuity of £40. In fact, she may have done even better. In June 1528 Gilbert's mother protested at being required to pay over another £100 in lands and rents and an annuity of £40, pointing out that the lands worth over £342 that Gilbert and Elizabeth already enjoyed were more than she and her husband were left with to provide for all their children.

It has to be said that Henry was not required to dig deep into his own pockets. These lands were part of those possessions which Gilbert stood to inherit as his patrimony. Nonetheless, in terms of reward, marriage to a baron was an auspicious match for Elizabeth. When her brother George married Constance Talbot, the daughter of Sir John Talbot of Grafton and his wife Margaret, the indenture dated 30 March 1533 allowed Constance a jointure of £40 out of lands in Staffordshire. The wedding was to be held at Kinlet and 'the cost and expense thereof as in meat and drink' to be borne by the Blounts. In return Sir John Talbot paid 525 marks for the marriage. The couple stood to inherit the entire parcel of Blount/Peshall lands in Shropshire, Staffordshire and elsewhere, save only lands to the yearly value of £20 each which were earmarked for George's younger brothers, William and Henry.[41] As the son and heir, George would normally be expected to have made the best marriage his family could afford. Since Talbot was a cousin of the Earl of Shrewsbury it was no mean match, but it did not equate with the wealth and status Elizabeth now enjoyed.

Significantly, Elizabeth's marriage would be one of the charges levied against Wolsey's governance in 1528. It was claimed that providing her with such a good match was a means to 'encourage the young gentlewomen of the realm to be our concubines'. The article was just one of a number of broadranging and potentially damaging accusations against Wolsey intended to secure his downfall.[42] Whatever the wider political import of the charges, it seems clear that Elizabeth made a far better match than she had a right to expect. Of her four sisters, only one, Albora, was still unmarried by 1540. Her older sister, Anne, married Richard Lacon, the heir of Sir Thomas Lacon of Shropshire; their family's interests remained purely provincial. Richard Lacon was John Blount's petty captain in the French campaign of 1513 and served as sheriff of the county in 1539. In comparison, Elizabeth had moved far from the geographical and social spheres into which she was born.

If Gilbert felt he was marrying beneath him, the union had other benefits. He wed Elizabeth secure in the knowledge that she was capable of bearing him sons and the legal fiction of the

Act of Parliament enabled him to enjoy much of his inheritance during his father's lifetime. Since the crown need not have surrendered control of his estates until Sir George died in September 1538, Gilbert stood to benefit from the arrangement at least as much as his new bride.

In the climate of 1519 Elizabeth Blount had reason to feel satisfied with her lot. The idea that she might have seduced the king into repudiating his wife and making her Queen of England, particularly before she took him to her bed, would have been seen as preposterous. The possibility that the queen could be put aside in order to legitimate Henry Fitzroy by their subsequent marriage, only slightly less so. It is true that the five-year age gap which had seemed so inconsequential in 1509 had now started to show. Henry pursued his revels with his customary enthusiasm, but the queen withdrew early. The king was still considered 'extremely handsome', however, Katherine was, at best, considered 'rather ugly than otherwise'. In 1518 her sixth pregnancy had ended in yet another failure and who knew how many more chances there would be? Yet few would have seen Elizabeth as a suitable replacement. However, Henry had reacted to Fitzroy's arrival with renewed hope that he and his queen would have a legitimate son. As long as that hope or expectation remained, Katherine's position was unassailable.

In the meantime, Henry's lack of male issue endowed his bastard son with a level of importance that he might otherwise have lacked. Henry Fitzroy could claim a unique importance in the history of English royal bastards. Unlike King Henry I, his father did not have twenty other illegitimate sons to provide for. Even more significantly, neither was there a brood of legitimate offspring to overshadow him. After ten years of marriage Henry VIII could boast only a single daughter. Equally significantly, as the only surviving son of an only son, he was not overendowed with other male relatives who might be called upon to share the burden of government in the king's name. The exact status allowed to the child would depend on what honours his father chose to bestow, although necessity as much as policy demanded that Fitzroy should have a more prominent part in affairs of state than was usual with bastard issue. Henry would need to produce a whole brood of sons before that importance was seriously affected. In contrast, it would take a single legitimate prince to secure the succession. Yet, as time passed and Fitzroy remained the king's only living son, it was perhaps inevitable that the ready-made heir increasingly attracted the attention of onlookers.

2

Heir Apparent

On the morning of 18 June 1525, six-year-old Lord Henry Fitzroy travelled by barge from Wolsey's mansion of Durham Place, near Charing Cross, down the River Thames, to the royal palace of Bridewell. In his company were a host of knights, squires and other gentlemen. At 9 a.m. his barge pulled up to the watergate and his party made their way through the palace to the king's lodgings, on the south side of the second floor. The royal apartments, which Henry had newly refurbished just two years earlier, included two great vaulted chambers running the length of the building. More like a church nave than a domestic residence, they stood two floors high with large windows set in either side.[1] As Fitzroy entered the royal apartments, preparations for the day's events were already well in hand.

The rooms were decorated with rich hangings of gold and·silk. At the end of the far chamber a canopy of estate 'of rich cloth of gold of tissue' was set over a matching chair, whose gold pommels glittered in the morning light. Trumpeters were waiting to take up their position in the bay window at the far end. The chamber would have been filling up with those who had come to witness this grand event. For the moment, Fitzroy was led through the chambers to an ante-room, where he could rest and be made ready for his part in the proceedings. Outside, the king and his nobility prepared to take their place under the cloth of estate.

The occasion was well attended by the court. At the right hand of the king stood Richmond's godfather, Thomas Wolsey. Beside him were numerous bishops, abbots and prelates. On Henry's left were the Duke of Norfolk and the Duke of Suffolk and standing behind them numerous earls, lords, knights and esquires. By now, the crowd of onlookers packed the chamber. Before the ceremonies could begin the gentlemen ushers were forced to clear a path so 'that three men might go arm-in-arm'. At last, everything was ready. At a signal from the king, there was a fanfare of trumpets and Henry Percy, Earl of Northumberland, entered the chamber, carrying a sword before him. He was followed by the eight heralds of the College of Arms, with the Garter herald bearing a patent and the Somerset herald wearing a newly designed coat-of-arms. Finally, flanked by John de Vere, Earl of Oxford and Henry Fitzalan, Earl of Arundel, Henry Fitzroy entered, dressed in the robes of an earl.[2]

The feelings of the assembled nobles can only be wondered at, as the diminutive lord came to kneel before his father. As Henry VIII raised his son to his feet, the voice of Thomas More echoed about the chamber, as he read the patent, which created the Lord Henry Fitzroy, Earl of Nottingham:

> and when it came to the words 'Gladdii Cuituram' then the young Lord kneeled down and the kings grace put the girdle about the neck of the young Lord the sword hanging bendwise over the breast of him when the patent was read the king took it to the said Earl and this Earl of Nottingham accompanied as before entered into the said Gallery.[3]

Not since the twelfth century, when Henry II had made William Longsword Earl of Salisbury, had a King of England raised his illegitimate son to the peerage.[4] Even now, the ceremony was far from complete. Before the assembled nobles and onlookers could catch their breath, the newly created Earl of Nottingham re-entered the chamber.

This time his attire and the badges of office borne before him, were those of a duke. The Earl of Northumberland carried the robes. Behind him came Thomas Grey, Marquess of Dorset, carrying the sword, the Earl of Arundel, carrying the cap of estate with a circlet and the Earl of Oxford with a rod of gold. The only two existing dukes in England, Charles Brandon, Duke of Suffolk and Thomas Howard, Duke of Norfolk walked on either side of the child. Once again he came to kneel before his father. As the patent was read he was invested with the trappings of a duke. This time, when he rose to his feet, he was Duke of Richmond and Somerset.

To be a duke was a significant honour. It was it the highest rank of the peerage and the office, originally devised by King Edward III for his son, Edward the Black Prince to be Duke of Cornwall, had retained its royal aura. The former Lord Henry Fitzroy was subsequently referred to in all formal correspondence as the 'right high and noble prince Henry . . . Duke of Richmond and Somerset'. As if to compound this sense of Royal dignity and endow the child with as much respectability as possible, Henry VIII had granted his son the unprecedented honour of a double dukedom. While he is commonly referred to as Richmond, some pains were taken to see that he bore both titles with equal weight. The bulk of his lands came from possessions which had formerly been held by Margaret Beaufort, the king's grandmother, as Countess of Richmond. These included estates which had been the rightful inheritance of King Henry VII when he was Earl of Richmond, and lands which had belonged to Margaret's father, John Beaufort, when he held the title Duke of Somerset.

Indeed, for all of those who strained to catch a glimpse of the new duke in the chamber at Bridewell, Henry's use of the Somerset title would have struck a particular chord. It was widely known that John Beaufort, created Earl of Somerset in 1397, had been a royal bastard, who was subsequently legitimated. John Beaufort and his siblings were the children of Edward III's son John of Gaunt and his mistress Katherine Swynford. The affair took place during his second marriage. After Katherine had borne him four children, Gaunt's wife died and they were free to marry. However, due to the complexities of the affair, not least that the children had been conceived in adultery, they were not automatically legitimated. Instead,

Gaunt and Katherine applied to the Pope for a special dispensation, which being granted was confirmed in England by Act of Parliament by Richard II. The Beauforts were henceforth to be considered legitimate 'as fully, freely and lawfully as if [they] were born in lawful wedlock'.[5]

The church at Corfe Castle, a long-time Beaufort residence and now part of Richmond's holdings, proclaimed for all the world to see this significant change in the family's status:

> The coats-of-arms at the side of the north doorway reflected through heraldry the importance of the family's legitimization. On the left the shield lay on its side, indicating a bastard line, whilst on the right it was placed upright.[6]

Few of those present can have been ignorant of this particular piece of English history. Seeing Henry's evident pride and affection in his sturdy little son, many of those who witnessed Richmond's elevation must have wondered if this was what the king had in mind.

Although some might remember that the Beauforts had been excluded from the line of succession, others might remind them that this had not originally been the case. Richard II had made no such stipulation when he had confirmed his cousin's legitimacy. Only when John of Gaunt's eldest son (by his first wife Blanche), Henry Bolingbroke, seized the throne as King Henry IV, did he look nervously to his half-brothers and sister. The Beauforts had done well for themselves and his own claim to the throne was not above reproach. Henry IV confirmed their legitimate status, but with the significant proviso that it was 'excepting the royal dignity'. Henry IV had good reason for his actions. Despite the legal fiction of their legitimacy, the stigma of illegitimacy was not erased from people's minds. Most importantly, Henry had four perfectly good sons of his own and had no need to complicate matters further.

Henry VIII was not so fortunate. In June 1525 Henry VIII's only legitimate child was his nine-year-old daughter, Mary.

Katherine was now almost forty years old and her last pregnancy had been in 1518. With determined optimism, Henry had continued to sleep with her for several years without any sign of conception, before reluctantly conceding she was past the age of child bearing. Gradually, the whole country came to agree with the Venetian ambassador that Katherine was 'past that age in which women most commonly were wont to be fruitful'. Only once Henry ceased having sexual relations with her, and estimates for this begin in 1524, was he forced to acknowledge that she would never give him a male heir. After sixteen years of marriage and at least six pregnancies, the hopes for the Tudor dynasty rested solely on the shoulders of one small girl.

In the spring of 1524, Henry VIII had organised one of the lavish tournaments that were almost a weekly occurrence at court. On this occasion he intended to show off his new suit of armour 'made of his own device and fashion'. Obviously the new design caused quite a stir. Henry was able to set off against his opponent, Charles Brandon, before he, or any of his attendants, realised he had not closed the visor on his helmet. The horrified crowd called out the danger, but it was too late. Brandon's spear shattered in the king's unprotected face. As the king fell to the ground the fate of England hung in the balance, yet Henry had a miraculous escape. Shaking off the splinters of wood, he assured his panic-stricken subjects that he was indeed alive, first by walking about and then by remounting his horse and competing six more times 'by which all men might perceive he had no hurt'. It was a very public reminder that the king, whatever he might wish to believe, was not immortal. Given Henry's love of dangerous sports, the next time England might not be so fortunate.

Unlike France where the law prevented the accession of a daughter, there was no reason why Mary could not reign as Queen of England, except that prevailing opinion was firmly against it. The motto of Henry VIII's third wife Jane Seymour – 'bound to obey and serve' – neatly summed up the perceived role of Tudor women. They were the weaker sex, physically less able, mentally inferior and morally suspect. They were subject to the authority of their husbands and fathers. They were not designed to rule. The admirable example of women like Margaret of Savoy, who acted as regent for the Emperor Charles V in the Netherlands, or the formidable career of Mary's own grandmother, Isabella, who ruled as Queen of Castile in Spain, did nothing to reassure. Even more worrying was the complex issue of female inheritance. After she married, a woman's lands and possessions belonged to her husband and no one could agree exactly how this would work if part of that inheritance were a kingdom. The English looked nervously to the example of other small countries, like Burgundy, whose independence had been lost when they had been left in the hands of a woman.

England's one experiment with a ruling queen was not an experience anyone was eager to repeat. At his death in 1135 King Henry I's only legitimate issue was his daughter, Matilda.[7] During his lifetime Henry I had made his barons swear to accept her as the heir to his kingdom, but his authority could not reach beyond the grave. After his death the barons chose her cousin, Stephen, Count of Boulogne, as a more acceptable male alternative. This, ultimately, plunged England into nine years of civil war, which decimated the land. When Stephen was imprisoned for seven months in 1141, Matilda briefly occupied the throne. It was not exactly a precedent. Stephen remained the anointed king and Matilda's 'extremely arrogant demeanor, instead of the modest gait and bearing proper to the gentle sex' helped ensure she was not crowned queen. Matilda eventually secured a victory of sorts when Stephen recognised her son Henry as his heir, but she never ruled as queen of England as her father had intended.

All things being equal, Henry VII's mother, Margaret Beaufort, Countess of Richmond, had had the better claim to the crown in 1485. However, such things were not equal. A king needed to be able to defend his crown, if need be, on the field of battle. It was quite possible that England might prefer to see a member of the peerage take the throne, rather than accept Mary as their queen. In 1519 the Venetian ambassador had seen nothing wrong in speculating on the chances of the Dukes of Suffolk, Norfolk or Buckingham, ruling the kingdom if Henry died without a legitimate son to succeed him. Shortly afterwards Henry himself wrote in great secrecy to Wolsey, requiring him to 'make good watch' on a number of the nobility. If this letter is rather too 'cloak and dagger' to be absolutely sure that Henry's concerns centred on the succession, the fate of one of those named, Edward Stafford, Duke of Buckingham, certainly seems to indicate that the king was increasingly anxious about the future of his dynasty.

At this time there were only three dukes in England. Two of them had been Henry's own creations. Charles Brandon was created Duke of Suffolk in 1514 for his part in the French War. He had begun his career as a mere esquire, owing everything he was now to Henry VIII, 'my sovereign lord and master who has brought me up out of nothing'. Since men had been amazed at his elevation to the peerage, they would perhaps have been reluctant to accept him as their king. His marriage to Henry's sister, Mary Tudor, in 1515, had brought him closer to the throne, but it could not overcome the disability of his birth. Mary continued to be known as 'The French Queen' by right of her first husband King Louis XII of France. As the contemporary inscription on their portrait openly acknowledged 'cloth of gold' (Mary) outranked 'cloth of frieze' (Brandon). Given his relatively humble origins the duke was perhaps fortunate he was not cast as canvas.

As part of the same ceremony in 1514, Thomas Howard, with rather more justice, had become Duke of Norfolk, in recognition for his victory at the Battle of Flodden. He had spent much of his adult life trying to recover the dukedom that had been bestowed on his father by Richard III in 1483. Unfortunately, the family had enjoyed the title for just two years before it was forfeited for fighting on the losing side at Bosworth in 1485. Thomas Howard had struggled to restore his family to their former glory for twenty-nine years. Despite the apparent splendour with which his son, also Thomas Howard, would bear the title, when he succeeded to the dukedom on his father's death in 1524, the house of Howard was built on fairly fragile foundations.

However, Edward Stafford, Duke of Buckingham was a rather different proposition. His family had been Dukes of Buckingham for four generations. His father had been executed by Richard III, for a rebellion that may have more to do with his own ambition than his support for the Tudors.[8] As the nephew of King Edward IV's queen, Elizabeth Woodville, and a direct descendant of King Edward III, Buckingham could boast an impressive royal pedigree. He was also a major landowner in his own right, with an impressive array of magnificent castles and an army of retainers. Perhaps most worryingly, he was the epitome of an over-mighty subject, with sufficient pride and ambition to give any monarch pause for thought.

Certainly, Buckingham was killed as much for what he might do as for what he had actually done. The charges levied against him in May 1521 were treasonous. Chief among them was the allegation that he had spoken of how he would kill the king. It was also alleged that he had proclaimed the death of Henry's infant son to be God's vengeance, that he had dabbled in prophecies that Henry would never have a male heir and that, instead, he himself would become king.[9] If he had said and done what he is claimed to have said and done, then Buckingham deserved to die. If his downfall was a plot, perhaps led by Wolsey to remove a powerful rival, then Buckingham's actions must have been sufficient to give colour to the charges. In the political climate of the time such behaviour was more than foolish, it was fatal.

Buckingham's conviction sealed his fate and his execution sent a chilling message through the ranks of the peerage. Significantly, from June 1525 the most senior noble in England was not Norfolk or Suffolk. The highest-ranking member of the peerage was Henry Fitzroy, Duke of Richmond and Somerset whose elevation to the peerage had been such a spectacular affair. The heralds' reports all testify to the splendour and gravity of the occasion. The ceremonies were followed by 'great feasts and disguisings' as Henry VIII celebrated his son's honours with customary extravagance. While we cannot be sure whether Elizabeth, now Lady Tailbois, returned to the court to witness the event, her husband was almost certainly able to give her an eyewitness account.[10]

As arrangements for Richmond's new dignity had taken shape, Elizabeth and Gilbert had been honoured with a spate of further grants. In April 1525 Gilbert was made bailiff and keeper of Tattershall in Lincolnshire, now part of Richmond's lands. His elevation to a knighthood also seems to be associated with his step-son's new rank, as he now appeared as Sir Gilbert Tailbois for the first time. However, the exact significance behind all this display was more elusive. Both contemporary and subsequent observers have been forced to speculate on Henry's motives for raising his bastard son to such unprecedented heights.

Henry may have been prompted into action by a piece of good fortune. On 14 February 1525, Charles V had inflicted a shattering defeat on Francis I at Pavia. The French forces were decimated and many of their foremost military leaders were killed. To Henry's great joy, one of the dead was the English exile, Richard de la Pole, which effectively extinguished any threat that family still represented to the security of the Tudor dynasty. While Richard was still at large and far from reconciled to the Tudors' occupation of the throne, the policy of advancing his illegitimate son to almost regal honours might have seemed too dangerous a gauntlet to throw in the face of a disgruntled, rival claimant. At the very least, Henry could now be reassured that that particular danger was laid to rest.

It has also been argued that Richmond's elevation was born more out of pique than policy.[11] During the battle at Pavia Francis I had been taken prisoner and his realm was now vulnerable to invasion. Henry was overjoyed. 'Now is the time for the Emperor and myself to devise the means of getting full satisfaction from France', he declared. His dream of regaining England's ancient rights across the Channel, and more besides, at last seemed within his grasp. England prepared to reap the spoils of war. Forces were to be mustered, armaments to be made ready and money to be raised for the enterprise, from the so-called Amicable Grant. Whatever the political realities of the situation, and Henry was objective enough to arm his ambassadors with a sliding scale of demands, he clearly believed that the French throne could be his for the taking.

Almost at once the King of England was being warned that Charles intended 'little or nothing to your commodity, profit, or benefit' and so it proved. More concerned with his own problems elsewhere, than indulging Henry's dreams of European expansion, Charles V agreed terms for peace in the Treaty of Madrid. Whatever Henry had expected, it was not that.

Not for the first time the King of England's ambitions were thwarted by Katherine's family. Like Ferdinand of Aragon before him, her nephew Charles V refused to co-operate in Henry's grandiose designs. The king was bitterly disappointed and Richmond's elevation has been seen as a deliberate snub to the queen and the Spanish alliance that she represented. Certainly, the ceremony did nothing to spare Katherine's feelings. To make some honourable provision for a natural son was normal and expected. To parade him around the court, almost as if he was a legitimate prince, would have been a trial to the most patient of wives. For Katherine, who knew she had failed in her most basic duty, the implicit rebuke must have been keenly felt.

Not only was there anxiety about the possible implications for her beloved daughter, Mary, but also Katherine's own pride and honour were at stake. In a private letter, one of the Venetian observers wrote:

It seems that the Queen resents the Earldom and Dukedom conferred on the king's natural son and remains dissatisfied, at the instigation it is said of three of her Spanish ladies her chief counsellors, so the king has dismissed them the court, a strong measure, but the Queen was obliged to submit and have patience.[12]

Henry may have been angry enough not to care whether he upset and embarrassed his wife and through her therefore exact some small revenge on the real target of his wrath, Charles V. However, the significant financial outlay involved in Richmond's elevation, at over £4,000 per annum, is evidence the king also had a far more serious purpose in mind than this transient satisfaction.

It might also appear that Henry was pushed into honouring his son by Charles V's decision, on 7 June 1525, to break off his engagement to Princess Mary. The couple had been betrothed since 1522 and their marriage could have offset many of the dangers of a female ruler. If Mary could marry and produce a son before Henry died, England's future would be far more secure. Even without this obvious benefit, Charles V was a proven soldier and leader who could support her peaceful succession and help her to rule. If the king had to be a foreigner, a Hapsburg was perhaps rather more acceptable to the English people than either a Valois or a Stuart. If Mary's marriage was a compromise from the ideal solution of a legitimate prince, then at least Henry could console himself with the thought that his grandson would one day rule over an immense empire.

Now Charles V demanded that the nine-year-old Mary should leave England at once to be brought up among her future subjects. Also her dowry should follow within four months. The terms were unreasonable and intended to be rejected. Charles was already well advanced with his own plans to marry Isabella, Infanta of Portugal and needed Henry to release him from his obligation to Mary. Yet the claim that Richmond's elevation was set in hand 'immediately after the news reached England that Charles meant to break his engagement',[13] rests on two assumptions. Firstly that Henry had not intended to raise Richmond to such high honour prior to the breaking of this news and secondly, that the king had come to rely on the union between Charles V and Mary as being the best means of securing her, and England's, future.

In fact, whatever Katherine might have hoped, there is nothing to suggest that Henry viewed this match as anything other than another diplomatic alliance. In 1518, the two-year-old princess had already been engaged to the infant Dauphin of France and no one was surprised when that betrothal did not endure until the children were adults. In the treaty it had been acknowledged that this betrothal would 'not prevent the Emperor from marrying any woman of lawful age before our daughter comes to mature years'. It had always been unlikely that Charles V, who was already twenty-five and eager for an heir of his own, would wait for Mary to grow up.[14]

Also, Charles's conduct towards his mother, as Queen of Castile, ought to have given Henry pause for thought. Juana had succeeded as Queen as Castile after her mother's death in 1504. When Charles V assumed the title of King of Castile from 1516, he did so in complete disregard of his mother's prior claim. Even if she was eventually deserving of the epitaph 'Juana the mad', and her virtual solitary confinement at Tordesillas Castle can only have contributed to her decline, legally Charles should have continued to rule as regent in her name. Such conduct did not speak well of his attitude towards the rights of ruling queens.

Certainly, Mary's betrothal had not stopped Henry negotiating for her possible marriage to James V of Scotland in 1524. Nor did it prevent him from considering the offer of a French match in March 1525. The manner in which Charles repudiated the betrothal was hardly designed to mollify the king, but his action cannot have been entirely unexpected.

In any case, the plans for Richmond's elevation seem to have begun well in advance of this particular disappointment. The first indication of Fitzroy's impending honours is generally taken from an undated note of Wolsey's to the king, usually assigned to May 1525:

> Your grace shall also receive by this present bearer, such arms as your highness hath devised . . . for your entirely beloved son, the Lord Henry Fitzroy.[15]

These included two heraldic beasts: a white lion representing the dukedom of Richmond and a silver yale symbolising the dukedom of Somerset. An escutcheon in the centre completed the honours with its chief design a castle and two bucks' heads for the earldom of Nottingham. Significantly, the arms of France and England, as borne by the king, were crossed with a 'baton sinister argent' a silver band which proclaimed his illegitimacy to the world. His motto 'Duty binds me' stressed his obligation to Henry VIII – his king and father.

A list of the 'wardrobe stuff appointed for my Lord Henry' gives some indication of the scale of these plans. There were hangings for six chambers, a closet, a chapel and a hall. The various furnishings included twenty-five different carpets and twenty-one assorted beds, each with their own pillows, sheets and counterpanes. Richmond's bed, with its canopy and a scarlet counterpane, was decidedly grand.[16] When the necessities for his household were finally assembled it would require a chariot and seven horse-draughts to transport them. Although the young duke's financial accounts do not begin until 12 June 1525 (just prior to the ceremony at Bridewell), all these goods and the two hundred and forty-five people thought necessary to attend upon a six-year-old duke could not have been brought together in a few short weeks.

At least one member of Richmond's household seems to have had more notice than this of his new appointment. If the experience of the duke's tutor, John Palsgrave, is in any way representative, then plans for the household were already in the pipeline by April 1525. Palsgrave apparently owed his selection to the influence of Sir Richard Wingfield, Chancellor of the Duchy of Lancaster. On this basis the arrangements must have been made before 18 April 1525, because on that date Wingfield sailed from England to Spain, where he died in July 1525 without returning to England.[17] It is unlikely that he would have been able to ensure that Palsgrave was chosen to bring the king's son up 'in virtue and learning' as the tutor would claim, if the composition of Richmond's household was not already well in hand before his departure, especially as Wolsey seems to have had his own candidate waiting in the wings, in the shape of Dr Richard Croke.

In fact, the timing of Richmond's elevation was probably not a knee-jerk reaction to the events of spring 1525. The simplest reason for the date chosen is almost invariably overlooked. All the accounts, with the exception of the Venetian Lorenzo Orio's wildly inaccurate report, agree that Richmond was six years old on 18 June 1525. A child's sixth birthday was an important milestone, marking the end of infancy and the beginning of adult life. Writing in his journal in 1547, King Edward VI would recall when he made the transition out of the nursery, being

> brought up [un]till he came to six years old among the women. At the sixth year of his age he was brought up in learning by Dr [Richard] Cox . . . and John Clerke . . . Master of Arts.[18]

At six, the dangers of death in infancy were past and the child was of an age when a father needed to address the care and education of his son. While Fitzroy had struggled through the perils of the first few years of life, Henry had had reason to be cautious: there might not be any future prospects. Since the date of the ceremony coincides so exactly with the most likely date for Elizabeth Blount's delivery, it does seem reasonable to assume that 18 June 1525 was in fact Richmond's sixth birthday. Now the child was old enough to take his place in the wider world Henry had an obligation to ensure his son was adequately cared for.

Admittedly, obligation could easily have been satisfied with significantly less than the honours and income that Henry heaped upon his son. However, perhaps Henry's honour could not. Putting aside for a moment the political implications of Richmond's elevation, this was Henry's 'worldly jewel', whom he 'loved like his own soul' and these feelings alone were surely sufficient to ensure that his son would be equal to no mere subject.

His elevation to the peerage was not the first honour Henry VIII had bestowed on his son. The child had already been elected into the Order of the Garter. Membership of this prestigious and ancient order of knighthood was a marked note of favour. Numbers were strictly limited to the king and twenty-five members and vacancies only occurred through death or dishonour. Despite the polite fiction of elections, the king's wishes dominated the choice of candidates.

According to one account, Richmond's election into the Order may have taken place as early as 23 April 1525.[19] Although according to the register of the Order it occurred on 7 June 1525, when all the knights present, not surprisingly, nominated the Lord Henry Fitzroy. At some point, the child must also have been knighted, since the discovery that Lord Roos had not been knighted had caused no small problem when he was elected into the Order. Fitzroy was duly nominated to the place formerly occupied by the Duke of Norfolk, who was moved down to make room for him. This placed him second only to actual royalty (namely, the king, Charles V and Francis I).

Henry's instructions for the installation of 'our dearest son' were drawn up on 18 June 1525 when he was at Bridewell. The ceremony duly took place on 25 June, in St George's Chapel at Windsor Castle, where his coat-of-arms can still be seen. Although the proceedings were not quite as lavish, nor as prominent as his elevation to the peerage, the chapel was decked out with his banners, helm and crest. Robes of the garter, including a mantle of purple velvet decorated with 'a great cross of St George', tassels of purple silk and buttons shaped like sundials, were laid out for the duke. This time, instead of trumpeters there were choristers to accompany the service and a host of clerics and 'officers of the King' to ensure that everything ran smoothly. Richmond arrivedin a gown of black satin, furred with sable, with gold buttons and gold laces, which he gave away in reward to the Garter Herald after the ceremony. As a knight of the Garter Richmond enjoyed an honour not bestowed on Henry's legitimate son, Prince

Edward, during his father's lifetime. Even so, it is unlikely Henry would have considered this alone was sufficient provision for his son.

Richmond's elevation to the peerage certainly seemed to herald great things. At this time the only other royal bastard in England was Arthur Plantagenet, Viscount Lisle.[20] The illegitimate son of Edward IV and his 'wanton wench' Elizabeth Lucy, 'my lord the bastard' had spent his youth living at his father's court. Yet, he was completely overshadowed by a host of legitimate male relatives and only achieved prominence under the Tudors. When Henry VIII made him an esquire of the body in 1509, he was already almost fifty years old. Richmond's grandfather, John Blount, also made an esquire of the body at that time, was half his age. Not until 1523 did Arthur join the ranks of the peerage, when he married Elizabeth, the daughter of Edward Grey, Viscount Lisle. Despite Henry's benevolence, the titles now showered on Richmond made Lisle's fortunes seem positively dismal. In addition, Lisle's lands were valued at £800 per annum, several thousand pounds short of the income intended for Richmond.

On 12 June 1525 Orio was already reporting that Henry VIII had moved to legitimise his son.[21] Although he was entirely mistaken, Orio was not deterred. He subsequently became so carried away by the prevailing rumours that he declared:

> The King has created his natural son by name Henry, aged seven years, Duke of Buckingham, with an annual rental amounting to 40,000 ducats, also Earl of Richmond and viceroy, so that he takes precedence of everybody.[22]

Although his sources were clearly so wildly inaccurate that it is amazing that he got the right name, the statement does reflect how far Richmond was perceived to have risen from his innate status as the king's natural son.

Around this time Richmond was also granted a number of offices. From 18 June 1525 he was Captain of the Town and Castle of Berwick upon Tweed and Keeper of the City and Castle of Carlisle, 'an office held by the heir apparent from the time of Richard the Second'. Shortly afterwards, on 22 July 1525, he became Warden General of the Scottish Marches, a post Henry VIII himself had held as a child in 1494. Not since William the Conqueror, in the eleventh century, had an actual bastard sat upon the English throne. However, here was Richmond apparently being asked to fulfil the duties of a bona fide prince. Surely it was only a small step from here to the real thing?

Orio was not the only person, then or now, to believe that Henry was grooming his son as a possible successor. Yet it is dangerous to place too much emphasis on the king's choices at this time. It must be remembered that for much of his young life Henry VIII was only the second son, not the heir apparent, and the offices he held reflected this. It was also a well-established practice for any monarch to employ family members in as many posts as possible and Henry did not have many on whom he could call. As a mere girl, Mary was ineligible for any of those public offices that a prince might have performed for his father. Not only could Richmond help to address this deficiency, but his youth was often a positive advantage. Image and honour would be satisfied by the appointment of the king's blood relative, but lesser men could do the real work at a fraction of the cost.

There were also other practical reasons to cloak Richmond in a mantle of respectability. Whatever Henry was thinking, and he was careful never to declare his hand, the events of 18 June 1525 must have been reassuring to his subjects. Even as they marvelled at the 'gravity and good manner' that the six-year-old could display, they must have been relieved to see that the king's son was sound and healthy. If he had any defects none of the keen eyed observers at Henry VIII's court ever reported them. It must have been a comfort to know that there was a viable alternative to Mary. Also, in 1523, while Mary was still betrothed to Charles V, Henry had been negotiating with the Scots, only to find he was being courted by the French. A betrothal was the traditional means to secure any diplomatic alliance. Yet with the best will in the world, Mary could only be engaged to one person at a time. An illegitimate son was not quite as valuable in the marriage stakes as a legitimate one, but given sufficient status, Richmond could be a useful tool in matters of matrimonial diplomacy.

Indeed, if these events were truly intended to signal Richmond's new position as heir to the English throne, Henry did not go about it in a very systematic or committed manner. Although Henry Tudor had been Earl of Richmond prior to his accession as Henry VII, it should be remembered that this was not an honour normally associated with the direct line of succession. Henry did not make his son Duke of Cornwall, the title traditionally bestowed on the heir apparent, nor did he create him Duke of York, the dignity usually reserved for the monarch's second son. Instead, his titles were those most intimately associated with the Tudor dynasty itself, rather than the estate of royalty. In a similar manner, Henry VII had honoured his mother as Countess of Richmond, without intending to imply that she was destined for the throne.[23]

Henry was clearly reluctant to use any of those lands which might be needed for his legitimate sons. The closest Richmond got to the inheritance of the legitimate heir was a collection of manors in Somerset and Dorset which had been annexed to the Duchy of Cornwall in 1421 by Henry V. These lands, formerly held by Sir Matthew Gourney and briefly granted under Edward IV to George, Duke of Clarence, were not, therefore, specifically part of the duchy. Despite this, in December 1490 they had been included in the charter drawn up by Henry VII for his son and heir, Arthur.[24] The king did allow Richmond to hold the lordship of Middleham in Yorkshire, which in 1534 was described as 'his second son's inheritance which is parcel of the Dukedom of York'. However, the impressive residence that was Middleham Castle was specifically excluded from the grant.

Rather than signalling his intention to place a crown on his head, it might be more accurate to suggest that Henry VIII wanted to provide for his illegitimate son in a manner which stressed their blood relationship, not his place in the succession.

Henry VIII was obviously not yet willing to abandon hopes of one, or even two legitimate sons. Should he have a male heir, that child would automatically take precedence over the unofficial Princess of Wales. An existing Duke of Cornwall or Duke of York would be a very different matter. At the very least Henry was keeping his options open. Indeed, the decision to bestow upon the young Duke of Richmond those lands traditionally associated with the Beaufort and Tudor lines neatly sidestepped any direct consideration of the child's exact status in respect of the succession.

Although it had sometimes been claimed that Richmond was given precedence even over Mary, his patent expressly stated that he outranked all but the king's (and his successor's) legitimate issue. In 1525 Henry's 'entirely beloved daughter' still outranked him. Although she was never formally created Princess of Wales, to all intents and purposes she held that position. When she was sent to Ludlow in the Welsh Marches, it was a tacit acknowledgement of her status as Henry's heir and she was spoken of as if she was Princess of Wales. In 1525 the Venetian ambassador wrote that 'the Princess went to her Principality of Wales with a suitable and honourable escort'. Even Charles V, who was keen to protect his cousin Mary's interests in England, so that he might use them to his own advantage, did not become unduly concerned about Richmond's honours affecting her rights for several years to come. Certainly, in marriage negotiations at least, Henry VIII was still prepared to offer Mary as England's heir apparent, if he had no legitimate son.

The spate of honours that accompanied Richmond's elevation is also evidence that Henry was keen to use the occasion for wider political advantage, as he replenished his depleted nobility.[25] Royal blood was much in evidence. The new Earl of Lincoln was Henry Brandon, the king's nephew by his younger sister Mary and her husband Charles Brandon, Duke of Suffolk. Although their elder son, who had been born with such commendable promptness in 1516, had not survived infancy, their second son was now a promising three-year-old. The new

Marquess of Exeter, Henry Courtenay, was the king's cousin, the son of Henry's maternal aunt, Katherine, from her marriage to William, Earl of Devon. Sir Thomas Manners, now to be Earl of Rutland, was a great-nephew of Edward IV. Henry Clifford, the new Earl of Cumberland, would subsequently cement his ties to the Tudor dynasty through his marriage to Henry VIII's niece, Eleanor Brandon. Even Sir Thomas Boleyn, who was created Viscount Rochford, was family too in a way, being the father of the king's most recent mistress, Mary Boleyn.

While Richmond's elevation was by far the most spectacular, these other creations were intended to do more than simply reflect his glory. After the death of Richard de la Pole, the last militant sprig of the Yorkist line, Henry Brandon's creation as Earl of Lincoln was particularly significant in signalling the eradication of their claim to the English throne and the ascendancy of the Tudors. At a stroke Henry demonstrated good lordship by rewarding his loyal nobility and created a network of kinship and alliances to help secure his dynasty. At best, these nobles would provide loyal support to his legitimate heir, although there was also the unspoken thought that one of these near relations might be a suitable candidate to follow him on the throne.[26]

From this point, despite being only six years old, Richmond also became an independent magnate in his own right. Like any other noble in the realm, he was now expected to support himself from his own estates and revenues. Although Henry covered a good deal of the costs, many of the expenses relating to Richmond's elevation, including £13 6s 8d 'for sealing and writing the patents of creation of the earldom of Nottingham and Dukedom of Richmond and Somerset' came out of Richmond's coffers. A large number of the 'necessaries for the household' now being assembled, including more than £63 on 'hangings for chambers and other stuff', were paid for by Richmond himself.

In contrast, Mary continued to be supported by their father, even after her legitimacy was called into question. The king may well have considered that his son could easily afford the bills. The £20 annuity that he received as Earl of Nottingham was just the tip of the iceberg. In the first year his income of £4,845 exceeded all expectations.[27] Yet, if Henry's goal was to gain acceptance of his son as heir apparent, it is curious that he chose to ennoble him in a manner which stressed his independence, rather than bring him closer into the Royal Household.

On 16 July 1525, Richmond's immediate prospects were made no clearer by his appointment as Lord High Admiral of England. This decision was not a case of needs must. The present admiral was the very capable Thomas Howard, Duke of Norfolk. Nor is it something that Henry can have done on a whim. Only eleven years previously Norfolk had been granted the office for life. Now Henry was required to mollify the disgruntled duke with a generous exchange of lands. Even then Norfolk was not exactly happy. He took his time in surrendering his patent, claiming, with rather bad grace a month later, that it had been among other papers. Because Richmond was so young, Arthur, Viscount Lisle took on the day-to-day responsibilities of the post as vice-admiral. While this may have been a cheaper option, not even Henry would have chosen to deeply offend one of his senior nobles purely in the interests of economy. A more plausible explanation is that the king wanted to make the new Duke of Richmond a more public figure. Most Tudor government was organised on a county-to-county basis and a national office like Lord Admiral was a rare commodity. Now, by his proclamations if not actually in person, the whole country would be familiar with the king's natural son.

Then, before the summer was over, it also became apparent that there was a more concrete and immediate reason for Richmond's lavish new status than a vague or future policy over the succession. As well as his appointment as Warden General of the Marches towards Scotland (another office recently relinquished by the Duke of Norfolk), Richmond was also granted several other posts which effectively placed the government of the north of England in the hands of the king's son.[28] The policy of employing wardens for the East, Middle and West Marches were to be brought under the auspices of a newly resurrected Council of the North, a council that Richmond would preside over in the name of the king.

This was obviously a significant aspect of Henry's immediate intentions. Several parts of Richmond's honours were clearly designed with this appointment in mind. The inclusion of manors in Westmoreland and Yorkshire gave him a personal interest in local affairs. To further support this process, Wolsey made him High Steward of the Bishopric of Durham and High Steward of the Liberties of the Archbishop of York. Finally Sheriff Hutton Castle, where his new household would be established, was a proven base for government of the north.

At the same time Mary was to go to Ludlow as the figurehead of a similar body for the Marches of Wales. Both the Council of the North and the Council of the Marches had evolved from traditional manorial courts. When Richard, Duke of York had established a court at Sheriff Hutton, he had been ensuring the peace and security of his own estates. It had only been brought under royal control when he seized the throne as Richard III.[29] The sparsely populated north of England, with its deep-rooted feudal loyalties and distance from the seat of government, presented particular problems for control.[30] Henry VII had made use of the authority of Margaret Beaufort's council as Countess of Richmond, but after her death in 1509 Henry VIII had made do with the appointment of local gentry to police the Marches as lord wardens. Unfortunately, their commission from the king was not always sufficient to ensure order. In February 1522, the Bishop of Carlisle, sent north to see to preparations for the anticipated war with Scotland, complained of so much theft and extortion that 'all the country goeth, and shall more, to waste'.

In the spring of 1523, Henry was still pursuing war with Scotland, rather than seeing to the state of the north. In between fighting the Scots the king's lieutenant, Thomas Howard, then Earl of Surrey, made some efforts to restore order in the north, sending a long and detailed report to Wolsey of what still needed to be done. In the end it was only the resistance to taxation that brought the danger sharply into focus, in particular the Amicable Grant of 1525. This demand for one sixth of lay income and one third of clerical income came hot on the heels of an especially heavy subsidy. The country's mood was far from generous and there was widespread opposition. Henry made as dignified a retreat as possible, claiming he 'never knew of that demand' and leaving Wolsey to bear the brunt of the blame for this unpopular measure. It was clearly time for central government to exercise a firmer hand over the far reaches of the realm.

The decision to send Richmond to Sheriff Hutton was derived from a number of factors, which were not related to the succession. To hand such power to an established feudal magnate, such as the Earl of Northumberland, might invite as many problems as it solved. The region needed to be brought under the king's control, not establish a rival centre of patronage and power. The use of a lesser noble, like Lord Thomas Dacre, had already brought its own difficulties. In February 1525 he had been imprisoned in the Fleet for his inability to keep order as Warden of the East and Middle Marches. Since both the most powerful church posts, Archbishop of York and Bishop of Durham, were held by Wolsey that option was also lost. In the circumstances, the decision to use Henry's six-year-old illegitimate son was probably derived as much from practical necessity as concrete political policy. Despite the documents and instructions 'signed with the gracious hand of the King's Highness' it is entirely possible that the original architect of this plan was Richmond's godfather, Wolsey.

The cardinal certainly seems to have had his own agenda for exploiting Richmond's usefulness. Many of Wolsey's political schemes and government initiatives would rely on Richmond, not necessarily for their success, but that they might be attempted at all. As the Duke's Council, headed by Brian Higdon, Dean of York, began to take shape, almost all of the senior officers had prior links to the cardinal. Only the treasurer, Sir Godfrey Foljambe, the vice-chamberlain, Richard Page, and the cofferer, Sir George Lawson, have been identified expressly as the king's men.[31] Richmond perhaps expressed something more than pro forma respect when he wrote to Wolsey in March 1529:

> to whose favour and goodness no creature living is more bound than I am. And like it hath pleased Almighty God and the king's Highness much part by the means and good favour of your Grace to prefer and advance me in honour.[32]

In fact, Wolsey was perhaps more beholden to Richmond, since this particular initiative in Tudor local government could not have been attempted without him.

However, Richmond was no John of Gaunt or Earl of Northumberland to rule over northern parts as a feudal lord. He had no existing power base or affinity in the north, and he was, after all, only six. Rather than his council being the executive arm of the duke's will, his youth allowed Wolsey to place the real business of the council in the hands of educated professionals, largely clerics and lawyers, who were accustomed to working at the centre of Tudor government. Wolsey's 'new men' were by no means unsuited to their task. Many of them had firsthand experience of the unique difficulties of the north, having served under Wolsey in his capacity as Archbishop of York or Bishop of Durham. Between them they had a wealth of clerical and legal experience, including canon, civil, chancery and equity law, which allowed them to exercise the same function as the king's courts in London. Significantly, none of Richmond's officers were above the rank of knight. It remained to be seen whether this new initiative would be successful in controlling the established northern lords.[33]

From the outset there were indications that more might be asked of them than they could deliver. In a significant departure from previous models the authority of Richmond's council was not confined to Yorkshire but extended right across the border counties, though it was not a complete departure from the traditional feudal form. The council was still responsible for the administration of Richmond's lands and household. In January 1527 the surveyor and general receiver of his estates, Thomas Magnus, arranged 'for divers great causes to meet with sundry my lord of Richmond's officers in Lincolnshire'. He then made a substantial detour through Northamptonshire and Cambridgeshire, in order 'to survey and see my lord's lands in those parts'. In a similar manner one of the council, William Franklyn, Archdeacon of Durham, was pressed into service to take a view of Richmond's lands in the north. In addition, all manner of domestic concerns, from the order in the kitchen to the arrangements for Christmas, were as much part of their duties as the government and security of the north.

It did not take long for these dual requirements to clash. Henry decided that Richmond should have a chapel at Sheriff Hutton 'because the Lord Dacre and the Lord Latimer have chapels'. The council begged to be allowed to put this matter off until they had tackled the instructions they had already been given 'for the good order as well of my said Lord's household, as of the north parts of this realm, which we esteem to be matters of no small importance'. The government of the north was bound to be a difficult and time-consuming task; and the administration of the large and complex community that was a ducal household was also a significant undertaking. If one was to be preferred to the other, then the envisaged model of justice and domesticity was going to suffer.

A second potential difficulty was the king's and Wolsey's evident inclination to use Richmond's patronage as if it were their own. The cardinal's role was by no means confined to setting up the establishment. In 1527 when the Duke of Norfolk wanted to place his servant in Richmond's household, he was required to ask Wolsey 'to write a letter unto my lord of Richmond's council to admit him' as he had been advised that they would not do so 'without your grace's letters to them directed for that purpose'. In his turn the cardinal, like any good lord, also assumed responsibility for promoting the welfare of Richmond's servants. When the duke's chamberlain, Sir William

Parr, hoped to secure a grant of lands from the king, it was Wolsey who pressed his suit. While it was natural that Richmond's officers should consult Wolsey regarding their role as the king's Council of the North, their eagerness to defer to him over other matters was rather at odds with Richmond's role as an independent magnate.

The role of the king in his son's affairs was even more complex. The creation of a separate household, financed from his own lands, did not stop Henry from regarding his son's possessions as his to bestow. There was, of course, an element of royal prerogative in this, since even the most established magnate would be hard pressed to deny the express wish of the crown. When Henry VII had taken a liking to a manor-house at Woking, even his mother, despite her obvious reluctance, had deemed it wiser to relinquish the property.[34] Richmond's position was much less secure; Henry was his father as well as his king. Despite his extensive possessions he was still a minor and his illegitimate status meant his reliance on Henry's favour was absolute. In March 1527, when a parsonage fell vacant in the manor of South Molton in Devon, Richmond's council meekly sent up a blank paper, already embossed with Richmond's seal, so that the king could chose the new incumbent. Yet if Henry truly wanted his son's authority as a representative of the crown to be effective, then it had to be seen to be respected, even by him.

While the child's existence may have been generally known in court circles, no one knew how the country at large would receive him. When the young duke began his journey northwards to take up his responsibilities at Sheriff Hutton, his council meticulously recorded how he had been greeted:

> My Lord of Richmond departed from William Jekyll's house unto my Lady Parrs, where his grace was marvelously well intreated and had good cheer . . . *and from my Lady Parr's unto Huntingdon no person of all the Country met with my Lord's Grace saving only at*

Huntingdon [author's italics], Dr Hall met his Grace without the town, and upon the bridge the bailiffs with the honest men of the town presented unto his grace, four great pikes and four tenches. And at Huntingdon the Abbot of Ramsey sent unto his Grace certain swans, cranes, and other wild fowl, in a present.[35]

Everything was done to ensure that Richmond's train would be an impressive sight as it wound its way across the country. His council, gentlemen and servants, were dressed in his livery of blue and yellow, crested with white. Each of them wore Richmond's badge, a demi-lion rampant, bursting out of a Tudor rose, bordered with gold embroidery. The horses were elaborately trapped in cloth of gold or silver or rich satins and velvets. Richmond himself rode in a lavish horse litter that Wolsey provided for the occasion. Padded with crimson velvet and cloth of gold, this was also embroidered with his arms. No casual observer was to remain ignorant of who had just passed by.

The sheer number of carts required to carry those things necessary to the state of a duke, including 120 sheaves of arrows, 20 gilt javelins in leather cases and 47 other javelins, must have added to the visual impact. The bill for carriage by land and water was over £90. Richmond's wardrobe alone consisted of numerous doublets, short coats, long coats, cloaks, shirts, hose, bonnets and eight pairs of shoes. For the household there were vestments and altar cloths for his clergy; pewter, board cloths and napkins for his table and for the kitchen more than forty types of pots and pans, which all cost £1,193.[36] Since they were so encumbered with bags and baggage, expedience alone must have demanded a leisurely pace, which also provided a perfect opportunity to show the duke off to the country in an appropriately stately manner.

Following his investiture into the Order of the Garter, Richmond spent some time with his father at Hampton Court. Members of his household, including his tutor, John Palsgrave, and his Master of the Horse, Sir Edward Seymour, as well as a number of his councillors, had already begun to assemble. The child finally left from Sir William Jekyll's house at Stoke Newington in Middlesex on 26 July 1525. From there he went to Northampton, where Lady Maud Parr (the mother of Henry VIII's last wife, Katherine Parr), gave the young Duke 'a grey ambling nag'. At this point the Duke of Norfolk and others, who were providing an honourable escort out of London, took their leave of Richmond, carrying messages from the duke and his company back to the king.

Leaving Northampton the following morning, Richmond travelled north in daily stages, passing through Buntingford, Shengay and Huntingdon, where there was a day's rest on the Sunday, until he reached Collyweston on 1 August. Once the favourite residence of Henry VIII's grandmother, Margaret Beaufort, this was one of the properties granted to Richmond at his elevation. In a letter of 2 August, his council assured Wolsey that the duke was not finding the journey at all arduous, being 'in better case [condition] and more lusty of his body, than his grace was at the first taking of his journey'.

However, Wolsey's expensive new horse litter, no doubt also intended as a concession for a small child over such a long distance, was not a success with the six-year-old duke. As his council apologetically reported:

> In all which journey my lord's grace rode not in his horse litter, but only from William Jekyll's house 3 or 4 miles, which riding in his said horse-litter his grace liked nothing; but ever since his grace hath ridden upon his hobby [pony], and hath been very well at ease.[37]

If the pony was the 'little bay ambling' which Richmond was given by the Marquess of Dorset, then perhaps the excitement of the gift fuelled his determination to ride like the grown-ups. From the beginning Richmond showed every sign of being a lively and somewhat demanding charge, one not above exploiting his status in order to get his own way. It is perhaps as well to remember that while it was not unusual for royal children to be expected to perform in an adult manner this did not make them grown-up. Almost as if this was a minority government, the tension between the power and authority vested in the duke and the freedom of action actually allowed to the child would be an ongoing source of problems and dilemmas.

The party broke their journey at Collyweston for a week. Not for the last time Richmond benefited from the extensive programme of improvements that Margaret Beaufort had made to her possessions. Collyweston boasted the particular comforts of a gallery, library and chapel. The gardens had been laid out with planted ponds and summer-houses, with an adjacent park for hunting and other sports. Richmond also seems to have reaped the rewards of another of his great-grandmother's legacies. Margaret Beaufort had always been a popular local patron. Now, in his turn, local dignitaries warmly received Richmond when the Abbots of Peterborough and Crowland sent him 'certain goodly presents of swans, crane and other wild fowl'.

If Richmond felt in any way overawed by recent events there is no sign of it. During his stay Davy Cecil, the Keeper of Cliff Park and Steward of Collyweston took him hunting. It was afterwards proudly recorded that the six-year-old had 'killed a buck himself'. Still mindful of exactly how Richmond was being treated the council also happily reported that Cecil, at his own expense, had 'made his Grace and all his folks right good cheer'. Given the size of the child's entourage this must have been quite a costly privilege for the steward.

On 7 August the party finally left Collyweston on their next leg towards York. Now, news of Richmond's impending arrival had begun to travel before him. Sir John Husse was eager to pay his respects and despite an affliction which left him barely able to ride, he expressed his intention of attending upon the duke when he passed through Grantham in Lincolnshire. The party continued on via Marton Abbey, near Stillington, until on 17

August the duke and his company at last arrived in York. They remained there until 28 August when Richmond was escorted from the city by his officers and members of the local gentry, who 'attended on his grace and brought him on his way towards Sheriff Hutton' to officially take up his new duties as the head of the king's Council of the North.

3

Sheriff Hutton

Sheriff Hutton Castle, where Richmond would be based for the next four years, was an imposing three-storey structure that dominated the local area from its elevated position. On his tour of England in 1534 John Leland 'saw no house in the North so like a princely lodgings'. Passing through the magnificent gatehouse emblazoned with Yorkist crests, three wards or courtyards led to the great sweeping staircase, which gave access to the duke's lodgings. However, the castle had last known greatness at the end of the previous century and had since fallen below the standard of a residence appropriate for a duke. While the chambers intended for Richmond were in reasonably good order, much of the rest of the castle had fallen into neglect and disrepair.

A survey of the castle found that the lead on the roof was thin and worn, the stonework needed attention in several places and the chimneys (which clearly needed sweeping) were 'very noisesome when they be occupied'. Even the apparently splendid towers needed patching or rebuilding. Large parts of the walls had actually fallen down and of the two sets of iron gates, one set was rusted and the other set was missing. A well of 'fair water' and a serviceable bakehouse and brewhouse were only small comfort to the duke's large entourage, who now had to make themselves as comfortable as possible. At once Richmond's council set about returning the castle to its former splendour, spending over £321 on repairs. As the new walls and chimneys rose above the horizon, this was as vivid a symbol as any that there was a new policy towards government in the north.

Sheriff Hutton was intended to be a visible symbol of royal authority. More like a small community than a domestic residence, 245 people, only slightly fewer than the establishment set up for the Princess Mary at Ludlow, were considered necessary to fulfil the needs of one small duke. Only two members of the prestigious new household, the schoolmaster and the nurse, were any real concession to the actual needs of a six-year-old child. All of the usual household departments were represented, including a cellar, slaughter-house, spicery and sausagery. Although not entirely self-sufficient, most basic needs could be met within the castle walls. The castle had its own stable, laundry and even its own barber. Below stairs there were cooks, labourers and menial staff. Above stairs there were ushers, grooms, pages and footmen for the privy and strangers' chambers, and cupbearers, carvers and waiters to attend upon the duke.

Richmond's arrival caused something of a stir. His council reported how 'all the noble men and other worshipful men of all these north counties daily resorted to his lordship in great number . . . and he [is] as highly esteemed in honour as ever was any young Prince in these parts'. The child seems to have been an object of some curiosity. His tutor expressed his concern that 'the time of learning by your Grace appointed be not interrupted for every trifle or resort of every stranger, but only strangers of honour'. Instead, he suggested that the little duke, who seems to have been quite the tourist attraction, might be encouraged to make some exhibition of his learning for the visitors 'as he was wont [accustomed to] and doth of his other pastimes'.

Visitors to the castle were conducted through chambers decorated with magnificent tapestries, woven into scenes of hunting and hawking or hangings of arras depicting biblical stories and popular allegorical themes, such as the Lady Pleasance accompanied by virtues and assaulted by vices. The rooms were furnished with chairs of crimson velvet, fringed with red silk, and gold, which were embroidered with Richmond's arms. Chairs of black velvet, fringed with green silk, held plump cushions of green velvet embroidered with the king's arms. Four gentlemen ushers were appointed to ensure that access to the duke's own lodgings was strictly controlled. Richmond received callers enthroned on his cloth of gold chair of estate under a matching canopy. Even in the supposed privacy of his bedchamber he slept under a crimson counterpane on a mattress of down. Anyone who had business with Richmond or his council was to be left in no doubt that power and authority resided here.

In practice, much of the real decision-making power remained in London. On the very day of their relocation to Sheriff Hutton further commissions and instructions arrived from Wolsey. Eager to be seen to be grasping the nettle, the council assured him that the king's subjects in the north would soon be free of all such crimes and injustices that 'as hithertofore they have been molested and disturbed with many ways'. Richmond's officers immediately set about giving form to their good intentions. They arranged court sessions at Newcastle, made enquiries into the state of the county of Northumberland and took recognizances of good behaviour from all the leading gentlemen in the locality, whether they had committed any offence or not. It was in many ways a good beginning, although perhaps slightly over zealous. Several of the local gentry, many of whom were loyal subjects, did not take kindly to being required by clerics and lawyers to give a guarantee of good behaviour. It was an early indication that their task would not be an easy one.

Richmond's council was always keen to ensure Wolsey's support for their actions and not just in matters relating to the government of the north. As the year drew to a close they were anxious that the duke's first Christmas in the north should be staged in an appropriate manner. In early November they wrote earnestly seeking Wolsey's advice over the important matter of New Year gifts. William Amyas was sent to London to see to the making of a suitable gift for the king. The council also suggested six senior members of the Royal Household, the queen, the French queen (Mary Tudor, now Duchess of Suffolk), the Dukes of Norfolk and Suffolk, and the Marquesses of Exeter and Dorset, as other possible recipients of gifts from the duke. If protocol required the inclusion of Katherine of Aragon, who was not best placed to appreciate an expensive present from her husband's illegitimate son, it is interesting that his half-sister Mary was omitted. In the end it seems most of the illustrious list were to be disappointed, since only £6 9s 5d was paid for the gifts that year.

In the event, Christmas at Sheriff Hutton seems to have passed off in some style. Despite the mild disappointment that the Earl of Northumberland and the Earl of Westmorland did not come, the council reported that he had passed 'a right honourable Christmas' with several members of the nobility, as well as many local people, coming to pay their respects. If Richmond's household was a true parallel to Mary's then the silver gilt 'ship for frankincense' found among his goods was set up as the centre-piece of the celebrations. The king's gift to his son was a gilt ewer 'with a star upon the cover, and my Lord's arms', which weighed just over 36 oz. Wolsey sent a garter of crown gold for which he paid £4 11s 4d. Nor were they the only ones to pay their respects to the duke. Richmond's accounts include the significant sum of £9 6s 8d paid out in reward to those who flocked to the castle to bring gifts.

Richmond's involvement with the actual business of the council was generally limited to specific episodes. However, he was the focal point of all formal occasions and expected to play a full part. As the king's representative in the north it was his duty to receive local dignitaries, like Lord William Dacre and Henry, Lord Neville, when they came to pay their respects. Perched on his chair of estate, and surrounded by his council, even this exuberant child seems to have been impressed by the gravity of the situation. When Henry Percy, Earl of Northumberland, first attended on Richmond at Sheriff Hutton he was suitably impressed. Having showered the child with praises he told Wolsey 'my dulled wit cannot disclose unto your grace how highly he excelleth in every virtuous pastime'. According to William Franklyn, Archdeacon of Durham, the diminutive duke was:

> a child of excellent wisdom and towardness; and, for his good and quick capacity, retentive memory, virtuous inclination to all honour, humanity, and goodness, I think hard it would be to find any creature living of twice his age, able or worthy to be compared to him.[1]

While some allowance must be made for the politics of flattery, the general tone of such reports does suggest that Richmond showed every promise of being the equal of his father.

Richmond's general care was the responsibility of his nurse, Anne Partridge, who received 50s as her quarter's wages in 1528. The officers of the household were exclusively male and although some of them were married, Anne and the maid who accompanied her were probably the closest thing Richmond had to a maternal influence in his daily life.

The duke's education was initially entrusted to John Palsgrave. Previously employed as schoolmaster to the king's sister Mary, Palsgrave was apparently well qualified for the task. He had graduated with a Bachelor of Arts degree from Cambridge in 1504. The author of a Latin play and a new approach to learning French grammar, his scholarship appears impressive. He later boasted that he had devised a new and simpler method for Richmond to learn Latin. A former secretary to the king, he claimed Henry VIII had personally endorsed his appointment.

Keen to make a good impression, Palsgrave enlisted the help of his friend and patron Sir Thomas More to ensure the duke would acquire the moral values thought to be imparted by a classical education. Stephen Gardiner also recommended the study of both Latin and Greek. As the author of *'Lesclarcissement de la Langue Francoyse'* Palsgrave was well able to teach French, and William Saunders, another former servant of Wolsey, was sent up to instruct Richmond in music and singing. One of the first entries in

Richmond's accounts was 40s for a pair of virginals, a favourite instrument of Henry VIII.

If this seems a fairly ambitious programme for a six-year-old, it was no more than was expected of many noble children. The little duke was not expected to be an instant scholar. The antiquary Thomas Leland presented Richmond with a book to help him to learn his alphabet. Following the practice laid down by Sir Thomas Elyot for the education of an infant prince, Palsgrave asked for a painter to illustrate his lessons. He made every effort to make Richmond's studies as pleasant as possible 'in so much that many times his officers wot [know] not whether I learn him or play with him', keeping the lessons short to accommodate the attention span of such a young child. Nor was his education confined to what could be learnt in the schoolroom. Richmond was to be a true renaissance prince. He was taught archery and the basic skills which might, one day, make him a fine jouster. He also developed a love of hunting, keeping hawks, greyhounds and bloodhounds in order to do so. As part of this well-rounded education he was also taught to dance.

Palsgrave's initial reports of the child's progress were promising. Writing to the king he praised Richmond as the best student he had ever had. They had studied Latin and Greek grammar and moved on to Virgil and other classical works. Despite some minor concerns over his lisp, which Palsgrave hoped would disappear as soon as Richmond lost his milk teeth, the child was doing well. Writing to Sir Thomas More, with whom Palsgrave might have felt at liberty to be more candid, he still claimed that he had never had a pupil to equal the duke, 'no man, rich or poor, had ever better wit'. Although there is no evidence that Mary had any companions in her schoolroom at Ludlow, Richmond was not taught in isolation. The boys who shared his studies included William Parr, the nephew of his chamberlain and his maternal uncles, twelve-year-old George Blount and his younger brother Henry. In both age and station the children were a rather mixed bunch, but no one could claim that Richmond lacked the company of other children.

In addition to his duties in the schoolroom, Palsgrave was also appointed as a member of Richmond's council, though exactly what other duties this entailed is not clear. While Palsgrave was a signatory to a number of letters concerning council business, it may simply have been a matter of prestige. In any case his tenure at Sheriff Hutton was destined to be rather short lived. P.L. Carver's claim that he remained a member of Richmond's council until December 1526 is based on the misdating of a letter, which properly belongs to 25 December 1525, the only Christmas that Richmond passed at Sheriff Hutton. By February 1526, merely six months after his arrival, Palsgrave had already been replaced as schoolmaster by Dr Richard Croke.[2]

Palsgrave's departure may have been hastened by the death of Sir Richard Wingfield on 22 July 1525. Deprived of his patron he soon found himself in financial difficulties. Even as he was seeking the assistance of his former pupil Mary Tudor, Duchess of Suffolk, to secure the benefice of Cawston in Norfolk, he instructed William Stevinson to ask her husband for a loan. As tutor he was entitled to a stipend of £13 6s 8d per annum and thanks to Sir Thomas More he also had a number of church livings to supplement his income. Yet now he pleaded with More 'for your accustomed goodness to continue until such time that I may once tread underfoot this horrible monster, poverty'. To make his point he also addressed similar pleas to the king and Richmond's mother Elizabeth Blount.

Palsgrave may well have had real problems. But it is difficult to separate his genuine difficulties from the general sort of complaints that were the common lot of most sixteenth-century tutors. He presented the fact that Richmond was surrounded by those who thought a young nobleman should spend his time hunting, hawking, riding or in 'many other devices found within the house when he cannot go abroad' as a personal slight. Yet his experience would have struck a chord with many tutors during this period. Although men were beginning to realise that a child needed more than a strong sword arm and a firm seat on a horse to succeed in this new age, the old feudal prejudices still lingered. Many preferred to see the king's son in the saddle rather than poring over books; that should be left to clerics. Palsgrave's claims that he was insulted and belittled, with even Richmond's mind being poisoned against him, until the child would soon not believe a word he said, was perhaps little more than the thinly veiled contempt endured by many clerics.

It is also possible that the tutor had a rather exaggerated sense of his importance in the household. He seems to have equated his role with that of Sir William Parr, the chamberlain, and Richard Page, the vice-chamberlain. Nevertheless the 'six sundry articles' that Palsgrave alleged had been lodged against him do suggest that moves were afoot to take advantage of his present precarious position and oust him from his post. Since the tutor was certain he still enjoyed the full confidence of the king, he had to look elsewhere for the author of his present difficulties. Such a person would have to be sufficiently powerful to deflect the combined influence of Mary Tudor, Sir Thomas More and Elizabeth. The obvious choice would be Thomas Wolsey.

The vast majority of those who taunted Palsgrave answered directly to the cardinal. If Wingfield had engineered the tutor's appointment, then Wolsey had no particular reason to come to his aid and perhaps every reason to wish to see him removed in favour of a candidate of his own. Tellingly, Palsgrave did not appeal to Wolsey to help him out of his difficulties, perhaps not least because in 1515 Wolsey had refused to grant Mary Tudor's requests that her old schoolmaster be made Archdeacon of Derby, or be given a living in the diocese of Durham. In contrast Richard Croke's first loyalty seems to have been to Wolsey. It is probably only coincidence that he was a distant blood relation of the Blounts of Kinlet. Since he had fallen out with his former patron, John Fisher, Croke had a far more pressing reason for entering Richmond's service and would have been suitably grateful to Wolsey for securing the appointment.

Certainly, subsequent events suggest that Palsgrave resented the cardinal. In April 1528 he was rebuked for his attitude towards the King's Council and a search of his papers revealed a number of charges against Wolsey's government. At various times it has been suggested that the articles, which were presumably designed as a basis for attainder, were drawn up under the instructions of, among others, the Duke of Norfolk or Suffolk, Sir Thomas Arundel or Lord Thomas Darcy. However, the enthusiasm that Palsgrave brought to the task also suggests that he had his own agenda. Such enduring bitterness may indicate that Palsgrave held Wolsey responsible for his ignoble and premature departure from the north.

As a Cambridge graduate and reader in Greek at the University, who had studied in Europe, Richard Croke may have anticipated that he was well able to meet the educational needs of a six-year-old. Yet it was not long before he too was complaining that Richmond was all too frequently taken out of lessons to practise archery and other sports. In some respects his complaints mirrored Palsgrave's battles in the schoolroom. His authority was being treated as if it was of no account and clerics in general were being openly demeaned, until even his own pupils felt free to insult him, calling him bastard, fool or rogue. Croke's efforts to reassert his authority by punishment were hampered by the intervention of other members of the household, until the boys had so little respect for him that they felt they could miss lessons whenever they liked.

However, his complaints also highlighted a more serious problem, one that might have repercussions far outside the schoolroom. Richmond probably never saw the vast majority of business handled by his council. A letter written on 3 March 1527 to his father about the state of the north and the 'right good rule and quietness [that] is in these parts' is clearly a school exercise rather than real news. In matters of policy and direction his role was limited to official correspondence issued in his name. For example, in April 1526 Sir Christopher Dacre advised Lord Dacre that he and the Archbishop of Glasgow had received letters from 'my Lord of Richmond'. For this purpose an elaborate seal of the duke's arms, some four inches in diameter, had been commissioned for attachment to all official documents. This made his signature a valuable commodity. Richmond's offices endowed him with a good deal of power and influence and when it came to his patronage the division between nominal and actual authority was much less clearly defined.

In his complaints Croke singled out Sir George Cotton, one of the gentlemen ushers, for indulging the duke so 'he might win the fullest favour for himself'. The tutor protested that Richmond was no longer studying before morning mass or doing any writing before dinner. Indeed, the whole timetable which Wolsey had devised for the duke's studies had simply been set aside. Richmond spent more time with Cotton than in lessons. The tutor's allegation that fools and players had been admitted to the privy chamber to sing bawdy songs is backed up by the £3 18s 8d in the accounts given to 'players and minstrels for rewards', although exactly what a child of Richmond's age made of the entertainment is not recorded.

As a result of these extracurricular activities Croke found the child was now often too tired to study. If Croke scolded him, Cotton made excuses. Worse, the usher had now taken it upon himself to set 'lessons' for the duke, which Croke saw as a thinly veiled excuse to encourage Richmond to write letters in his own hand to abbots and other local figures 'to the great dulling of his wits, spirits, and memory, and no little hurt of his head, stomach, and body', in order to obtain hawks or other small favours for Cotton and his cronies. While the tutor worried that Richmond's handwriting would suffer, he was also careful to remind Wolsey that this was not in keeping with the carefully crafted aura of dignity and status that had been constructed around the duke.

Any hopes that Croke had of improvement were also hampered by the actions of Richmond's chamberlain, Sir William Parr, who Croke alleged was also interfering in Richmond's schedule. On his orders the duke was no longer repeating his lessons after supper and he had arranged for his nephew to hear the daily religious offices of matins and vespers with Richmond. Worse still, the duke was happily exploiting the disunited front displayed by the adults around him and now refused to mind either his usher or his nurse. With some justice Croke predicted that 'a disposition of the best promise . . . may at last be ruined under such masters, who measure everything for their own pleasure and profit, and nothing for the advantage of their lord'. At his wits' end Croke rather dramatically declared that Richmond's education was finished unless something was done.

His solution was a series of five articles that were designed to increase his control over what Richmond learnt, at what times and in whose company, so that he might 'be induced most highly to esteem his book of all his other studies'. A lofty ambition perhaps for a child whose preference for sport over study proclaimed him very much his father's son. All of this was a far cry from the pursuit of virtue and learning originally envisaged for Richmond. Now neither threats nor praises could encourage him to settle to his books. If Croke raised the prospect of chastisement Richmond simply responded 'Master if you beat me, I will beat you'.

Although the idea that a royal child was not subject to corporal punishment has become a popular tradition, with Barnaby Fitzpatrick being cast as the whipping-boy for Edward VI, this was not the case. Other children of rank, such as the Earl of Surrey and Lady Jane Grey, were certainly beaten. Even royal status was no protection. Edward VI's tutor, Richard Cox, was certainly prepared to hit his charge when necessary. On at least one occasion, finding his efforts met with nothing but boredom, and after coaxing and threats had proved ineffective, Cox gave a final warning then hit the child and 'gave him such a wound that he wist [knew] not what to do'. If Edward could be so sharply punished, Richmond's confidence was slightly misplaced.[3] Yet equally there was an increasing reluctance to punish any but the dullest pupils in this manner, if another form of inducement could be found.

Eventually a more suitable solution was found. In a letter probably written in January 1528, Richmond was enthusiastically advising his father:

that I effectually give mine whole endeavour, mind, study, and pleasure to the diligent appliance of all such sciences and feats of learning, as by my most loving Councilors I am daily advertised to stand with your most high and gracious pleasure.[4]

Such keenness was not provoked by a sudden injection of intellectualism. Richmond wanted the king to send him 'a harness [suit of Armour] for my exercise in arms' so that he might practise the warlike exploits he had read about in the commentaries of Caesar. Anxious not to miss out, Richmond also addressed an almost identical letter to Wolsey as his godfather 'to be means for me unto the Kings highness in this behalf'. A combination of texts designed to appeal to the warlike enthusiasms of an active young boy and what looks suspiciously like a little bribery was evidently an effective teaching technique.

While Croke's antagonism towards Cotton rumbled on, his relationship with Richmond clearly improved. When the king recalled him in October 1527, the young duke supplied him with a gracious letter of recommendation. Beautifully written and elegantly phrased, the letter itself was perhaps the best possible testimony to the tutor's 'labour and diligence to induce me in learning'. For his part Croke honoured his promise not to forget his royal charge. Writing from abroad he asked to be remembered 'most humbly to my most dear lord and master, my lord of Richmond' and promised on his return to bring the young duke presents of a replica of Caesar's bridges and an unusual model galley 'such as few men have seen' that had five oars. Whatever intellectual tastes Croke had been able to instill in his pupil were obviously still more practical than contemplative, but it was a sign of his willingness to learn.

Whether Croke anticipated a return to the schoolroom at Sheriff Hutton is not clear: perhaps he welcomed the opportunity of a dignified exit, perhaps no one was quite sure how long the king's business might keep him away. In any case, his departure necessitated the appointment of another tutor.

While Richmond refers to him simply as 'a new schoolmaster' this may have been George Folbury, a contemporary of Croke's at Cambridge. He graduated in 1514 and become a fellow of both Clare and Pembroke Colleges. He took his Master of Arts in 1517 and was preacher to the University in 1519, graduating Bachelor of Theology in 1524. This appointment could have coincided with his return from Montpellier, where he is believed to have obtained his Doctorate in Divinity. This time there are no complaints. Either whatever measures Wolsey had implemented were effective or this tutor had fewer illusions about his proper place in the duke's household.

If things were quite as bad as either Palsgrave or Croke claimed, it is amazing Richmond ever learnt anything at all. Yet the child could boast elegant handwriting, not unlike that used by his half-sister Elizabeth, which was a refreshingly legible change from the scrawl favoured by many of his elders. Unfortunately, many of the letters he wrote at this time were formal set pieces to the king or Wolsey designed to 'make a demonstration of this my proceeding [progress] in writing', no doubt penned with his tutor breathing down his neck. Others are either a formal request for some favour for himself or a recommendation for one of his servants. Unlike Edward VI, who found endless pleasure in schemes and papers, Richmond was perhaps more like his father: willing, even eager, to attend to business when there was a discernible goal, but lacking the patience to pursue a project purely for its own sake.

Richmond's tutors clearly felt the burden of educating the king's only son. Perhaps they worried that a good mind was not being stretched to its full potential and that they might be called to account. Perhaps they had a vision of the perfect, learned prince and were being frustrated in their attempts to mould Richmond in this image. Certainly, Croke's desire that Richmond 'should write no thing of his own hand but in Latin' was out of step with an age that increasingly preferred to use the vernacular for personal correspondence. Only one of Richmond's surviving letters was written in Latin and that, a eulogy for his late servant,

Matthew Boynton, was written when Richmond was about eleven. His tutors may have forgotten that if Richmond was truly intended to grow up to emulate his father, as he showed every sign of doing, he would need several strings to his bow. Since their concerns were not echoed by any other members of Richmond's council, it seems safe to assume that things were not so bad. While his outdoor pursuits may have offended the sensibilities of his tutors, to his council they were obviously part of the necessary education of a virtuous prince.

When it was first decided that Richmond should go to the north as the king's lieutenant little can have been known about his capabilities. In a sense it did not matter. His blood relationship to the king, his titles and his physical presence all served the required purpose. However, he gradually began to attract notice from abroad. In April 1526 when James V, King of Scotland, sent some papers to Wolsey he desired to be recommended to his cousin. The following month Richmond was included in a list of nobility drawn up by the members of the Cognac League to whom they offered pensions out of any lands conquered in Italy, as part of their plan to persuade Henry VIII to take up arms against Charles V. Richmond was to receive 30,000 ducats per annum. His inclusion was more than an obvious piece of flattery, it reflected Richmond's role as the premier magnate in England. Wolsey was only promised 10,000 ducats, although, in this case, their generosity may also have been prompted by Richmond's presence at court.

The duke's own movements are often poorly documented. Reliance on the correspondence of his council has perpetuated the view that he was continually resident in the north. However, Richmond's person was not required for the day to day running of his council, which frequently decamped to Newcastle or Carlisle without him. Even the various removals of his household are only a general guide to the actual location of the duke. Such speculation is not helped by the fact that Richmond's own correspondence is seldom dated to any particular year. However, just as Mary did not spend all her time in the Welsh Marches during this period, so Muriel St Clare Byrne offers reasonable grounds to suggest that Richmond was back at Collyweston in Northamptonshire by February 1526.[5] Furthermore, his name on a charter drawn up at Westminster raises the possibility that he was at court in May 1526. He seems to have been back at Sheriff Hutton by September 1526 when Thomas Magnus included his request for the Cardinal's blessing in his letter. Yet, it is entirely possible that the king's Lieutenant-General north of the Trent spent at least some of 1526 in the south.

In common with any large household of the sixteenth century, the needs of health and hygiene required that Richmond and his entourage should move at regular intervals to allow Sheriff Hutton to be thoroughly cleaned. However, since he lacked any other suitable manor in the vicinity, another lodging had to be found. From 1526, he habitually spent the winter months at Pontefract Castle. Rather like Sheriff Hutton this also required extensive repairs, which cost in excess of £198. It was here that Richmond spent Christmas in 1526, sending to his father for his New Year's gift two little gilt pots, engraved with branches. In contrast to their anxiety the previous year, the council's obligatory letter to Wolsey reflected a certain satisfaction:

his said Grace hath kept a right honourable Christmas and to visit see and attend upon his said Grace here hath been good number of honourable and worshipful personages both spiritual and temporal and many honest folk of the commonalty.[6]

This year Richmond was also persuaded to write to his father in thanks for his present, a large gilt bowl with a cover, 'pounced with great drops', which weighed 48 ounces.

His letter is as brief as any modern parent might expect from a young child struggling to express his gratitude for a heavy, expensive gift that had far more to do with status and prestige than the interests of a seven-year-old boy. In a very elegant hand he politely asked his father's blessing, delivered up his thanks for the 'honourable and goodly' gift before closing 'humbly beseeching your grace to accept and take this my letter penned with mine own hand for a poor token at this time'.

This period also marked Richmond's initial foray into the myriad waters of diplomacy. Sir Thomas Magnus received letters from James V and his mother, Margaret Tudor, asking for a selection of hunting dogs. Suspecting that this was simply a ruse for the King of Scotland's messenger to inspect Richmond and investigate the 'manner, form and fashion' of his household, Magnus decided to turn the situation to Richmond's advantage and foster good relations between the young Warden-General of the northern borders and his cousin, 'trusting no thing but much goodness, perfect love, and favour, by this means shall increase'. He showed the letters to Richmond. The duke reacted with enthusiasm and on 11 February 1527 'ten couple of hounds of the best that I have' were dispatched to Scotland along with Nicholas Eton, his yeoman of the hunt and a groom to show the correct method of using the dogs.

The Scots warmly received the overture. James V thanked Richmond for his present and reciprocated with a gift of two brace of hounds and a promise of red hawks. As Magnus advised Wolsey, James had formally expressed his gratitude 'for inducing acquaintance between him and my lord of Richmond's grace', although the king was perhaps most keen to obtain the bloodhounds Richmond had mentioned. Nevertheless, Magnus considered the matter important enough to send copies of all the letters to Wolsey. He was particularly pleased that Richmond's servants had been lavishly entertained and well rewarded while in Scotland, since their treatment reflected the respect and esteem in which the duke was held across the border.

Before the month was out this blossoming relationship underwent its first political test. On 26 March 1527 Richmond wrote, in his official capacity as Warden-General of the north, to the King of Scotland about the refusal of the inhabitants of Liddesdale in the border country to comply with an order for redress in respect of several robberies that had been committed by the Scots. James V's reply was co-operative, promising to send the Earl of Angus to see to the matter and Magnus had every reason to hope that the initiative had been beneficial.

On a personal level, James V was probably very pleased with his new hunting dogs and Margaret was almost gushing in her professed affection for her nephew. After all the effort which had gone into creating an aura of power and dignity around the duke, it must have been gratifying to see Richmond being treated with such respect by the ruler of another country. However, if the relationship was to bear real fruit, this in itself was not enough. Unfortunately, tangible rewards were more elusive. A case in point was the fugitive Sir William Lisle and his supporters. In the autumn of 1527 Lisle, who had long been a thorn in the side of Richmond's council, escaped from Newcastle jail. It was believed he had fled into Scotland. Richmond's council wrote time and again to the Scots to secure his arrest, but to no avail.

Fuelled by the belief that the Lisles were being aided by the Armstrongs, some of whom were the Earl of Angus's own servants, the council persevered. After more than a year they advised Wolsey rather wearily:

My Lord of Richmond's grace hath often and many times written . . . for the apprehending taking and delivering of the said Sir William Lisle . . . and at all times we have had right pleasant answers but as yet nothing is done by them to any good effect or purpose.[7]

The personal relationship between the two young princes, rooted in a mutual love of sport and hunting, gave an added lustre to Richmond's position, but it was not strong enough to achieve any real progress in Anglo-Scottish relations. For all their fine words the Scots continued to follow their own agenda and Richmond's tenure in the north was not of sufficient duration to effect any long term gains.

About this time Richmond also made his first foray into the world of matrimonial diplomacy. This in itself was not surprising. Henry was not overendowed with marriageable issue and Richmond was older than most royal infants when launched into the marriage market. However, in this case the circumstances were a little unorthodox. In February 1527 a letter from the English ambassadors in Spain, Sir Gregory Casale and John Russell, advised Wolsey of the competition for the hand of Catherine de Medici, known as the Pope's niece.[8] With Scottish and French interest so strong, the ambassadors, who stressed they had acted 'upon our own mind' rather than by commission from the king, had made some discreet enquiries. Presenting Richmond as 'a Duke in England' who might spend twice as much as any of the present candidates, they said it had been known at once who they meant and it was thought the Pope would be happy to have such an alliance.

Such a bold step would not have been taken unless they were sure that it would be well received by Henry. If Richmond's usefulness as a tool in the marriage market was indeed a factor in his elevation, it is perhaps surprising that negotiations had not already been put in hand. However, this was rather a delicate situation. Catherine de Medici was a valuable prize. Those interested in the bride who was eventually won by Henri, duc d'Orléans, the second son of Francis I, included James V of Scotland. While English diplomats might claim that Richmond was a comparable match, there was no guarantee that the Medicis would feel the same way. While royal bastards had their place in the marriage market, their illegitimate status was expected to be taken into consideration. Henry VIII's recent gift of 30,000 crowns had no doubt encouraged the Pope to look favourably on England, but this gift was intended to secure his support for a marriage between Mary and Francis I and was unlikely to stretch to cover this alliance as well. Better perhaps for the ambassadors to make enquiries, rather than for the king to make an official overture, only to have it ignobly and embarrassingly rebuffed.

In the event, this match was not pursued, perhaps because by March 1527 Wolsey was lobbying for a marriage between Richmond and Charles V's niece, the Infanta Mary of Portugal, born in 1522. Wolsey claimed his chief interest was that the children were of a similar age. Yet, as Wolsey was very well aware, the infanta in question was already betrothed to the Dauphin of France. Under the terms of the Treaty of Madrid, Francis I was due to wed the emperor's sister, Queen Eleanor of Portugal, and her daughter Mary was to marry Francis' heir. From the English point of view such a close alliance between France and Spain could only be detrimental, if not outright dangerous. There was a firm possibility that England would be isolated from European affairs. Wolsey and the king had already taken steps to counter this arrangement. Their initial proposal that Mary might marry the duc d'Orléans had become a suggestion that she might marry Francis I himself. Henry's terms were tempting[9] and in February 1527 a marriage between Mary and Francis had begun to seem a very real possibility.

However, by the time the negotiations for Richmond's marriage were broached, Mary's match was looking increasingly fragile. The sticking point was the Treaty of Madrid. If Francis decided to honour his commitment and marry Eleanor, then the English needed to find another way to ensure their participation at the centre of European affairs. If Richmond married Mary of Portugal, not only would it keep England in the game, but also it would break her engagement to the dauphin, which would free him to marry Mary Tudor. At a stroke England would secure both a French and an Imperial alliance, which would do much to realise Wolsey's dreams of becoming the arbiter of Europe. The danger was that England was not the only player in these games of dynastic diplomacy and when the stakes were so high an illegitimate son was not exactly a trump card.

Anxious not to cause offence, the English ambassadors assured Charles V that if there had been a suitable Hapsburg prince for Mary to marry, they would have offered him the princess. Nevertheless, Richmond was a close blood relative of the king, full of excellent qualities and with the wealth and status of a great prince. Significantly, Mendoza, the Imperial ambassador in England, was satisfied that Henry's affection for his illegitimate son was so strong that Richmond's marriage would be treated with the same 'honour and regard' as any match of his daughter's, the princess. The English ambassadors' further claim that Richmond 'may be easily by the King's means exalted to higher things' has sometimes been taken as an indication that he would be made Henry's heir. Neither Henry nor Wolsey was above attempting to encourage Charles V to believe that the English throne was a prospect in the negotiations. However, in the climate of 1527, it seems far more likely they had something else in mind.

For all of their efforts in singing Richmond's praises the English ambassadors had been unable to extract more than a vague promise from Charles V that he would try and think of some female relation for Richmond to marry. Then a rumour emerged that Henry and Wolsey were hatching a plan to make Richmond King of Ireland. Whether or not this move was ever seriously entertained, the speculation certainly seems timed to enhance Richmond's desirability in the marriage stakes. According to the rumour, prior to her marriage to Francis I, Mary and Henry would both renounce all their rights in Ireland, in favour of the duke. It was obviously supposed to be an attractive idea. With Mary allied to the French, the emperor might see some advantage in having a political interest right on England's shores.

If this was the case, the ploy was not entirely successful. It was immediately assumed that 'it would be tantamount to having a second King of Scotland', making Ireland as great a threat to England as Scotland already proved to be. Since the Archbishop of York, Dr Edward Lee, was quick to reassure that the king and Wolsey could take steps so this would not happen, it does seem the plan was being seriously considered. Even so, it was full of pitfalls.

The Imperial ambassador's claim that it was 'most unwelcome' among the English people was part of his ploy to represent the country as ripe for rebellion, as he was also hinting broadly (and unsuccessfully) that Charles V should launch an invasion of England in order to protect the interests of his aunt and cousin. However, Katherine was predictably annoyed at this apparent diminishment of her daughter's prospects and, more seriously, Mary was presently being offered to the French as Henry's heir apparent. Francis I was not likely to take kindly to the alienation of any part of her inheritance. Finally, Cardinal Grenvelle, who often directed Imperial policy when bouts of illness or depression left Charles V indisposed, had no trouble seeing through the whole plan as a 'wicked scheme' to fracture the Treaty of Madrid.

Grenvelle suggested that Charles should wait until Henry was as good as his word. If he went through with this outrageous idea, they could easily find some other Hapsburg princess for Richmond to marry, one rather more suited to his age and bastard status. Unfortunately for Henry and Wolsey, the Imperial court was only prepared to accept Richmond in a possible marriage alliance when it was to its advantage. In the present circumstances the Infanta of Portugal was too valuable a prize to be sacrificed in such a way. Grenvelle was scornful of the very idea:

> The cardinal's overtures to Don Inigo respecting the king's illegitimate son, and the intention of conferring upon him the title of king, together with the proposal for his marriage, might be considered in the light of a joke, were it not that the cardinal's presumption and folly are well known.[10]

However, Grenvelle was reluctant to reject the proposal out of hand and suggested to Charles that he should make all the right noises. He could easily take refuge in the fact that he was bound by the Treaty of Madrid and the not unreasonable point that Mary of Portugal was not his daughter to bestow. Her father should decide whom she married. The idea of an alternative marriage for Richmond could be couched in vague enough terms to hold English interest, without needing to mention any names. Grenvelle himself confided that he thought one of Charles V's other nieces, the daughters of Isabella, Queen of Denmark, or one of the emperor's illegitimate daughters might make a suitable match.

This, of course, was not what the English wanted at all. The suggestion of one of Isabella's daughters was rapidly brushed aside. The ambassadors countered once again with Mary of Portugal, only to be met with the old protest that she was already betrothed to the dauphin. The English ambassadors stood firm, audaciously suggesting that if Francis I did not marry Eleanor, then Charles V would be looking for another dauphin to marry her daughter. This attempt to equate Richmond with the heir to the French throne was not well received and the Imperials did not scruple to point out that the English 'dauphin' was illegitimate and not quite the prize he was painted as. The ambassador's protestations that the prospective bride and groom were of similar age was not well received either. It was bluntly suggested that Mary's dowry of 300,000 doubloons was the real attraction. In fairness, the English ambassadors' persistence probably owed more to alarm over the increasing likelihood that Francis I intended to honour the treaty and marry Eleanor after all.

By the middle of April 1527 it seemed all too possible that England would lose all prospect of either a French or an Imperial alliance. Wolsey's stipulation that Mary, who everyone agreed was rather small for eleven, could not go to France for another ten months, gave the French an excuse to stall. The emperor's unwillingness to match Richmond with Mary of Portugal and the English unwillingness to consider anyone else brought the Imperial talks to a standstill. The fleeting suggestion that Richmond should marry a French princess was clearly a fall-back position. The French ambassador had already suggested to Francis I that a match with the Duke of Richmond might be a means to salvage negotiations with England. Yet, given that all the unmarried Hapsburgs were female and the French king had three sons, Richmond would have been wasted on a French match. When the English and French finally came to an agreement on 30 April, Mary looked destined for the lesser prize of the duc d'Orléans. Richmond did not feature in the arrangements.

In fact, negotiations for his marriage now came to a grinding halt. Even though Charles V's proposal for one of the daughters of the Queen of Denmark was still on the table, it now looked as if the young duke would not be marrying after all. On 18 May, Mendoza sourly reported that Wolsey seemed to have lost all interest in the marriage of 'the bastard of England'. The ambassador believed this had all been a ruse to free the dauphin to marry Mary and it is hard to see any other explanation. A union with either of the Danish princesses would have been a more than respectable match for the young duke. These were the nieces of an emperor and the daughters of a king and unlike Richmond they were legitimate. If a grand European alliance was a consideration in Richmond's elevation in 1525, this was a lost opportunity. It can only be justified if the purpose of these negotiations was not so much to find Richmond a wife, but to secure the best marriage for his half-sister.

Any idea that Wolsey hoped to see Princess Mary safely married and dispatched to France in order to clear the way for his godson to ascend the throne in England is at odds with his terms for the French match.[11] Also, any such policy would have endangered the French alliance which Wolsey had taken such pains to forge. The French might accept the possibility that Henry could still have a legitimate prince as a calculated risk. They are not likely to have viewed the accession of his illegitimate son with the same equanimity. Nor would it explain why the Imperial match was simply brushed aside. Whatever Richmond's destiny, such a marriage would have enhanced his status. If he had any hopes of the throne this union would have gone a long way to ensure Charles V's natural concerns for his cousin's inheritance were replaced with healthy self-interest in the fortunes of his niece, especially if his gain was at the expense of the French.

Certainly, Charles V was not as disinterested as he had pretended. As England and France moved towards the Treaty of Amiens, he viewed the prospect of their closer alliance with concern. Suddenly, on 17 July, the English ambassador in Spain wrote that the longed-for daughter of Portugal might be bestowed on the Duke of Richmond after all. It was proposed that Richmond might have the eldest daughter, with a dowry of 400,000 ducats and, since there was a danger the Duchy of Milan might fall into the hands of Francis I, it might be better to give that to the duke as well.[12]

The emperor had gained possession of the Duchy of Milan through the defeat and surrender of Sforza, the present duke. Although he was preoccupied with battles with the Turks, Charles V was loath to give up the land. France, fearing encirclement, was equally reluctant to see it remain in Hapsburg hands. To be fair, the possible benefits of this plan were not simply to the advantage of the English. It had all the makings of a grand European alliance with Charles V, Henry VIII and Francis I all bound together in a single accord that 'should be indissoluble'. This was exactly what Wolsey had hoped for. A marriage between Francis and Eleanor might bind France and Spain, but the union of Richmond with Mary of Portugal would allow Mary to marry the dauphin, and all of this would ensure that England's future interests were central to the politics of Europe.

However, it seemed too good to be true and so it proved. On 21 July Lee might have believed that, with careful handling, it could come to pass. Wolsey remained realistic, informing Henry VIII of the progress of the negotiations on 31 July when he wrote of:

the blind and doubtful overture made by Mons Bouclans [John Almain] for the alliance of the duke of Richmond to the daughter of Portugal, with the gift of the Duchy of Milan in contemplation of the same alliance; meaning thereby to interrupt and let [leave off] the conjunction of your highness with the French king.

Unfortunately for Wolsey, Henry was keen to see his son married to a Hapsburg princess, with his own independent kingdom, especially if it came at no cost to himself. Wolsey persevered 'by all ways and means' to ascertain Charles V's good faith and what conditions might apply to this 'gift'. On 5 September he broke the bad news to the king. The Emperor 'mindeth nothing on earth less' than to bestow the Duchy of Milan on Richmond, it was simply a ploy to prevent the English from coming to terms with the French. Henry was not convinced. On 8 September the cardinal was still instructing the English ambassadors to pursue the possibility, although since Wolsey had no wish to upset the primary goal of the French negotiations, they had to be careful 'setting forth in such wise and matter as the French ambassador take no jealously or suspicion thereby'.

Wolsey was convinced that once Charles V knew the treaty between England and France was fully concluded, the proposal would be discreetly dropped. For the Imperials it was a defensive, rather than a proactive policy. The prize of the Duchy of Milan and the hand of the sought-after infanta would only be delivered at the cost of fracturing the French alliance. Accordingly, the next time the English ambassadors put forward Richmond's name they were politely rebuffed on the grounds that the duchy was too small for him. In the end Sforza was restored to Milan in 1529 once he had been safely married to Christina, the second daughter of the Queen of Denmark, who had been offered as a possible bride for Richmond in October 1527.

The Imperial delegation at the court of Henry VIII was obviously feeling the affects of Wolsey's preference for a French alliance. When Margaret of Savoy, Regent of the Netherlands, enquired about sending over an embassy to discuss friendship, commerce and a marriage between the Duke of Richmond and one of the daughters of the Queen of Denmark, she was advised that she might be wasting her time. The ambassador thought it was probably best if he first discovered whether Wolsey would actually deign to entertain the proposals. It was entirely possible that her envoys would have had a wasted journey, as the cardinal was so busy with his French friends it might be some time before the Imperial ambassador could even arrange an interview with the minister.

In fact, Wolsey had a rather more important marriage to broker – a new wife for his king. In 1527 rumours began to circulate that Henry was thinking of putting Katherine aside. No one can have been entirely surprised. While Henry was still young enough to produce a legitimate son, it was political suicide to remain married to a queen who was so obviously past the age of child bearing. Of course, the idea was broached rather more diplomatically. At first it was claimed that Henry's concerns over the validity of his marriage had been sparked when doubts were raised by the French about Mary's legitimacy during negotiations for her marriage to the duc d'Orléans. In 1528 this was amended to the idea that the English ambassadors in France had stirred up the doubts. As matters progressed even this account was discreetly dropped. In truth the impetus came from the king.

Henry now turned his full attention to a matter which (so he claimed) had been concerning him for some time. Against all good sense he latched on to the prohibition in the Old Testament book of Leviticus (20:21), that 'if a man shall take his brother's wife, it is an unclean thing . . . and they shall be childless'. However, a contrary text in the book of Deuteronomy (25:5–7) positively encouraged a man to take on his brother's widow, but Henry persuaded himself that this was Judaic custom rather than God's law. Even though Katherine and Henry had a perfectly healthy daughter, the king was obligingly advised that the original Hebrew had said they would be without sons. Henry's desire for an annulment was not in itself unusual. When marriage was as much a business merger as a domestic arrangement, sometimes the partnership had to be dissolved. Unfortunately, Henry's belief in Leviticus would set him on a collision course with the pope. The King of England believed his marriage was so sinful that the papacy had no authority to allow it. However, the pope would not accept an argument that diminished the power of his office.

Perhaps hoping to ensure a quick and speedy resolution, Henry did not begin by seeking to repudiate Katherine. Contrary to modern opinion, bigamy was generally regarded as less heinous than divorce, even when the separation was disguised as an annulment, due to some hitherto unknown impediment. Erasmus agreed, 'far be it from me to mix in the affairs of Jupiter and Juno' he wrote, 'but I should prefer that he should take two Junos than put away one'. Henry's initial applications to Clement VII concerned permission not to put away Katherine, but to take another wife. In the difficult years to come, as Henry was taken to task by Katherine for not spending enough time with her, only to be rebuked by his mistress for paying too much heed to the queen, he must have felt rather like a man with two wives. As a domestic arrangement, it was clearly unworkable. As a political solution, the issue of a bigamous marriage might well invite more problems than it solved.

By the autumn of 1527 moves were afoot for the king's 'great matter'. The timing could not have been worse. Henry had good reason to hope for a favourable hearing from the pope. Monarchs even more than ordinary men needed sons to succeed them; the peace of Christendom could be said to depend on it.[13] However, Charles V's sack of Rome in 1527 meant that Pope Clement VII was virtually his prisoner. The emperor was unlikely to co-operate in any approaches from the English king to put aside his aunt, one of many factors which would make Henry's case rather more complicated than it might have been.

If Richmond realised the significance of Richard Croke's departure, to help provide evidence to support Henry's case that his marriage was unlawful, there seemed no immediate cause for concern. Henry could easily provide for a Prince of Wales and a Duke of York, without affecting Richmond. Nor did it automatically mean Mary's position would change. There were ways and means for Henry to put aside his wife without prejudicing his daughter's rights. If Katherine could be persuaded to retire into a nunnery, it could be argued that Henry was free to marry again, without any need to address the legitimacy, or otherwise, of their daughter. Even if their marriage was annulled on some technicality, it could be claimed that her parents, who had been accepted as man and wife in the eyes of the world for the past two decades, had been unaware of any impediment at the time of her birth. Such issue, born in good faith, was not automatically bastardised, even if their parents' union was subsequently discovered to be unlawful.

Since Henry so desperately needed legitimate issue, the idea that he would deliberately set out to debase any child of his, when there was a viable alternative, seems absurd. For the moment at least, the marriage negotiations of 1527 indicate that Mary was still the heir apparent. Yet the failure to secure her marriage to the dauphin perhaps strengthened Henry's resolve that his daughter was not the best means to secure England's future. His concern for his dynasty is demonstrated in his abrupt rejection of a French alliance. Even as Wolsey was in France to enquire about a marriage between the king and Renée of Anjou, Henry spoke to the Hungarian envoy, who had just rejected Renée as a suitable bride for his master on the grounds that she might not 'bring forth fruit as it apperith by the linacion of her body' due to a hereditary deformity. The king eventually found his own replacement rather closer to home, in the shape of Anne Boleyn.

The question has often been asked whether Henry pursued Anne as a man who believed he would soon be free to marry or whether it was her refusal to yield that spurred him on. The answer must be both. To be fair to Henry, he had always believed, albeit with increasingly impressive optimism, that God would eventually grant him a legitimate male heir. Once it was clear that Katherine would bear no more children, the shrewd political move would have been to take immediate action to put her aside and try again. Instead Henry seems to have concentrated on finding a suitable marriage for his daughter. If Mary had been betrothed to Francis I or the dauphin, Henry might have been satisfied, or maybe not. His attraction to Anne

Boleyn was a significant and unpredictable factor that she was well placed to exploit.

When Henry's pursuit of Anne became apparent in the spring of 1526, there was no reason to suspect that this would be anything more than a conventional affair. Far from being a ready alternative to Katherine, very little about Anne Boleyn suggested that she would be a suitable queen. The daughter of a mere knight, Sir Thomas Boleyn of Blickling in Norfolk, being the niece of the Duke of Norfolk, on her mother's side, was scant compensation. Anne was no European princess whose marriage would secure a diplomatic alliance or a substantial dowry.

Unlike Henry VII's union with Elizabeth of York, which had been designed to promote accord, it was all too possible that this pairing would encourage discord. Few of the nobility would enjoy seeing the House of Howard accrue further power and influence, especially since many saw Anne as their social inferior. At twenty-six Anne was also much older than most Tudor women when they first married, significantly reducing her time in which to produce the desired heir. Also, her volatile temperament made it clear that she was unlikely to conform to the ideal picture of the pious and devoted consort. Devoted Anne Boleyn might well be, but it was to be strictly on her own terms.

At one point in the summer of 1527 Henry was content to offer her the role of 'my only mistress, rejecting from thought and affection all others save yourself', which Eric Ives has translated as something akin to the role of 'maîtresse en titre' employed at the French court. Somewhat at odds with her reputation as a wanton, Anne reportedly responded that her virginity belonged to her husband. If Anne was bidding for the higher prize of becoming Henry's queen, then she was also adhering to the same moral stance for which Jane Seymour was so admired, and it is perhaps rather unfair that she should be blamed for that. At her age it was a risky policy. While she held Henry's interest there was no possibility of other suitors. Yet this path had no guarantee of success. Her fears that Henry might return to Katherine and 'my youth and time spent to no purpose at all' betrayed more than a simple desire to goad Henry into action. Fortunately for Anne, Henry's commitment to Leviticus was at least equal to his passion for her.

For the moment the gathering storm clouds that would become the English Reformation had no impact on Richmond. Instead, the spring and summer of 1528 saw a drama of another sort. The north of England did not escape the sweating sickness, which swept across the land. Richmond was, for the moment, in good health. But the death of six local people, which his council described with lurid detail, and the dreadful news 'that many young children be sick of the pox near thereabouts' was not reassuring. As a precaution, in May Richmond was taken from Pontefract Castle to Ledstone, some three miles away. Here he waited out the pestilence with a train of just five attendants, at a house of the Prior of St John's, within his manor of Pontefract. The emergency also highlighted another shortfall in Richmond's apparently illustrious household. The list of officers drawn up in 1525 had included Dr William Butts, one of the king's physicians, as resident doctor. Yet it seems that position had never been filled.

In July 1525 the duke's council had written to remind Wolsey 'to send a physician unto my lord's grace for the preservation of his person'. Now the council worriedly pointed out how dangerous it was for Richmond to be without a doctor 'in this time of such strange infirmities'. Thankfully, by October the danger was past. Magnus wrote to Wolsey to reassure him that Richmond and his small company had remained perfectly healthy throughout the crisis. To everyone's undoubted relief he was now safely back in his own house surrounded by all his servants. Richmond himself wrote to thank his father for his concern.

There is nothing to suggest that Henry's focus on his matrimonial affairs caused any diminishment of his affection for his only son. While Richmond was at Sheriff Hutton, Henry maintained regular contact with him by letters and messengers, which passed to and fro. Richmond thanked his father for his 'most honourable letters' or gifts of 'goodly apparel' sent from court. One of the 'tokens' sent by the king, via Thomas Magnus, was a gold unicorn horn set with pearls and turquoise. Another was a collar of gold 'for my Lord's neck' set with seven white enamel roses. Now the king responded to the present emergency by forwarding a selection of medical remedies. Richmond assured his father that these 'preservatives' had made all the difference, ensuring his continuing good health.

The duke also continued to be a focus of patronage and power for the local nobility. In the autumn of 1528 William, Lord Dacre called to pay his respects on his way south to the king. The Earl of Northumberland went one better and invited Richmond to visit with him at his house at Topcliffe near Thirsk. No doubt with some trepidation, Richmond's council agreed to a single night's stay for the nine-year-old boy. They need not have worried. Richmond rose to the occasion and 'did use himself, not like a child of his tender age, but more like a man in all his behaviours'. About this time the Earl of Westmorland and his wife, perhaps as a means of storing up favour for the future, also brought their son and heir, Lord Neville, to live in Richmond's household.

Unlike Mary, who was recalled from Ludlow in the Marches of Wales in the summer of 1528, Richmond was allowed to remain at Sheriff Hutton. Nor was this a simple case of out of sight, out of mind, since it is clear the whole enterprise was costing far more than had originally been planned.

When he was first sent to Yorkshire it was envisaged that the income from Richmond's lands and offices would pay for the duke and his household. It was estimated that his ordinary expenditure would be just over £3,000, which was well within Richmond's anticipated revenues of £4,000. Yet while the first year's accounts submitted by George Lawson, for the period 12 June 1525 until 31 July 1526, appear healthy with a clear balance of £484, in fact the year's expenses could not have been met without the loan of £500 from the Abbot of St Mary's in York. In fact, they were fortunate that the revenues were higher than expected. In the first six months they had already managed to spend £2,650, which made them approximately £1,150 over budget.

The setting up of the household had been an expensive business. As well as repairs to the buildings, there had been the huge outlay on fixtures and fittings, elaborate furnishings, twenty-six horses and their equipment, as well as travelling expenses. All this before the basic expenses of diet, fees, rewards and wages had been addressed. In addition to his household expenses, the duke's council were also called upon to defray official costs in their role as the king's Council in the North. In October 1527 they paid for a band of sixty soldiers, both horse and foot, to be stationed at Felton, a lordship of Sir William Lisle, in an attempt to capture the outlaws. The plan was to arrest Lisle and his men when they came for supplies, but at 4d per person, per day, over two months, the policy was expensive. The council apologetically explained that this was not their fault, but that 'horsemeat and all other victuals be very scarce and extreme dear in those parts'.

The council were also expected to discharge the various fees of local officers of the crown. Yet they quickly found themselves short of ready cash. In September 1526 the Earl of Westmorland complained to Wolsey that he had not received his fee as Vice-Warden of the East and Middle Marches. Wolsey referred him to Richmond's council and they referred him to the king. As they apologetically explained, they had had some difficulties collecting the duke's rent and fees, in fact they admitted they 'could not obtain any part of the revenues'. So far they had only received £400 from Richmond's estates. In the spring of 1527 Magnus was nudging Wolsey to think of his godson's expenses when re-distributing the lands of the Lord of St John's, even as the poor man languished on his deathbed. More than once the duke's council applied to Wolsey, hoping that he would 'remit, pardon and forgive' the £500 borrowed from the Abbot of St Mary's.

The magnificent style of a ducal household made no concession to Richmond's tender age. On an ordinary day the entire household would sit down to two main meals consisting of ten different sorts of meat, including such delicacies as half a lamb or a kid, veal, rabbits, chickens and geese, as well as bread, pies, custards and fruits, all washed down with ale or beer. On fish days salmon (both salted and fresh) cod, pikes, shrimps, turbot, sturgeon, eels, whelks, crayfish and other sea and freshwater fish graced his table. Each of his principal officers had a special menu costing 6s 5d a day and were also allowed bread, beer, wine and beef in their chambers for breakfast and supper. Candles to see by and kindling to keep them warm were another perk, with others of Richmond's servants, such as gentlemen waiters, chaplains and grooms, enjoying similar privileges on a sliding scale, according to their rank.

In such an establishment it was perhaps inevitable that there would be some below stairs pilfering. Wolsey's instructions had ordered that access to the wine and beer should be strictly regulated. Despite this, the opportunity for self-enrichment proved too much for some. In April 1526 the council advised Wolsey that Simon Prior, a yeoman purveyor (appointed by the cardinal) had obtained 230 beasts worth £60 from a widow named Agnes Clerc 'surmising then untruly that they should be for the use and expenses of my said lord of Richmond's household'. In fact none of them found their way to the duke's table. Hearing that Prior, who they belatedly declared was a rogue, had been arrested at Tottenham on some other charge, they asked that Mistress Clerc should be recompensed out of his confiscated goods. Human nature being as it is, the occasional incident of this kind was no doubt an occupational hazard in even the most well-ordered of households. Unfortunately, Sheriff Hutton was far from being the most well-ordered of households.

Matters were not helped by the fact that a 'clerk of the green cloth', the officer responsible for the accounts, was not appointed until August 1526. Once he arrived he and Thomas Magnus drew up a programme to assess and review the household expenses. What they found was a history of poor accounting where books and inventories were not regularly kept. They realised Richmond's household was living far beyond its means. In February 1527 it was decided that only drastic measures would suffice and eighteen members of the household were discharged, some as being superfluous to requirements and a few for their (unspecified) misconduct.

If the council were pleased with their decisive handling of the situation, the king was not. Not only did Henry tell them to re-admit several of the dismissed officers, but also to pay them greater wages than before. Declaring themselves to be 'much perplexed', Sir William Bulmer, steward of the household and Sir Thomas Tempest, the comptroller, defended their actions, protesting that these new instructions made 'all our orders and directions to be of little regard; and we and all other officers and Councilors here be lightly esteemed among my Lords servants'. They claimed the books were now in order and there was no wastage. However, since expenditure had not been sufficiently reduced they had taken the only possible action. Now there was the further worry that all of those who had been dismissed would be encouraged to return, hoping for better terms than before.

In the same letter, Bulmer and Tempest confidently asserted that the improved accounting and 'many other good and politic devises daily practiced' had brought the household into much better order. They assured Wolsey that the high costs were not due to 'great waste or unreasonable expense'. They could not have been more mistaken. Only six days later Magnus made his own calculations and broke the bad news to Wolsey. The clerk of the green cloth had estimated that, not including wages and liveries, the household's weekly expenditure did not exceed £25. In fact, they were spending over £50 a week. The clerk of the green cloth 'some deal confused' declared he would look at his figures again. Before he could do so he caught cold and promptly died.

Magnus had no hesitation in attributing his demise to the stress of the financial situation. He advised Wolsey that in future he thought it was best if he handled the finances himself. With careful management and regular accounts he hoped to make some headway before Easter, but things remained tight. Somewhat ironically, he advised Wolsey not to be too hasty in sending up a new clerk of the green cloth. Not only had the last one been more a hindrance than help, but also the duke could not afford to pay any more wages.

The council certainly seemed to believe that over-manning was the root cause of their financial difficulties. The following October Magnus was successfully able to discharge several of Richmond's servants, this time reminding Wolsey that if they were re-admitted the king would have to bear any charges that could not be met. However, Richard Croke laid the blame for the spiralling costs firmly on the shoulders of Sir William Parr and George Cotton, who, along with Cotton's brother Richard, who served as comptroller of the household, were openly accused by the tutor of embezzlement. According to Croke all manner of goods had been siphoned off from Richmond's kitchens for their personal use, only a fraction of which ever appeared in the formal accounts. He also alleged that Parr was often absent and on the few occasions when he was present, he spent more time hunting or hawking than attending to business.

In view of their conflict over control of Richmond, Croke may have hoped to engineer his enemies' dismissal. Procuring the odd cut of meat or spare haunch of venison was one thing, but making sufficient provision for the needs of one's entire family was quite another. Croke's willingness to defend his claims in front of the council certainly suggests he was sincere, and the fact that these men remained in Richmond's service is not necessarily proof of their innocence. The charges, which Croke was confident could be substantiated by the clerks of the kitchen, never seem to have been formally investigated. Since by Croke's own admission the fraud did not appear in the accounts, it was probably difficult to judge the extent of the abuse, although the possibility exists that some of those dismissed for misconduct paid the price for their superiors' misdeeds.

Even allowing for a certain amount of bias, Croke's charges appear to be borne out by the disordered state of the household. No one seemed to be quite sure what proportion of the rich velvets and expensive fabrics that were Richmond's cast-off wardrobe should be re-used, which should be given in lieu of fees or which should be granted to Hugh Johns, the yeoman of the wardrobe of robes. Certainly, when Wolsey sent up a new set of articles intended to curb overspending the measures included firmer controls over the procurement of food stuffs and stricter rules over what were legitimate perks of the job, such as the droppings from the roast meat, and those things that were not, like table cloths.

Slowly, things did improve. A year later in October 1528, Magnus was still reporting on his progress, sending, of all people, Sir William Parr to Wolsey with the details. To be fair they were not alone in their difficulties. At this time Sir John Neville, Sheriff of Yorkshire, also complained to Wolsey that recent shortages in the north had substantially added to his expenses. Richmond's council were obviously at fault for their shoddy accounting and dubious management. But they were hampered by Wolsey's failure to ensure good practice or to appoint a clerk of the green cloth. In addition, the king's use of Richmond's household as a source of patronage as well as a political statement resulted in a greater number on the payroll than the revenues could support. While the question of financial irregularities did not arise again, things were not completely resolved. In April 1529, the duke's council was still trying to avoid repayment of the £500 borrowed from the Abbot of St Mary's in 1526.

Richmond remained at Sheriff Hutton until 16 June 1529, when he was almost ten years old. If his return was linked to Henry's 'great matter' and a corresponding decline in his fortunes, it is hard to see why he was not recalled with Mary. Nor does it seem that the council's ability to govern was the deciding factor. The complaint that the council should be removed on the grounds that these clerics were 'sore moved against all temporal men' suggests their intervention was effective enough to be resented.

The council had made strenuous attempts to bring the north to good order. They did not sit complacently in Yorkshire: officers were sent out to assess the less hospitable regions and assizes were held at Newcastle and Carlisle. Richmond's councillors also sat on Commissions of the Peace for Cumberland, Westmorland and Northumberland, as well as Yorkshire. They were even prepared to intervene in disputes within the palatine of Durham, despite its privileged status. Their actions produced clear improvements. In August 1527 Magnus reported that the York assizes had been very quiet with 'but little business and so few things to be done as have not been seen afore'. In November 1527 they held the largest and most well-attended assize that Newcastle had ever seen.

Not every aspect of the experiment was a resounding success. It had originally been hoped to extend the council's jurisdiction right across the northern counties, using deputy wardens to oversee the West, Middle and East Marches. Instead, in December 1527, responsibility for the East and Middle Marches was ceded to the Earl of Northumberland and Lord William Dacre became Warden of the West March. Technically, this was a failure for Richmond's council, but the plan had never been implemented before and came with no guarantee of success. They had repeatedly advised Wolsey of their own misgivings about the arrangement and it is perhaps unfair to blame the council for the shortcomings of others.

The policy had not begun well. The cardinal took several months to appoint the three wardens. Once they were in place, the Earl of Cumberland apparently tried to rule the West March from his castle at Skipton in Yorkshire. Lord Eure openly admitted that he lacked the support of the local gentry and could not ensure order and the Earl of Westmorland's sole interest in his position seems to have been his fee of £1,000.[14] That the fault did not lie entirely with the council is demonstrated by the fact that a number of Richmond's officers were seconded to assist Northumberland and Dacre in carrying out their new responsibilities as wardens.

Nevertheless, the council did have its limitations. Thomas, Lord Dacre, despite his prominent role at Richmond's elevation, refused to surrender the town and castle of Carlisle to the duke's council without confirmation from the king or Wolsey. After his death in October 1525, a dispute between his heir, William, Lord Dacre, and the Earl of Cumberland got so out of hand that the council was forced to refer the matter to Wolsey. Such events highlight the difficulty these new men of the cardinal's faced in getting their social superiors to toe the line, although it has to be said that even the king's personal intervention did not effect any immediate improvement in Dacre's conduct. The council's decrees could be ignored, defendants might fail to appear and at least one man from Tynedale, who was placed in Richmond's household as a pledge of good behaviour, absconded.

Yet no sixteenth-century court, not even the king's courts in Chancery or Star Chamber in London, was immune to such disobedience. The chief problem faced by Richmond's council was a handicap shared by Mary's council in the Marches of Wales. Any party dissatisfied by their order could and did decide to try their luck in London. When Nicholas Rudd discovered that the judgment of Richmond's council 'should weigh and pass against him' he obtained a subpoena in the Court of Chancery. When Wolsey recommitted the suit to the north, Rudd failed to appear. Having been told that Rudd was again intending to try his case in the king's courts, Richmond's council were clearly anxious that Wolsey should not allow the duke's authority to be openly flouted:

> may it therefore please your Grace if he shall come before the same to put him in some further order so that it shall not appear in the county of Westmoreland that my lord of Richmond's precepts and commandments or other decrees be contempted and disobeyed.[15]

Although this did affect the council's ability to act as the fount of all justice and power in the north, it was a general weakness of sixteenth-century government, rather than a direct reflection on the personal standing of Richmond himself.

Nor does it seem that Richmond's recall was linked with Wolsey's increasingly precarious position. As the cardinal failed to secure the much-desired annulment of the king's marriage, his enemies began to circle. However, none of the changes in the composition of the government of the north seem designed to root out those who had connections with Wolsey. Several of Richmond's officers, including Thomas Magnus, remained attached to the Council of the North.[16] However, if there was an intention to make it specifically less clerical in character then Bishop Tunstall was a curious choice to head the new body. In fact Tunstall's appointment signified yet another experiment in northern government. This time all pretence at the traditional style of a nobleman's council was dropped. Tunstall was known as the President of the Council and he answered directly to the crown.

Richmond's tenure as the king's lieutenant in the north has sometimes been dismissed as a little more than a farce, incapable of bringing the area under proper control. His council did experience a number of difficulties. At various times they complained of a lack of goods and provisions. They suffered from poverty, severe weather conditions and areas so sparsely populated that they had trouble finding sufficient numbers of people to undertake the commissions with which they had been entrusted. Such conditions could not fail to hamper the effective implementation of justice. Yet the records kept and the precedents established under their authority continued to be used.

By 1532 Tunstall was also recalled and Richmond surrendered his role as Lord Lieutenant to Dacre. That this admirably bureaucratic solution would also falter tends to support the idea that the feudal and isolated character of the north of England made it particularly difficult to govern, rather than the argument that Richmond's council was especially flawed. When the question of the government of the north was again addressed in 1536, the example of Richmond's council provided the solution. This time the Duke of Norfolk was to be dispatched as the king's lieutenant 'and shall have a Council joined with him, as was appointed to the Duke of Richmond at his lying in those parts'. Perhaps, at least in comparison to other models, the council was rather more successful at a difficult task than has generally been acknowledged.

4

Lord Lieutenant of Ireland

Richmond's return to the court in June 1529 passed entirely unnoticed. All attention was focused on the legatine court being held in the parliament chamber at Blackfriars to determine the validity of Henry and Katherine's marriage. By now the king was utterly convinced that his union with his dead brother's wife was against God's law and that no pope had the power to effectively allow him to live in sin with his sister. Cardinal Lorenzo Campeggio, who had recently arrived as an envoy from the pope, admitted that he thought 'an angel descending from heaven would be unable to persuade him otherwise'. For her part, Katherine had believed in 1509 that God had rescued her from seven years of dismal widowhood because it was His divine will that she should marry Henry. She had stood firm then and she saw no reason to change now. It is doubtful that Richmond was even aware that his father had also considered a rather more unorthodox means of securing the succession, one which would have ensured that his bastard son could ascend the throne of England, with a royal princess as his bride.

Privately, Wolsey now admitted to Campeggio that they had thought of marrying Richmond to his half-sister Mary and thus uniting the two claims. In theory the policy had much to recommend it. It offset the danger of domination by a foreign power by marrying Mary to an undeniably English lord. It also reduced the danger of civil war. Although it was incestuous, canon law actually allowed that sexual intercourse between a brother and sister using the missionary position was less sinful than intercourse with an unrelated partner, using any other position.[1] If Henry was prepared to forgo all this talk of divorce and more importantly the associated questions of papal jurisdiction, Clement VII may well have been persuaded to accede to such a request.

Certainly, Campeggio, rather than protesting at such a sinful and unnatural solution, agreed that he had also thought of this at first. However, having seen Henry he could not believe that even this drastic step 'would suffice to satisfy the king's desires'. Ironically, Richmond himself may well have contributed to Henry's unshakable belief that his second, or in his eyes his first, canonically correct marriage would give him a legitimate male heir. After all, he was evidence of Henry's virility and if God would grant him a son in a supposedly sinful union, yet withhold that blessing in an apparently lawful marriage, the implication was clear. The marriage was not lawful.

Actually, it may not have been. Dispensations for marriage were most commonly issued in cases of consanguinity, when two blood relations (usually distant cousins) wished to marry. With much of the nobility being related in some way or another this was a necessary expedient. The dispensation which had been issued at the time of Henry and Katherine's marriage, was for affinity. This was the relationship created when one of the partners had already slept with a member of the other's family. In this case the assumption was that Henry's brother, Arthur, had slept with Katherine. Yet if their marriage had not been consummated, as Katherine claimed and Henry never dared to deny, then the dispensation for affinity did not apply.[2]

What the couple had actually needed was a dispensation for public honesty, which recognised the legal connection made by marriage or betrothal and nothing more. Since a dispensation for affinity did not automatically cover the lesser offence of public honesty, Henry could have accepted Katherine's protestations that she was a virgin and still been at liberty to argue that their original dispensation was flawed. Henry's unshakable belief in Leviticus would be a rod for his own back, and one that would set him against both the papacy and his queen.

As the legatine court convened at Blackfriars, Henry spoke eloquently of his pangs of conscience. If he expected this was a mere formality, the required prelude to granting his desires, he was wrong. Katherine's impassioned defence, on her knees before her husband, took the wind from everyone's sails. Far from being childless, she pointed out that they had been blessed with several children 'although it hath pleased God to call them from this world'. Rather than being Prince Arthur's tainted relict, she asserted that she had come to the king 'a true maid without touch of man' and dared him to deny it. Neither then, nor at any other time, did he in fact contradict her, which certainly seems to indicate that he knew it to be the truth.

In other circumstances Henry's commitment to the Leviticus argument might have seemed noble, even pious. If his sole aim had been to put aside his aged and barren wife for a younger model, then it would have been far easier to use the technical, but perfectly valid, point that the original dispensation for consanguinity rather than public honesty had not covered their actual relationship. Instead, he had chosen to fight the papacy for the moral high ground on this point of divine law. Despite the inconsistencies in his arguments, surely men had to admire his righteous intent?

If Henry had planned to replace Katherine with a French princess or some other suitable consort, this might have been the case. There were after all viable political reasons for Henry to put aside his wife. In other circumstances Katherine might well have been censured for her selfish obstinacy. A queen had a duty to provide the kingdom with an heir and if she could not then surely her duty should be to step aside. Even her nephew Charles V might have been more sympathetic to the troubles of a brother monarch if his 'solution' had not been such a flagrant insult to his aunt. Much of the sympathy and support for Katherine's position was engendered by the fact that by the summer of 1529 everyone was very well aware that Katherine's intended successor was Anne Boleyn.

It was widely known that Anne's sister, Mary, had already

been Henry's mistress in the 1520s. This gave all Henry's pious protestations a rather hollow ring. Reginald Pole, the clerical son of Margaret, Countess of Salisbury, himself a man of royal blood, was perhaps more direct than most when he rebuked the king:

Are you ignorant of the law which certainly no less prohibits marriage with a sister of one with whom you have become one flesh than with one with whom your brother was one flesh?[3]

Even before it was brought to his attention it is doubtful that Henry was unaware of this. An oblique admission of guilt is found in his request for a dispensation from 'the first degree of affinity from forbidden wedlock'. At the same time as Henry was disputing the pope's authority to validate his sinful union with Katherine he would have welcomed a similar dispensation for himself and Anne.

It became clear in April 1530 that Henry was now motivated by his desire for Anne. Since the birth of her eldest son, Elizabeth Blount had been living in Lincolnshire with her three other children, Elizabeth, George and Robert. On 15 April 1530 the death of her first husband, Gilbert Tailbois, left her a widow and available. If the king needed to ease his conscience and secure the succession, on balance, Elizabeth was a better replacement than Anne. What would have seemed unthinkable in 1519 appeared positively ideal just a decade later.

As the case of the Beauforts had illustrated, children conceived in adultery were not automatically legitimated by their parents' marriage. If, as Henry so vehemently claimed, his union with Katherine was not lawful, then he had been a bachelor when he wooed Elizabeth. In such a scenario a child born out of wedlock was widely accepted as being legitimated if the parents subsequently married.

This solution had numerous benefits. Henry would have been guaranteed his son and heir. An heir who had already shown himself to boast numerous good qualities and whose burgeoning athletic prowess boded well for the future. Also he would have acquired a wife who was already the mother of three fine sons and a daughter and at thirty was no older than Anne Boleyn and still young enough to provide Henry with more children.

Elizabeth and Henry had remained on good terms. Although Elizabeth was at pains to assure her mother-in-law that 'she did never make any request to the King's Highness, or to my Lord's grace', moves were afoot in April 1529 to give the couple an even greater share of the Tailbois estates than they had previously enjoyed. Henry had continued to remember his former mistress with a New Year gift and it was not a simple pro forma obligation. In 1532 Elizabeth's present, a gilt goblet with a cover, was one of the heaviest and therefore most expensive. While she did not come to attend the festivities in person, her servant received 13s 4d in reward for bringing her gift to the king.

In June 1532 Loys de Heylwigen, a member of Charles V's household, was convinced Henry's repudiation of Katherine was 'to legitimate by subsequent marriage a bastard son of his' and provide the kingdom with an heir. He was startled to discover Henry would consider marrying anyone else, assuming 'that the King's love for another than the Queen' had to be the mother of his son. Attempts to persuade him that Anne was 'eloquent, gracious, reasonably good looking, and of a good house' fell flat. De Heylwigen dryly suggested that perhaps the king had been charmed by potions. Certainly the advantages of the match were not sufficient to turn the affection Henry evidently still felt for Elizabeth into the type of ardour he now felt for Anne Boleyn. In that at least De Heylwigen was correct. Henry had fallen under her spell and could not conceive of marrying another.

The King of England was unusual among monarchs in choosing his queens for love. During his one attempt at true matrimonial diplomacy with Anne of Cleves in 1539, Henry might grumble that in matters of matrimony 'princes take as is brought to them by others, and poor men be commonly at their own choice and liberty', yet in five out of his six marriages he had no one to blame but himself.

If Henry had any thoughts of legitimating Richmond by sub-sequent marriage, there is no sign of it. When Henry's cousin, Lord Leonard Grey, courted Elizabeth in May 1532, he stressed that he would not have pursued her if the king had objected, 'as I am well assured he doth not'. Perhaps Henry was so convinced that Anne would be his saviour that he did not see any need to pursue the option. Perhaps he also harboured concerns that Richmond's title (and legitimacy) would not be fully secured by such means. The best case scenario was an annulment of his marriage from Katherine, leaving him free to make an unimpeachable second match, which would give him an heir whose title was beyond reproach. In default of that, Richmond was an insurance policy, one perhaps whom Henry had begun to take for granted.

In the end, this particular opportunity was lost. At some point between July and September 1532, Elizabeth chose Edward Fiennes, Lord Clinton, the son of Thomas Fiennes, Lord Clinton and his wife Jane, the illegitimate daughter of Sir Edward Poynings, as her second husband. Born in 1512, Clinton was rather younger than Elizabeth. He would marry twice more and the most glittering aspects of his career, as Lord Admiral and Earl of Lincoln, would occur after her death. Nonetheless, Elizabeth made a very respectable marriage. The family hailed from Amington in Staffordshire and had had established interests in Warwickshire since the early fourteenth century. Edward's father, Thomas, Lord Clinton, had succeeded to the title in 1514 and had begun a successful career as a courtier, attending the marriage of Mary Tudor to the French king and serving at Tournai, before his sudden death from the sweating sickness in 1517.

There is nothing to suggest that Henry had a hand in arranging this marriage. Elizabeth's interest in the Tailbois lands made her a wealthy widow who could expect to make free choice of her own husband. Although Clinton became a ward of the crown after his father's death, by June 1518 his wardship and marriage had been purchased by his maternal grandfather Sir Edward Poynings at a cost of £135. In his will in July 1521 Sir Edward had also allowed that his grandson might:

marry at his own proper choice and free election when he commeth to full age without interruption or impediement of my said Executors or any other in his name for the same.[4]

Edward, no doubt, took full advantage of his grandfather's benevolence to pick Elizabeth as his bride. Although, since the couple may have been brought together by their respective landed interests in Warwickshire, which Elizabeth owed to the king's bounty, perhaps Henry was the unwitting agent of their union after all.

However, if Clinton hoped to reap the continuing rewards of Elizabeth's royal liaison, he was to be very disappointed. In February 1535 'Lady Tailbois, now the wife of Lord Clinton' was granted three tuns or barrels of Gascon wine, but Clinton himself was not specifically included in the grant. In 1536, when he lobbied for some lands in Kent, his suit was blocked by Thomas Cromwell. A grant of the office of bailiff and keeper of the park at Tattershall in Lincolnshire in February 1537 went jointly to Elizabeth with her second son, George, Lord Tailbois, rather than with her husband. Not until April 1538 would Clinton earn the first of a series of grants given to him in his own right.

In another respect also, this marriage would not bring Clinton all the benefits he might have hoped for. Even as he enthusiastically supported the king's moves against the English Church and all the former monastic lands it brought him, Clinton must have been equally anxious to secure his own dynasty. Instead, Elizabeth provided him with three daughters, Bridget, Katherine and Margaret, and he had to wait for his second wife, Ursula, the daughter of William, Lord Stourton, to provide him with his male heir.

Richmond would weather the next few uncertain years of the king's divorce far better than his half-sister Mary. Openly acknowledged by all as illegitimate, yet comfortably arrayed in rank and wealth, he enjoyed a degree of security that Mary would not. The possibility of a legitimate prince may have cast a small cloud over the hopes and aspirations of some of those who had attached their star to his, as with each legitimate son Richmond's political importance would correspondingly decline. Yet such a prospect was by no means certain. William Tyndale cannot have been alone in questioning the king's certainty. 'Who hath promised him a Prince?' he demanded. Even if the king produced a boy there was little immediate cause for concern, as the death of an infant was all too possible and if the king should die before the child reached its majority, Richmond, being at least ten years older, might still seem the better candidate for the throne. As it was, Henry would need to produce a whole host of sons before Richmond's usefulness as a land and office holder was seriously impaired. For the moment a male blood relative was far too valuable to be seriously affected by the mere anticipation of an heir.

In fact, the duke's return heralded a new development in his fortunes. On 22 June 1529, he was appointed Lord Lieutenant of Ireland. More than a face-saving manoeuvre, this appointment was probably a major factor in his recall. The governance of Ireland had posed at least as many problems to the Tudors as the turbulent north. They were loath to trust the Irish nobility and equally unwilling to bear the cost and charge of an English deputy, especially since neither method had ever proved really successful. An arrangement made by Henry VII with Gerald Fitzgerald, Earl of Kildare, that the earl would serve as Lord Deputy in return for confiscated lands had worked well enough to be confirmed by their respective heirs. Yet by 1515 Kildare was being called before Henry VIII's council to answer a number of complaints.

By 1520 Henry VIII had decided to place his trust in the English nobility, sending Thomas Howard, then Earl of Surrey, over to Ireland to serve as Lord Lieutenant. This was also not an ideal solution. The posting was not exactly popular among the English lords and (more importantly) it was very expensive to the crown. Furthermore, Howard grumbled that Ireland would not easily be brought to order, declaring that the country would be more difficult to quell than Wales.

For a time, Kildare's rival, Sir Piers Butler, later Earl of Ossory, was substituted as a return to a cheaper option, even though Thomas Howard had expressed the opinion that Butler was not up to the task. Eventually, in May 1524 things came full circle when Kildare was restored as deputy, with Ossory acting as treasurer. Henry VIII may have been hoping for the best of both worlds, especially since Kildare had more power in the north of the country while Ossory's influence was mainly in the south, but he was disappointed. The rivalry between the two created more problems than it solved and, partly in response to Ossory's urgent pleas for English assistance, Henry was again forced to look to the state of Ireland.

The result was a complete re-organisation of government with the Duke of Richmond at its head. Richmond would hold his office as Lord Lieutenant directly from the crown. Instead of a deputy, there was to be a three-man executive board made up of members of the Irish Privy Council. John Allen, recently made Archbishop of Durham, was chancellor, with Patrick Bermingham as Chief Justice of the King's Bench, and John Rawson as treasurer.

Known as 'the secret Council' these three men were instructed to rule in Richmond's name.[5] The duke's attestation 'Tested by our beloved cousin Henry, Duke of Richmond our Lieutenant of Ireland of our blood at Dublin' was attached to all writs and warrants. The arrangement was clearly reminiscent of the Council of the North and the appointment of John Allen, a former servant of Wolsey's, strongly suggests that the cardinal had a hand in devising the policy. Once again Richmond's tender age was a positive advantage, allowing the use of his innate authority as the king's son, while relatively minor officials conducted the daily business. This solution allowed Henry VIII to forgo the expense of sending over an English deputy, yet still ensure the authority of the crown was upheld. It may even have been hoped that this executive board, made up of men with a more personal interest in Irish affairs, would prove more successful as a means of control.

Significantly, these concerns of government were not in the forefront of everyone's mind. This desire to stress Richmond's personal authority so strongly instantly made many men's thoughts return to the rumours of 1527. Perhaps Henry did intend to endow Richmond with an independent kingdom after all. For the first time Charles V expressed his concern over Richmond's possible future prospects. Henry was:

> now trying to get a divorce from our Aunt, the Queen of England, his legitimate wife, and give the kingdom of Ireland to his bastard son. These are things which we can in no wise tolerate, as they might be the source of much scandal among Christian Princes, very detrimental to England itself, and besides injurious to the Queen and the illustrious Princess Mary, her only daughter and heir in that kingdom.[6]

Royal offspring had been used as caretakers for Ireland before. Most famously Henry II had sent his son Prince John to rule in regal splendour in 1185. As a child Prince Henry's own role as Lord Lieutenant of Ireland, from September 1494 when he was three years old, was more of a titular position. Exactly which role Henry intended for his own son is not clear. At this stage he may not have been sure himself. Certainly, the door was now open for Richmond to assume a greater role in Ireland, as and when the king should desire it. As far as the plan to make him King of Ireland was concerned, while Henry did nothing to confirm the speculation, neither did he deny it.

Richmond's appointment certainly seemed to indicate a new policy towards Ireland. Regrettably, this era of executive government was short-lived. This was almost certainly largely due to Wolsey's fall from power in the autumn of 1529. When the pope ordered that any further hearings concerning the King of England's marriage would be held in the courts at Rome, Henry's hopes for an annulment before the summer was out were immediately shattered. A bitterly disappointed king needed a scapegoat and Wolsey was the obvious choice. Others at court, including the Dukes of Norfolk and Suffolk, who had resented the cardinal's monopoly of Henry's attention, were more than willing to encourage the king's wrath towards his beloved servant. Even Anne Boleyn, who had once echoed Richmond's sentiment that she was 'most bound of all creatures, next [to] the king's grace, to love and serve your grace', now shared and perhaps encouraged Henry's anger and frustration. Without Henry's support, Wolsey's position was no longer tenable.

Thomas Wolsey's career would come to its ignoble end in November 1530, when he died before formal charges could be brought against him. In the interim his fortunes faltered and were revived by hopes of reconciliation and recovery, only to falter again. Isolated in the north, Wolsey would now play no further part in orchestrating his godson's life. Richmond's reaction to the loss of one of the guiding forces of his formative years is not known. Any feelings of loss may well have been cushioned by the king's grant of Wolsey's former manor and park of Cheshunt, in Hertfordshire, valued at £20 40s per annum. Less cynically, Henry's grant was a stark reminder to his son where the real power lay. Henry was lavish in his affections and generous in his bounty to anyone who was riding high in his favour, but he was equally ruthless to anyone who fell from his grace. The uncertainty of Richmond's birth apparently taught him an early lesson, which Henry's legitimate daughter Mary would only learn by bitter experience. Obedience to the king's will was the only sure route.

With other things on his mind Henry may well have been content to wait and see if the cardinal's initiative in Ireland was effective. Once Wolsey had fallen there was no one to argue for the plan's long-term implementation. On 22 June 1530 Henry fell back on more traditional means of enforcing control. Sir William Skeffington was appointed as Deputy Lieutenant to the Duke of Richmond and sent across the water with an armed retinue to govern in his name. The reason given in his patent for the appointment was that it was because of Richmond's youth.

However, since the duke was at least a year older than he had been when the scheme was originally implemented, there must have been other reasons for a change of policy.

Skeffington's appointment was probably related as much to the situation in England as to the mood of Irish politics. The gathering storm clouds of the king's increasingly desperate efforts to secure an annulment of his first marriage threatened a breach with the papacy, which would make England vulnerable to attack and foreign invasion. Ireland was an obvious marshalling point for any such enterprise and a stronger government presence there must have seemed prudent. Certainly Skeffington was well equipped with troops and armaments in case of any disturbances.

There was also the question of Richmond's envisaged role in Ireland to be considered. While in practice the appointment of a deputy made no material difference to his power and authority as Lord Lieutenant, a return to the old policy subtly shifted power back to the authority of the king. Instructions from Henry addressed Skeffington as 'our deputy', leaving no doubt that he was Henry's man. It is hard to say how far Henry VIII's increasing conviction that Anne Boleyn would bear him a son had any direct influence on Richmond's position at this stage. That Henry had been happy to use Richmond's personal authority in the summer of 1529, when he was convinced he was very close to taking Anne as his wife, tends to suggest that this was not Henry's primary motivation. Yet it might have made given him pause for thought. In the present circumstances, creating another independent kingdom on his own doorstep would not have been the wisest course.

Now that Richmond was back at court he was treated with every respect and the deference due to him as the most senior nobleman in England. On 9 August 1529 the king called the first parliament since Richmond's elevation. Despite being only ten years old Richmond was duly summoned to take his place among the peers. Dressed in his robes of crimson velvet, edged with ermine and laced with two flat, gold laces, with a matching kirtle and hood, topped with a large scarlet and ermine cap, this duke in miniature must have been an incongruous sight, sandwiched between the magnificent bulk of the king and the impressive physical specimens of Thomas Howard, Duke of Norfolk and Charles Brandon, Duke of Suffolk.

As was the custom, the Lords processed to Westminster Abbey for a service, before returning to sit in the White Chamber of the Palace of Westminster. Traditionally, dukes occupied the inner bench, on the left hand side of the throne and were ranked according to the date of the creation of their title. A more public demonstration of Richmond's continuing political importance can hardly be imagined. Even more surprisingly, the child also attended when the parliament was actually in session. Since much of the business was not likely to appeal to the natural interests of a ten-year-old, this was probably intended to be educational. Richmond did infact have a personal interest in some of the proceedings, not least the Act 22 Henry VIII c.17, which confirmed on the duke all those lands and possessions which had been granted to him at the time of his elevation. Rather than seeking to diminish Richmond's continuing importance in the scheme of things such moves served to further secure his title.

However, in the climate of the time, Richmond did not attract a great deal of gossip or attention from the various ambassadors. If he attended the Christmas festivities at Greenwich in 1529, the ambassadors were too busy reporting that Anne Boleyn had been given precedence at table over the Duchess of Norfolk and the king's own sister to mention his presence. The king, however, did not forget his son, presenting Richmond with a two-handled gilt cup with a cover and engraving, decorated with serpents and flowers, a 'great, flat standing cup', and two little gilt pots as his New Year gifts.

Sometimes the foreign observers were also a little confused by the embarrassment of riches Henry had heaped upon his son. In September 1529, the newly arrived Imperial ambassador, Eustace Chapuys, advised Margaret of Savoy that the Lord

Admiral was one of those being considered to go as an envoy to the court of Charles V. In the climate of 1529 he is unlikely to have meant the king's ten-year-old illegitimate son. In a letter three days later writing to Charles himself, Chapuys mistakenly associated the former Lord Admiral, Thomas Howard, Duke of Norfolk, with that office, who would certainly have been a much more feasible candidate as an official ambassador.

Yet Richmond continued to be treated with every mark of respect by Henry's subjects. While he was in London attending the parliament, Walter Devereux, Lord Ferrers, presented the duke with 'a grey trotting nag'. A headboard of yellow and blue damask was 'cut at the head, behind the bolster' when Sir William Courtney enjoyed Richmond's hospitality at the duke's Manor of Canford. Richmond also continued to spend a good deal of time with his father. In the spring of 1531 they were together at Hatfield, presumably for the hunting, since Richmond was given the present of yet another steed, this time 'a proper roan trotting horse'. The following year Richmond was again 'with the King's grace' at Grafton, which was one of a number of the king's properties that boasted the added diversion of a bowling alley.[7]

For the moment, Richmond still spent most of his time at his studies. His formal education did not cease on his return from the north. George Folbury appears to have continued as his tutor until he was twelve. However, others were not so fortunate. On his return from Yorkshire the scale of Richmond's household was correspondingly reduced. The original 245 listed in 1525 had been whittled down to a body of 94 by his death in 1536, although the actual number of the household was probably closer to 150, if the duke's officers were allowed the same quota of personal servants which had boosted the total at Sheriff Hutton. In part, this reduction was a response to the fact that his household was no longer required to support the king's Council in the North, although some of his officers, notably Sir George Lawson, who remained in the north also continued to draw their fee as members of his household. Although it is easy to see this as an unsubtle downgrading of his princely magnificence, it was perhaps nothing more than an entirely sensible economy measure, one that Thomas Magnus, at least, would have wholeheartedly agreed was well overdue.

It may have been envisaged that Richmond would sometimes return to Sheriff Hutton. It remained as one of his principal residences and his council had already invested a significant amount of money in making the property habitable. Certainly, when the Duke of Norfolk went north to assume his duties as the king's representative in 1537 he found a good deal of baggage and ordnance left behind by Richmond's household, as well as something of a skeleton staff. Casting around for some gainful employment for them Norfolk suggested that they might be used to supervise an armoury at the castle since 'the servants of my said Lord of Richmond I am sure will not go into the south with me, having their wives and livings here'. Whatever the original intention, there is nothing to suggest that Richmond ever again ventured any further north than Sheffield.

With Wolsey's fall from grace, Henry now needed some other man to oversee the general administration of Richmond's household. Norfolk immediately saw this as an opportunity he could use to his own advantage. His own son, Henry Howard, Earl of Surrey, was a most promising child and an excellent horseman, who later proved himself to be a fine soldier. Norfolk boasted to Chapuys of his 'proficiency and advancement in letters', even producing an example, which the ambassador acknowledged was written in very good Latin. Norfolk then confided that he hoped Surrey 'may in time become [Richmond's] preceptor and tutor that he may attain both knowledge and virtue'. Surrey was just old enough to provide Richmond with an example to emulate, although any hopes that this might encourage Richmond towards a broader love of learning may have been in vain. He is far more likely to have been impressed with Surrey's talents on the tennis court or in the joust, than his skill with a pen.

When Norfolk expressed the hope that the friendship between the two boys might prove to be 'very strong and firm', he was no doubt thinking of the political advantage he might gain from their relationship. In agreeing to allow Norfolk's son to become Richmond's companion, Henry VIII perhaps hoped, as Richmond grew to manhood, to provide him with a more fitting influence than he had known at Sheriff Hutton. Born in 1517, the twelve-year-old earl was both of a suitable age and an appropriate rank, criteria that were not so easily met. The only real alternative would have been Richmond's cousin, Henry Brandon, Earl of Lincoln, who, at only seven years old, was a little young for a role model.

Richmond and Surrey's relationship seems to have blossomed into a warm and enduring friendship. They would spend much of the next six years in each other's company. The exact details of Norfolk's association with Richmond are less clear. Any comparison with the role played by Margaret, Countess of Salisbury as lady governess to Princess Mary is misleading. After his return from the north George Cotton served as Richmond's governor and Norfolk held no official position in his household. Yet his involvement in Richmond's affairs extended beyond his general care and education, into areas relating to his lands and servants.[8] In fact, all those matters which Wolsey had formerly handled.

At least Wolsey had been in the privileged position of being the child's godfather. Norfolk appears to owe his involvement in Richmond's life to Anne Boleyn's influence with the king.[9] Nor was this in any sense a traditional wardship, not least because Richmond's father was still very much alive, but also because Richmond was already an independent magnate in his own right. In every outward respect he was treated as if he was already of full age.

Even so, as Richmond approached his twelfth birthday, the year 1531 does seem to have been something of a watershed. If the grant of the canonry and prebend of North Newbald, Yorkshire, issued to George Folbury on 17 March 1531, was in reward for his services, then the duke's formal education must now have come to an end. As if to herald a new stage in his fortunes, Richmond's household seems to have made a particular effort to celebrate Christmas 1531 in appropriate splendour. Hugh Johns, the yeoman of his wardrobe, ordered new carpets to decorate the windows and cupboards, on which were displayed the gold and silver which was a visible symbol of his rank and wealth and his habitual New Year gift from his doting father. The Lord of Misrule, who would preside over the festivities, was also given two old cushions of crimson velvet 'sore worn and almost spent' to trim his outfit and another cushion from which to fashion his doublet, so that he could conduct the entertainments in appropriate style.

This new stage in Richmond's life may also account for the timing of an inventory of his goods taken in June 1531. Such an extensive list of clothes, furnishings, household goods and personal belongings was most commonly used to ensure the proper distribution of assets after the subject's death.[10] However, it was now clear that a number of the items bought at Richmond's creation in 1525 were beginning to look decidedly shabby. After six years a great many of the tapestries that had decorated his chambers had frets and holes 'very needful to be amended'. After many removals a number of the beds could 'not be set up in no place to do service'. Many of the fabrics and furnishings were patched, frayed, or otherwise showing their age. Several items had been lost during the duke's various travels and his magnificent chair of estate was now 'sore broken with carriage in divers places'. Of the twenty-five horses Richmond had acquired since his elevation, seven had been given away, three were 'so sore worn' that they were only fit to draw the beer cart and six had already died, leaving just nine serviceable for use.

Hugh Johns had made valiant efforts to keep pace with the duke. No expense was spared on the lavish gowns, rich doublets, frocks, riding coats, hose, hats and bonnets that Richmond outgrew at an alarming rate. All of the best quality, his clothes were cut from silk, velvet, cloth of gold or silver and other rich fabrics, lined and decorated with expensive furs, trimmed with gold and silk, and embellished with elaborate embroidery. The attention to detail was stunning. His buttons of gold or enamel were shaped like roses, daisies, sundials or triangles with roses set in them, although even here, the overall impression of splendour was slightly misleading. It is doubtful that the twelve-year-old duke still got much use out of the robes of estate which had been made for his creation when he was six in 1525 and many of the other pieces were also now well worn or outgrown.

Some items, such as the covering of black velvet for Richmond's saddle (which had probably seen a good deal of use) had already been replaced 'at his coming out from Yorkshire'. Four new geldings were purchased to carry his goods from Pontefract to London. However, it was obvious that a significant overhaul of his wardrobe and furnishings was well overdue. Some matters were handled by Hugh Johns himself, who bought a number of items, including new leather chairs and several new mattresses to replace worn goods. However, much of the responsibility seems to have been shouldered by Norfolk, who was heavily involved in organising the re-distribution of Richmond's cast-offs. Several pieces went to Richmond's half-brother George, Lord Tailbois, born in 1523. Norfolk also oversaw the repair of damaged articles and even dismissed several items as being beyond use.

Unusually, a significant number of replacements were paid for from Norfolk's own purse. Fifteen pieces of material were provided to make new hangings. For the bedchambers there were several wooden bedsteads, new curtains of red and yellow and coverings of cloth of gold, velvet and silk. Since Richmond was supposed to be financially independent it is not clear whether Norfolk expected to recoup his financial outlay from the duke's officers or whether he was anticipating a different sort of return on his investment.

The marriage of the Duke of Norfolk's only surviving daughter, Mary Howard, to the king's only son, has often been put down to Howard ambition. Yet from the outset Norfolk maintained that it was Henry's idea. In December 1529 he had told Chapuys 'the King wishes the Duke to marry one of my daughters'. Norfolk and Mary would always maintain that Henry ordered the marriage. In fact, the true architect of the arrangement seems to have been Anne Boleyn.

The Duke's actions are evidence that he had other plans for his daughters. If he was lobbying for a match with the king's son, it might have seemed prudent to offer his eldest daughter, Katherine Howard, as the more glittering prize. Instead, within weeks of Norfolk's conversation with Chapuys, she was married to Edward Stanley, Earl of Derby. There is no doubt that this was entirely Norfolk's idea. The earl was a minor under the authority of the king and, on 21 February 1530, Norfolk was obliged to seek a pardon 'for the abduction of Edward Earl of Derby and [his] marriage to Katherine daughter of the said Thomas without royal license.'

Of the family of five children born to Norfolk and his second wife, Elizabeth, a daughter of Edward Stafford, Duke of Buckingham, Mary Howard, born in 1519, is generally thought to be their only daughter. However, Katherine was at least twenty-two years old when a few weeks later, on 16 March 1530, Chapuys informed Charles V that Norfolk's eldest daughter, the wife of Edward Stanley, Earl of Derby, had died suddenly of the plague. Anxious not to lose this alliance Norfolk arranged for his half-sister Dorothy Howard to become Derby's second wife. Indeed, far from engineering the royal match it was believed Norfolk considered the Derby marriage to be so important that 'had [he] not had a sister to offer, he would have proposed his other daughter, who has been promised to the Duke of Richmond.'

Even without the Derby match, it does not seem that Richmond was Norfolk's first choice as a husband for Mary. The duke was later to claim that the king's proposal had interrupted plans for Mary to marry Lord Bulbeck, the heir of the Earl of Oxford.

The marriage was made by his commandment, without that ever I made suit therefor, or yet thought thereon, being fully concluded then with my lord of Oxford.[11]

For her part, Mary's mother, Elizabeth, Duchess of Norfolk, seems to have been positively unwilling that her daughter should marry Richmond. According to Chapuys she preferred the Derby match and had had her wishes rather forcefully overruled by Anne Boleyn.[12] The Duchess of Norfolk had no doubt that Anne was the true author of events declaring 'queen Anne got the marriage clear for my lord my husband, when she did favour my lord my husband' and Henry's subsequent reluctance to acknowledge the union strongly suggests that he was persuaded into it by Anne, who cannot have viewed the prospect of Richmond making a sparkling European marriage with any pleasure. Despite the Duchess of Norfolk's objections the arrangements were finalised by the spring of 1531, when Chapuys was content to refer to Richmond as Norfolk's son-in-law. The child was now formally betrothed and as soon as he turned fourteen in June 1533 the union could be solemnised and Richmond would be safely married within England.

In the meantime, Richmond was often at court. As a duke he was not only entitled to food and lodgings at the king's expense, but a generous provision of candles, coal and other necessaries for the comforts of life. Yet while official business, or his father's pleasure, could find him at the royal palaces of Greenwich or Hampton Court, it was neither customary nor practical for both him and his household to be permanently resident at court. The grant made to Richmond in 1525 had included a suitable London residence. Coldharbour Mansion on the banks of the Thames had formerly belonged to his great-grandmother, Margaret Beaufort, Countess of Richmond. Unfortunately, after her death in 1509, the king had granted the property to George Talbot, Earl of Shrewsbury, which allowed Talbot to enjoy the property rent free, for the term of his life; he did not die until July 1538.

On his return from the north, Richmond had spent some time at Wolsey's manor of The More in Hertfordshire. This was a pleasant enough property, which had been substantially extended and improved by the Cardinal as befitted one of his principal residences. It could boast a great chamber and a privy chamber, as well as a 300-foot gallery. Wolsey had even modernised the plumbing. After his fall, the property returned to the king's hands. Henry could simply have continued the arrangement on a more permanent basis. Instead, it seems he already had something more suitable in mind for his son.

Richmond was installed at Windsor Castle, which seems to have been his main residence while he completed his education. As part of a programme of general improvements to the castle a 'new lodging called the prince's lodging' was subsequently built for his use on the western side of the north front. As at Sheriff Hutton he was joined in his studies by other youths, including Henry Howard, Earl of Surrey, although it seems unlikely that their time was spent exclusively in the carefree round of sports, courtly love, dancing and tennis, later described in Surrey's poetry. Richmond still had a role to play in the wider world and he had to be well equipped to shoulder whatever duties his father chose to bestow.

Although there was a traditional belief that Richmond and Surrey went together to study at Cardinal College, Oxford, this has long since been disproved. The idea that Richmond studied under Richard Croke at King's College, Cambridge is also mistaken. The disorder of Richmond's schoolroom at Sheriff Hutton with its bawds and fools has sometimes been taken as an account of Richmond's activities at university. However, there is no indication that Richmond attended either university and his increased profile at court is evidence to the contrary.

Indeed, in April 1530 the pomp and ceremony of the court came to him. On 23 April, the king held a chapter of the Order of the Garter at Windsor Castle to mark St George's Day. While he was in Yorkshire, Richmond had been excused from participating in the business of the Order by the king's letters. Now he was expected to play his part. With Norfolk, Suffolk and other knights of the Order, he donned his robes to attend mass in the king's private chapel. After the formalities, Henry spent some time with his son. Richmond obviously impressed his sporting father with his skill with a bow, since Henry paid 20s out of his privy purse to his fletcher to purchase some new arrows for the duke.

Since he also paid out 40s in reward to Richmond's nurse, the king was clearly satisfied that his son was fit and well and being well cared for. The £20 annuity which was awarded in May 1530 in reward for her services probably marked Anne Partridge's retirement as Richmond's nurse. At eleven years old Richmond was perhaps judged not quite old enough to entirely dispense with a woman's care. In 1538 a widow, named Joan Brigman, would receive an annuity of five marks out of the manor of Cheshunt, 'in consideration of her services to Henry, Duke of Richmond, in his childhood.'

The king clearly enjoyed a warm and loving relationship with his only son. Even amid the foreign ambassador's fascination for every detail of his affair with Anne Boleyn, this did not go entirely unnoticed. In 1530 the French ambassador was roused to comment that the king was very fond of his son. The following year the Venetian ambassador was of much the same opinion, going on to describe Richmond as 'a youth of great promise so much does he resemble his father'. Richmond visited Henry at Hampton Court and in May 1531 the king was again with his son at Windsor. This time Henry paid out 20s to buy the young duke a lute. The amounts were not lavish. Anne Boleyn and Mary both did significantly better in financial terms, but neither of them had Richmond's independent income. Also the gifts reflect a genuine interest in the child's activities. Even when they were not together the king continued to think of his son. A gold collar, enamelled with white roses, was blithely recorded as being 'sent from the King's highness for a token'.

Perhaps not surprisingly, relations between Anne Boleyn and the young duke do not appear to have been quite as warm. On his return from Yorkshire she presented Richmond with the gift of a bay horse and a saddle made of spruce leather, decorated with black velvet. If it was intended as a ploy to secure the boy's goodwill, the horse was rather ill chosen. Described as 'very ill to ride, and of worse condition',

Richmond did not risk his neck by keeping it, but passed it on to Gerald Fitzgerald, the Earl of Kildare.

Anne's relationship with Mary would seesaw between genuine attempts at reconciliation, in an attempt to negate her influence, and episodes of anger, frustration and fear at the danger she represented. With less reason for personal bitterness her relationship with Richmond was probably more formally correct. However, Henry's willingness to suspect in 1536 that Anne had conspired to poison Richmond hardly points at an affectionate relationship. They were no doubt a thorn in each other's sides. If she was a shadow on his favoured position as the king's only son, then he was a constant reminder to her of what Henry expected.

In general Richmond seems to have been healthier than many of his contemporaries. None of the surviving correspondence from his time at Sheriff Hutton mentions him contracting any illness at all. His enjoyment of hunting certainly indicates that he was usually fit and healthy. Richmond was also keen to follow in his father's footsteps at the tilt. Surrey's poetry later recalled the mock tournaments they had staged at Windsor. When Richmond fell ill in January 1532, the event was not widely reported and the cause of his sickness is not known. Henry sent one of his own physicians to attend upon the duke, but since the doctor's fee was only 40s the illness was probably neither too serious nor very prolonged. Nothing more is heard of this particular illness. Subsequent reports of his good health indicate that he recovered well and there is no reason to suspect any lasting effects. He was evidently quite fit by June 1532, since it was soon being reported that he was to be included in the king's train for his father's proposed meeting with Francis I.

Arrangements for this summit occupied much of the summer of 1532. It was agreed that Francis I would entertain the King of England at Boulogne, in return Henry VIII would receive the King of France at Calais. Despite strenuous efforts to keep the plans under wraps, by the end of July the Imperial ambassador reported that the six or eight ships being equipped under the guise of use against Scotland were in fact intended to carry the king to France.

Richmond's inclusion in a party that ultimately comprised almost every available nobleman in England, was not in itself particularly significant. However, rumours were soon circulating of a plan which would see Richmond being sent to reside at the French court, while Francis I's second son, Henri, duc d'Orléans, would come to England. Chapuys was quick to point out that this was 'an unequal exchange' but the proposal, this time involving Richmond, Orléans and Surrey, was also picked up by the Venetian, Carlo Capello. From the outset it seems that Richmond's role in the proceedings was to be more than to provide a suitably noble escort to the king and his lady.

The issue of the English and French king's respective entourages was a delicate matter, not least because Henry intended to parade Anne Boleyn as if she were indeed Queen of England. Despite the fact that Henry was legally no closer to securing the annulment of his marriage to Katherine of Aragon, he had effectively separated from her on 14 July 1531 by the simple expedient of leaving her behind at Windsor. For some time now the English court had been accustomed to seeing Anne dressed and treated 'more like a Queen than a simple maid'. Despite this, Anne was not only not the queen, but born merely the daughter of a knight, every peeress and princess in England and abroad felt that they outranked her.

The king's wish that the ladies of the French court would acknowledge Anne Boleyn was politely rebuffed. Francis I's suggestion that his own mistress should accompany him was not exactly what Henry had had in mind. The question of Anne's own train threatened to be equally problematic. A number of the English ladies, not least Henry's own sister, Mary, Duchess of Suffolk, refused to accompany her. In the end the issue was diplomatically avoided when it was decided that ladies would not take part in the actual summit. However, since Henry VIII was determined that Anne would accompany him to Calais, the problem of her status remained.

It was at least in part to address this issue that, on 1 September 1532, Anne Boleyn was created Marchioness of Pembroke, making her a peeress in her own right.[13] The carefully orchestrated ceremony was held at Windsor, with Anne's cousin, the future Duchess of Richmond, thirteen-year-old Mary Howard, playing a prominent role. Although Mary's mother Elizabeth, Duchess of Norfolk, was pointedly absent, Mary carried Anne's mantle of crimson velvet, furred with ermines, and passed the gold coronet to the king. Anne's elevation to the peerage endowed the queen-in-waiting with rank, wealth and a degree of future security. Henry also bestowed on her land worth £1,000 per annum and even illegitimate issue could succeed to the lands and dignity she now held.

This compares more than favourably with the fortunes of Henry's other known mistresses, not least because she received her reward before she had bestowed her favours. However, it was obviously only an interim step. Richmond's titles included two dukedoms, an earldom and revenues in excess of £4,000 per annum. In comparison, as a marquess with an income of £1,000, any male issue produced by Anne Boleyn would have felt rather hard done by.

The royal party set sail for France on 11 October 1532. The Duke of Richmond was allowed a train of forty attendants. Over the next ten days Anne lived 'like a Queen . . . and the King accompanies her to mass and everywhere, as if she was such'. On 21 October, reality intruded on this idyll when Henry and a small retinue left to meet the King of France. The Venetian ambassador, writing from England, assumed that Richmond accompanied his father. In fact, it seems to have been agreed that the children, like the ladies, would play no actual part in the summit. Henry VIII was introduced to Francis I's three sons at Boulogne, but they did not accompany their father to Calais.

In the meantime, Richmond was not exactly left cooling his heels among those ladies who had accompanied the new Marchioness of Pembroke.[14] Much of the English nobility, including Richmond's stepfather, Edward Fiennes, Lord

Clinton, also remained behind at Calais. Richmond may have been slightly put out that the Earl of Surrey was included in the king's party. However, not only was Surrey two years older than him, but since his wedding to Frances de Vere, the daughter of John, Earl of Oxford, in April 1532, he also had the added dignity of being a married man. Although Surrey did not live with his wife until 1535, this was evidently sufficient to class him among the adults.

The king's departure ensured that Richmond (rather than Anne) was the highest ranking noble at Calais. Perhaps this as much as any impatience at his exclusion explains why he was at the forefront of the welcoming committee when Henry VIII and Francis I returned to Calais. As they approached the town, Richmond hastened to meet them:

> without the town about the distance of two miles, the duke of Richmond, the King's base son, with a great company of noble men which had not been at Boulogne met them, and saluting the French King, embraced him in a most honourable and courteous manner.[15]

Francis I entered Calais to a 3,000 gun salute. In the lavish accounts of the feasting, music, dancing, and wrestling that Henry organised for the entertainment of the French king, Richmond features only briefly when the King of England hosted a special chapter of the Order of the Garter and Richmond was placed next to Francis. However, the duke was about to embark on what was, in effect, his first diplomatic mission.

The events at Calais were not solely about entertainment and extravagance. Even as the two kings attempted to outdo each other in spectacle, display and outfits encrusted with jewels, their respective ministers attended to the business of the summit. By 29 October, when Francis finally took his leave in a lavish exchange of gifts, it had been agreed that Richmond should go to the French court. It is fair to say that the news was not very important to the French who laconically reported:

The King of England yesterday gave unto the King his bastard son, who is a young child of fifteen or sixteen years, and the same day he made him a present of six horses.[16]

It is hard to know which gift the Frenchman held in more esteem. Slightly more accurately, the Venetian ambassador relayed that Henry VIII 'gave as servant to the most Christian King [Francis] his natural son'. He, at least, knew that Richmond was only thirteen years old.

Despite the earlier rumours about an exchange with Francis I's second son, Henri, duc d'Orléans remained firmly in France. The only envoy the King of France sent to the English court was a gentleman of his privy chamber. It was hardly a reciprocal arrangement. Admittedly, the French king had struggled to be reunited with his children, who had been held hostage in Spain to ensure their father's good faith in respect of the Treaty of Madrid, and he was perhaps naturally reluctant to give one up now.

By 10 November 1532, when Richmond had expected to have taken his final leave of his father, he was still trying to make provision for those of his servants who would not be accompanying him. It had evidently been decided that those who remained in England would be lodged in various religious houses that would provide them with 'meat and drink for themselves, horse meat for their geldings and chambers for their lodgings' apparently at the monasteries' own expense. The prior of Tutbury monastery, in Staffordshire, was informed that he was expected to accommodate Robert Amyas, the clerk of Richmond's jewel house, together with his personal servant and their two horses. The prior was not given much choice in the matter. Richmond signed his letter 'trusting you will show yourself conformable . . . like as all other religious fathers doth, as the King's trust and mine expectation is you will be'.

Since the decision to send Richmond into France had been under consideration for the last five months, such last minute urgency suggests a change of plans. If Richmond's absence had been envisaged as a matter of weeks, then nothing like this would have been necessary. Apparently Richmond's *séjour* in France was now to be considerably longer than had been originally planned.

It is often assumed that Richmond went to France primarily for the sake of his education: perhaps to attend the university, but largely so that he could acquire the manners and polish of the French court. Somewhat incongruously, given the English people's fairly xenophobic dislike of the French nation, one of Anne Boleyn's most admired attributes was the grace and style which she had acquired as a child on the continent so that 'no one would ever have taken her to be English by her manners, but a native born Frenchwoman'. The French language had been part of Richmond's studies since Palsgrave's appointment in 1525, and while the court of Henry VIII would have provided some opportunity to practise his skills, this was obviously a perfect opportunity to increase his fluency. When the two courts were discussing a mutual exchange, perhaps the educational benefits were a factor in the arrangement; however, by 12 November 1532, contemporary observers were speculating that the true motive behind Richmond's journey was rather more political.

It was reported that Henry and Francis had agreed that Richmond should go to France 'for the greater security of the matters treated between them' at the summit. Events certainly seem to bear out the idea that something discussed during the nine-day meeting had affected both the purpose and duration of Richmond's trip. With the benefit of hindsight, the proposed marriage between Henri, duc d'Orléans and the pope's niece, Catherine de Medici, which was due to be celebrated the following year, seems the most likely explanation. On such a happy occasion Francis I would be well placed to persuade Clement VII to grant Henry VIII his long desired annulment. In return, Henry could offer not only his profound gratitude, but also a possible alliance against Charles V.

As the king's only son Richmond was a powerful, physical surety for Henry's good faith, although the child, the spitting image of his father, may also have been chosen for another

Knights of the Garter, from the *Black Book of the Order of the Garter, c.*
1534. *Top*: The Duke of Richmond is standing to the right of the king in
the front row. *Bottom*: Richmond is on the far right. His red hair can
clearly be seen in the original painting. (*Reproduced by permission of the
Dean and Canons of Windsor*)

Henry Howard,
Earl of Surrey.
(*National
Portrait Gallery*)

Cardinal Thomas Wolsey.
(*National Portrait Gallery*)

The Lady of Richmond.

Mary, Duchess of Richmond and Somerset.
(*The Royal Collection, copyright © HM Queen Elizabeth II*)

Richmond's seal. (*Public Record Office*)

A letter from Richmond to his father, Henry VIII. (*Public Record Office*)

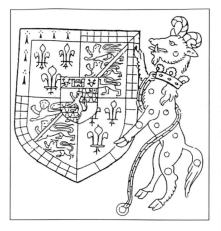

Right, framed: Richmond's arms,
St George's Chapel, Windsor, detail
above. (*Reproduced by permission of
the Dean and Canons of Windsor*)

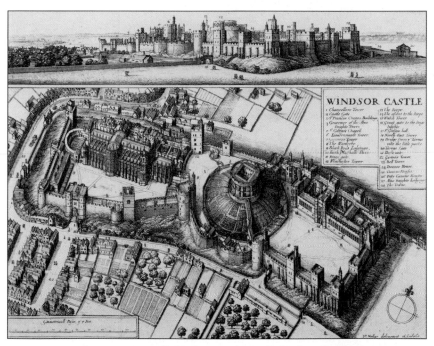

An engraving of a bird's-eye view of Windsor Castle.
(*The Royal Collection, copyright © HM Queen Elizabeth II*)

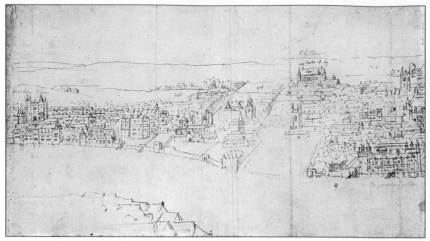

Durham House to Baynard's Castle. (*Ashmolean Museum, Oxford*)

Sheriff Hutton. (*Hazel Pierce*)

Lady Margaret Beaufort, Countess of Richmond. (*By permission of the Masters and Fellows of St John's College, Cambridge*)

Funeral brass of Elizabeth Blount. (*British Museum*)

Richmond's tomb, St Michael's church, Framlingham, Suffolk. *(Derek Clifton)*

reason. Richmond was living proof that Henry's marriage to Katherine had been an offence to God. Here also was the underlying promise that his union with Anne would prove fruitful. Richmond's presence was conclusive proof of the validity of the king's position.

If Richmond was merely a token of Henry's good intentions, or simply a physical demonstration of the present alliance between the two kings, then Francis I was curiously unwilling to accept him. The gentleman of his privy chamber that Francis I sent over to England was entrusted to ensure that Henry made good his promise of 'the present and gift' which the king of England had apparently promised to the French princes. This sounds suspiciously like a bribe, something that would not be necessary if the arrangement was to their mutual benefit. If Richmond's visit to the French court was primarily to serve Henry's own interests, then his generosity was perhaps instrumental in securing Francis I's agreement.

Nevertheless, Richmond was received by the French king with every outward sign of cordiality and affection. Accompanied by the Earl of Surrey and perhaps as many as sixty attendants, he finally left Calais in the second week of November. As he made his way through the countryside to rendezvous with the French court, it was happily reported back to England that Richmond was being 'very well welcomed and in all places have had presents of wine with other gentle offerings'. Although Surrey fell ill, Richmond suffered no ill effects from his first trip abroad, finding the food and climate 'very natural unto him'. By 5 December 1532, the Venetian ambassadors in France reported that Richmond had arrived and 'resides at the court, living at very great expense and very honourably'. Richard Tate, the duke's almoner, wrote to inform Henry that Francis had greeted Richmond with a warm embrace and 'made him great cheer' even saying that he now considered himself to have four sons.

Francis I was as good as his word. Once the dauphin, his two brothers, and the assembled nobility had welcomed Richmond, he was granted the status of one of the king's privy chamber. When the French court returned to Paris for the winter, Richmond was placed in the dauphin's own lodgings. Every day he took dinner and supper with the French princes. Although Tate was not entirely satisfied, grumbling secretly that 'I find great fault in [the] setting forward of my lord's train which as yet is out of f[rame]' he was optimistic that this would soon be amended. That small protocol aside, it does seem that Richmond was being accorded every outward mark of respect by the French.

Richmond spent the rest of the winter in Paris with Francis I's three sons. The young princes made their guests welcome, the splendid tournament hosted by the dauphin in January 1533 being exactly the sort of thing Richmond would enjoy.[17] Francis, the dauphin, was just over a year older than Richmond, having been born in February 1518. His brother Henri, duc d'Orléans was born in March 1519 and their younger sibling Charles, duc d'Angoulême on 22 January 1522. Richmond probably had most in common with the duc d'Orléans, the future Henri II, who was almost exactly the same age as him.

It is easy to imagine these two young royals getting on well. Henri was a lively child, the one most likely to take Richmond out riding or to play tennis. In the winter months he liked to go sliding on the ice on the pond at Fontainebleau or if the weather turned to snow he would make snow forts to hold snowball fights. The dauphin, described as colder and more reserved, preferred to keep himself to himself. He habitually dressed in black and was perhaps not always the best of company. Charles was not only considerably younger than Richmond, but also widely reputed as having a rather quick temper.

While he was in France, Richmond's circle of associates was not confined to a choice between the company of the three French princes or his English entourage. Not unlike the model envisaged for him at Sheriff Hutton, children from several eminent French families lodged with the dauphin and his brothers. The houses of Lorraine, Bourbon, Cleves and Guise were among those who had sent their sons to the court to share the royal princes' sports and studies.

Surrounded by sons of the highest nobility in France, Richmond seems to have made a good impression and been well liked. Several years after his death when Henri and his brother Charles were at a banquet with the English ambassador, Sir John Wallop, Henri suddenly 'began to speak of my lord of Richmond, lamenting his death greatly, and so did mons d'Orleance likewise'.[18] The ambassador was quick to point out that they had brought up the subject of the duke without any prompting from him, and the brothers' spontaneity, as much as their warm words, seems to indicate fond childhood memories of the duke. However, unlike at Sheriff Hutton, Richmond was far from being the centre of attention. When the French court began its summer progress he was quickly swallowed up in its train.

In general, the French displayed very little interest in Richmond's presence at court. When Montmorency, the dauphin's governor, wrote to his cousin, the arrival of the duke was mentioned only in passing and it was clear which piece of news was more important to him:

> The King of England has sent here his bastard son, and the son of the lord of Norfolk, who are being nurtured with the King's children. I assure you that the dauphin is now nearly as tall as I am.[19]

Direct or indirect references to Richmond's activities in any contemporary French sources are extremely rare. A passing mention in a letter to Arthur, Viscount Lisle does not exactly count, as it might be expected that he would be interested in news of his king's only son.

While the French chroniclers record in endless detail the pageantry, speeches, spectacles and gifts which accompanied the progress of the court, describing the separate entries of the king, the queen, the dauphin and other persons of note, not one of them saw fit to mention Richmond's presence. A contemporary account of the court's entry into the town of Béziers gives an exhaustive list of those who followed in the

French king's train. Even so, Richmond is lost among the great number of nobles that the author frankly admitted that he had left out. Whatever importance Richmond was accorded by the English people, to the French he was simply the King of England's bastard son and of small account in their affairs. His exact status, hovering somewhere between private magnate and royal offspring, was in a delicate balance. Yet, whatever importance Henry VIII set by Richmond's embassy, it seems it was not shared by the French people.

On 23 April 1533, Francis I celebrated the feast of St George's Day 'with much ceremony' at Fontainebleau. Since only a handful of his court were members of the Order of the Garter, this solemn observance of its major festival was no doubt staged in honour of Richmond's presence. Shortly afterwards the whole court departed on the first leg of their journey towards Marseilles. Their progress was designed to culminate in the celebration of the de Medici marriage and that meeting with the pope. However, this was also the first opportunity that the French king had had to visit much of his realm in person. As the train wound its way across France it was greeted with pageants, processions and presents from the inhabitants of the various towns en route.

Although Richmond never succeeded in attracting the attention of the French chroniclers he seems to have fared rather better with their king. When the lumbering train that was the French court and all its necessaries and attendants split up, the French princes went with their stepmother, the queen, towards the plains of Languedoc. Richmond and Surrey stayed with Francis I, travelling through Lyons and Toulouse until they came to Montpellier. He had now been in France for ten months and whatever the benefits to his education, the long-awaited meeting with the pope had yet to take place. However, in Richmond's absence, the situation in England had changed.

Henry and Anne's courtship was anything but simple. Everything about 1532 suggests that they were on the brink of matrimony. Anne dressed and acted as if she were queen. The king stepped up his attack on the pope's authority to be head of the Church in England. What had probably begun as a none-too-subtle blackmail attempt to get his own way became by March 1532 'A supplication against the Ordinaries' which set out Henry's claim that he was the right and proper head of the Church within his own dominions. The death of the incumbent Archbishop of Canterbury, William Warham, in August 1532 removed a major opponent of their marriage. Rumours abounded that the couple would marry before they embarked for the French summit. Then it was widely believed, even by Charles V, that they would marry while they were at Calais. Henry was certainly reassured to have Francis' backing in case of retaliation by Charles V or the pope. Ever the optimist, he was also newly hopeful that the pope could be persuaded or pressured into making what he considered to be the only right and proper decision. Yet still Henry and Anne did not marry.

If Anne's decision to consummate their relationship was intended to 'bounce' Henry into a decision, it worked. The discovery that Anne was pregnant in January 1533 gave matters an urgency that had previously been lacking. On 23 January, alleging a licence 'which if it were seen, should discharge us all' (and perhaps he actually meant his unborn heir), Henry married her. For several weeks this momentous step remained a secret, even though Anne could not resist making fairly blatant references to her pregnancy. The strange dance between Henry and Clement VII continued, when the king somewhat incongruously applied to the pope for a licence to appoint Thomas Cranmer (a known supporter of Anne) as Archbishop of Canterbury and the pope, equally curiously, approved the request. On 5 April the English clergy agreed that Henry's marriage to Katherine of Aragon was not lawful. The woman who had reigned as Queen of England for the last twenty-three years was bluntly informed she was now merely Prince Arthur's widow, the dowager Princess of Wales.

Anne's star, on the other hand, was firmly in the ascendant. On 12 April she appeared dressed in gold and silver finery and 'loaded with jewels', that until recently had been Katherine's, and went to mass as Queen of England. Once again she was attended by her young cousin, Mary Howard, the future Duchess of Richmond, who carried her train. In June, Henry put aside any concerns about her delicate condition and spared no expense on her coronation. Given his track record, the decision to subject her to such an ordeal was a sure sign of his determination that she alone should be revered as England's anointed queen.

Henry was not quite as sure of himself as this might indicate. In July 1532 the Act in Conditional Restraint of Annates stopped just short of abolishing papal power in England. Even at this eleventh hour, Henry was not yet ready to forgo the possibility that Clement VII would be persuaded to declare in his favour.

As the crucial meeting with the pope drew near, Thomas Howard, Duke of Norfolk was sent to France ostensibly to press Henry's case. As an experienced diplomat and Anne Boleyn's uncle he was the ideal choice. Anne's brother, George, Lord Rochford, accompanied him. When Norfolk's party arrived at Riom on 10 July, Richmond and Surrey rode a mile and a half out of the town to greet them. This display of filial affection, also allowed them to discuss recent developments in relative privacy. As late as 13 July, Robert Aldridge wrote from France that he was confident that they would yet 'accomplish our most desired purpose'. Back in England, there was mounting cause for concern.

The pope had recently indicated that the long awaited marriage between the duc d'Orléans and Catherine de Medici would now be delayed until September, which raised the dreadful possibility that the longed-for prince would arrive before the decision about his legitimacy could be secured. Now Norfolk's instructions encouraged him to mutter darkly about those who 'play and dally with kings and princes' and issue dire warnings about an alliance between Clement VII and Charles V, in the hope of persuading Francis I to abandon the meeting. The ploy was not entirely effective. The French king privately complained he was extremely bored by the duke's pestering.

This might explain why Norfolk remained in Lyons, when Richmond and Surrey accompanied the French king on to du Puy. As he awaited the return of the royal party, Norfolk received the news he least wanted to hear.

The pope's judgment on 11 July 1533 declared that Henry's separation from Katherine was unlawful. He was given until September to take her back or face excommunication from the Catholic Church. In addition, there was the dreadful sentence that any child born to Henry and Anne would be illegitimate. Norfolk immediately sent Anne's brother, Lord Rochford, back to England for instructions. Norfolk was told to make one last effort to persuade Francis not to meet with Clement. When that failed Henry recalled not just Norfolk, but Richmond and Surrey as well.

Given the King of England's efforts to get Richmond invited to the French court and Francis I's generous hospitality over the last eight months, this abrupt departure must have been awkward on both sides. Fortunately, Richmond had just celebrated his fourteenth birthday, which provided the ready excuse that he was now old enough to celebrate his marriage to Norfolk's daughter. This 'pretence' did not fool the Venetian ambassador, or anyone else. The pope's decision had ensured that Richmond's presence at the feast would be an embarrassment rather than an asset. However, the excuse contained enough truth to be an effective face-saving device. On 25 August at Montpellier, the trio formally took their leave of the French king and Francis sent them back to England with assurances of his continued devotion to Henry's cause ringing in their ears.

Norfolk proceeded with impressive haste to England, having made arrangements in advance for horses to carry him to Calais where 'I will not tarry . . . one half hour if the wind and tide may serve'. He was already in London by 30 August, although according to the town's chronicle, Richmond and Surrey did not even reach Calais until 25 September.

While at Calais they had the opportunity to enjoy the hospitality of Arthur, Viscount Lisle, who had been Richmond's vice admiral, until his appointment as Lord Deputy of Calais in

March 1532. Lisle and Richmond also shared the dubious honour of being the only living illegitimate royal offspring. If Richmond harboured any concerns about being overshadowed by a legitimate prince, Lisle was perhaps not the best person to reassure him. Completely eclipsed by his legitimate brothers and cousins, he had received no significant honours from his father, Edward IV.

Richmond could take some comfort from the knowledge that his position was different. He already enjoyed a significant degree of rank and privilege. None of his lands or titles was in any immediate danger of being hijacked for a newborn Prince of Wales, who was traditionally given the title Duke of Cornwall. How the new arrival would affect his personal relationship with Henry was rather more difficult to judge. A father can love more than one child and Richmond was exactly the sort of intelligent, able and athletic son to make any sixteenth-century king proud. Even so, as he made his way back to England, Richmond must have been one of the very few of Henry's subjects who was not praying for a prince.

If so, his prayers were answered, at least for the moment. News of the birth on 7 September 1533 of a princess did not rule out the prospect of a prince. Anne had conceived easily and the baby was healthy. Yet the arrival of a daughter was also a reminder that there were no guarantees. Anne's pregnancy had not been entirely trouble- free in the latter stages and she was not getting any younger. Legally, Elizabeth's arrival had no impact on Richmond's position. He remained the only male candidate for a throne which his illegitimacy ensured he was not eligible to inherit.

In all these years Henry had never given any indication as to which of his relatives would be his preferred heir if the direct line of succession were to fail, and he did not do so now. This either indicates his supreme conviction that God would grant him a legitimate son or the quiet confidence of a man who knows that if all else should fail he has an ace up his sleeve. Although public hopes were for a legitimate prince, as

Richmond came to pay his respects to his infant sister, private thoughts may well have turned to the ready-made alternative.

It had taken Henry VIII more than five years to put aside Katherine of Aragon and marry Anne Boleyn. It was a process that had risked the security of the realm at least as much as it promised to ensure it. Many men could have been forgiven for thinking that they had not endured such turmoil for the sake of a princess. It was still early days, but if Anne could not fulfil her part of the bargain, some other solution would ultimately be needed. In the last few years Henry had moved heaven and earth to get his own way. The 're-discovery' of the Royal Supremacy had taken the power of the king, parliament and statute law to a whole new level. In 1534 parliament would confirm Henry VIII as Head of the Church in England. In the circumstances, the legitimisation of the king's bastard son can no longer have seemed such a daunting prospect.

Richmond's claim was further strengthened by the repercussions of Elizabeth's birth for his half-sister, Mary. If Henry and Anne had had a prince, his claim would automatically have taken precedence as the male heir. Mary had seen her mother put aside and her father remarried, but so far her position as princess had been unaffected. Cromwell had considered that it might be better to keep her in 'the estate that she is now, and to avoid war, than to diminish anything'. Henry chose to act. As soon as possible, Elizabeth's position as the heir apparent would be secured by statute. For now Mary was verbally informed that she was no longer to use the title of princess. Henceforth, she would be known as the Lady Mary as befitted the king's natural daughter.

After eighteen years as the king's only legitimate child, Mary did not take the news well. She declared 'her conscience would in no wise suffer her to take any other than herself for Princess'. She assumed, or at least pretended to believe, that her father did not know of the order. She was wrong and her stubbornness and disobedience (perhaps rather too reminiscent of her mother's conduct) provoked Henry into ever more drastic action. Mary's household was disbanded. Her governess, Margaret Pole, Countess of Salisbury, was dismissed from her service and she was sent with a small band of attendants to live in the household being established for the Princess Elizabeth at Hatfield. This public reduction of Mary's status was designed to remind her, and all who had business with her, that the only true princess in England was Elizabeth. Everyone, from the servants in the household, to the ambassadors who came to pay their respects, to the common folk who stood by the road as their household passed by, were witness to her new position as merely the king's natural daughter.

Mary made her own opinion of Elizabeth's true status clear, when she conceded she would acknowledge her as her sister, just as she had always called the Duke of Richmond brother. However, it was not her opinion that mattered. In the eyes of their father both Elizabeth and Richmond now outranked her. Not only did Richmond's patent give him official precedence over all but the king's legitimate issue, which no longer included 'the Lady Mary', but the new disparity in their households and retinue made that distinction startlingly and publicly apparent. As Mary's stubborn refusal to acknowledge her 'true' status increasingly served to keep her from court and her father's good graces, Richmond was increasingly prominent.

If Elizabeth was not at court, and the infant spent a good deal of her time in her own household, the only people who took precedence over Richmond were the king and queen themselves. People must have become accustomed to seeing Richmond treated almost as if he was the heir-apparent. Even if Elizabeth was present, comparisons between the infant girl and the lanky fourteen-year-old, who was the image of his father, may not have been entirely in Elizabeth's favour.

On 26 November 1533 Richmond took a further step towards adulthood when his marriage to Mary Howard finally took place at Hampton Court.[20] The wedding did not attract a great deal of attention. Even the Imperial ambassador relegated the occasion to a footnote in his dispatch, noting only 'I have nothing more to say, save that tomorrow the marriage of the Duke of Richmond to the daughter of the Duke of Norfolk is to take place.' Perhaps he was not invited for there is no account of the festivities.

It was a political match. Although Mary had been at court for several months as one of Anne Boleyn's most favoured attendants (most recently carrying the chrism 'of pearl and stone' at Elizabeth's christening), Richmond had spent much of that time in France. They are unlikely to have had more than a passing acquaintance when they met at the altar. Even after the wedding they were not immediately expected to live together. Indulging in sexual intercourse before the body was physically mature was believed to be dangerous to the health of both partners. Katherine of Aragon's brother, the Crown Prince Juan, was widely supposed to have died because he consummated his marriage to Margaret of Savoy with rather more fervour than his adolescent body could stand. Henry was not going to risk Richmond like that. For the time being Mary returned to her duties as a member of the queen's household, while her husband resumed his informal apprenticeship in government.

That Richmond did not, after all, make a grand European alliance was more a reflection of the current political climate in England than his status as merely an illegitimate son. The negotiations of 1527 had proved there was scope for a suitable diplomatic alliance. A number of factors, not least Henry's preoccupation with his own matrimonial affairs and the resulting repercussions of that process, kept Richmond out of the international marriage market. In the circumstances, Henry may well have been more receptive to the idea of a domestic match than would otherwise have been the case. For Anne there were obvious benefits. Even as she acted the dutiful niece in sharing the benefits of her ascendancy with her uncle, she was securing her own position. Given Henry's obvious affection for his son, a marriage within England, to a member of her own family, was her best hope of limiting the political danger Richmond represented.[21]

However, the wisdom of this plan yet remained to be seen.

Anne may well have needed all her charms to induce Henry to forgo the money Norfolk would usually have paid for such a match. Nevertheless, in many ways Mary was an eminently suitable bride. The daughter of a duke, she could also boast her own share of royal blood on her mother's side as granddaughter to Edward Stafford, Duke of Buckingham, who had been executed for his regal pretensions in 1521. If she was rather too intelligent for her own good, 'too wise for a woman' as her father would put it, Richmond was not one to suffer fools gladly, and her skills in the more traditional graces required of a noble Tudor wife can only have been polished in the last few years at court in a post the envy of girls older than she.

Whatever Anne's attractions, Henry was unlikely to be persuaded to bestow his son on anyone he felt was unworthy to be the mother of his grandchildren. In 1529 it may have seemed like a good idea. By 1533 Anne must have realised that she had handed her uncle a loaded gun. Even if the marriage was not originally Norfolk's idea, the benefits of sharing a grandchild with the king must have seemed increasingly tempting. Rumours of conflict between him and Anne were already circulating by 1530. When the birth of Elizabeth was followed by the reduction in Mary's status, it would have taken a less politically astute man than Norfolk not to realise the potential value of his newly acquired son-in-law, if his niece did not produce an heir.

Richmond's own feelings towards his marriage are more difficult to assess. It was not a love match. The suggestion that he presented Mary with an anthology of poetry as a wedding present is as romantic as it is groundless.[22] Yet the couple had a good deal of common ground to draw them together and it was in their own best interests to achieve at least civility, hopefully affection and maybe even love. While many such political matches, including the Earl of Surrey's union with Frances de Vere, did develop into successful relationships both the king and Elizabeth, Duchess of Norfolk were testimony to the hardship which invariably followed if they could not make it work.

Although Richmond and Mary were not permitted to live together, their paths would have crossed now that Richmond was back in England. According to Surrey's poetical description of life and courtly love at Windsor, they saw enough of what one would hope were their respective wives to compare notes on their attributes. Allegedly very beautiful, apparently very intelligent, Mary's wilful character and sharp tongue may have made her rather too like her cousin Anne Boleyn for most people's comfort, but Anne was also sufficiently witty, charming and gracious to capture the king's heart. There was no reason why Mary could not follow her example with his son.

Norfolk's burgeoning ambitions for his son-in-law were perhaps already apparent by the autumn of 1533. Even before Richmond had returned from France, rumours had begun to circulate that now he was to go to Ireland. On 3 September 1533 Chapuys reported 'it is said the King will send him to Ireland as Governor'. Until now Richmond's role in Irish affairs had been purely symbolic. The sum total of his active involvement seems to have been the warrants issued in his name and the isolated incident in May 1530 when one of his servants received 5s in reward from the king, as he crossed over the water to Ireland.

Since Skeffington's appointment, the situation in Ireland had continued to deteriorate. He had arrived in Dublin on 24 August 1530, well armed with instructions, 200 marks and 200 troops. He was given authority to grant offices and call parliaments, but he was no great lord and his ability to control the Irish rested solely on his military prowess and his commission from the king. Despite his best efforts, he often lacked the support he needed, especially from the Earl of Kildare, who did everything he could to discredit him. Kildare also tried to curry favour with Richmond by presenting him with a bay horse, valued at £8. For good measure, a sorrel horse worth twenty nobles was also provided for Norfolk. Complaints regarding Skeffington's conduct reached the king's Privy Council in England and in another shift in policy he was replaced as deputy to the Duke of Richmond on 5 July 1532 by Kildare.

Unfortunately, rather than establishing order, Kildare's own disputes with his old enemy the Earl of Ossory merely added to the ongoing disturbances. As tensions increased the council summoned Kildare back to London to answer for his actions. His unwillingness to obey did not reassure them. It was therefore proposed that Richmond himself, in his capacity as Lord Lieutenant of Ireland, should go in person to see order restored. Rumours reached Charles V that Henry was even intending to resurrect his plan to make Richmond King of Ireland.

In fact, the plan to send Richmond to Ireland was largely due to Cromwell and was intended to reinforce changes he was already making to the way Ireland was governed, although it is tempting to imagine that Anne Boleyn would have fully supported any plan that sent her step-son into almost certain danger. The Imperial ambassador was confident something was going to happen and reported that Richmond 'is to leave soon for Wales, at the head of a force', although he was unable to discover if he was actually going across the water, or merely maintaining a military presence in Wales. In the end he did neither. The plan was commonly supposed to have been blocked by Norfolk. Certainly, when events in Ireland erupted into the Geraldine Rebellion of 1534, Cromwell was only too happy to blame him.

As had been the case with Wolsey, relations between Thomas Cromwell and the nobility were often strained. As the facilitator of the king's will, they had often needed his assistance. This was true even of the king's own children. Richmond regularly solicited Cromwell's support and assistance, thanking him 'for your manifold and approved friendship in times past'. The secretary was also the principal architect of Mary Tudor's return to her father's good graces after the death of 'that woman' Anne Boleyn in 1536. Yet Thomas Cromwell was not a knight or even a gentleman and many of the established nobility must have been put out as they resented this man's influence, as they had Wolsey's and were jealous of his relationship with the king.

Now the Imperial ambassador reported with some glee how the animosity, which Cromwell and Norfolk had previously been at some pains to disguise, now exploded into dispute:

> I am told that, amongst other accusations which Cromwell brought on that occasion against the Duke, one was that he was the real cause of the present disasters, from his wishing to keep the Duke of Richmond near him, and near his daughter, his wife, and that had he allowed him to go to Ireland eight months ago, as he was told to do, nothing of what has since happened would have taken place.[23]

Norfolk may well have been unwilling to endorse the plan, but he probably did not have to argue very hard to get Henry to agree. The situation in Ireland was too volatile to risk his son. Also, the Duke of Richmond would require an appropriately splendid retinue and a suitably magnificent household. Henry knew how incalculably expensive that policy might become, as the experience of Sheriff Hutton had shown.

In addition, as long as Anne had not produced a male heir, the king's son could be more usefully employed at court, even if only as a reassurance to his increasingly anxious subjects that the prospect of a prince was not an unattainable goal. Certainly, Norfolk could not have blocked the plan if the king had wholeheartedly supported it and although Cromwell could not blame Henry for the frustration of his plan, Henry was more than likely to blame Cromwell if order was not restored. By blaming Norfolk for interfering with his proposals, Cromwell perhaps hoped to line up a useful scapegoat to divert the king's wrath from himself and at the same time engineer the disgrace of one of his main rivals for the king's attention.

Although Richmond remained the Lord Lieutenant for the rest of his life, there is no evidence that he ever set foot in Ireland. The possibility of sending either Norfolk or Suffolk also came to nothing, mostly because neither of them wanted to go. In contrast, others, although certainly not Kildare, were eager to see Skeffington re-instated. In 1534 it was claimed he had 'gained the esteem of all. If he had remained until now, he would have found no one to resist him'. Eventually, Skeffington was sent back as the king's commissioner, although in October 1535 it was still being hoped by some of the Irish chieftains that Richmond himself would be sent:

> if it would please your highness to send your son, the duke of Richmond, to this poor country, I assure your grace that I and my brother and all my kinsmen, with all my friends, shall do him as lowly service, and as true as any man living, and I, my kinsmen, and all my friends, shall right gladly receive him to our foster son, after the custom of Ireland, and shall live and die in his right and service for ever.[24]

This was not to be. When Skeffington died on the last day of the year his post was given to the king's cousin, Leonard, Lord Grey, who had courted Richmond's mother. In yet another experiment in government it was perhaps hoped to marry Grey's military skills with his family connections in Ireland. If not an ideal solution, it was at least an attempt at a compromise between English and Irish overlords. However, after his death in July 1536 Richmond was not easily replaced. Not until the appointment of Thomas Radcliffe, Earl of Sussex, in 1560 was there to be another Lord Lieutenant of Ireland.

5

Young Courtier

In January 1534, Henry VIII was once again confidently expecting his legitimate male heir. The news of Anne Boleyn's pregnancy, which was known by December 1533, must have given an added air of festivity to the traditional New Year celebrations. This year the customary exchange of gifts was something of a family affair for the duke. Richmond gave his father 'a great spoon of gold' weighing more than 4 oz, which Henry promptly deposited in his jewel house. In return, the king gave him the usual collection of silver gilt so the duke could display the weight of his father's affection on his sideboard. Now that his wife's cousin was Queen of England she also gave him a formal gift. This time Anne's choice of a silver salt and a ring was rather more successful. Richmond particularly liked the ring, keeping it with him to wear. To round off proceedings, Richmond's new bride gave her father-in-law 'a tablet of gold' and in return the king gave her something out 'of his own store'.

However, Henry's mind quickly turned from the celebrations to more weighty matters. As Anne's pregnancy advanced, he took steps to set his realm in order. The spring session of parliament passed two more important pieces of clerical legislation on the road to the establishment of the Church of England. In addition, Katherine of Aragon was legally reduced to the position of Prince Arthur's widow, as Dowager Princess of Wales, and Henry's marriage to his wife of fourteen months was ratified in law.[1] The pope's final decision on Henry's marriage to Katherine declared it 'always hath and still doth stand firm and canonical', but it no longer mattered. The 1534 Succession Act vested the crown in the expected male heir – 'the first son of your body between your Highness and your said lawful wife Queen Anne'.

Even if there were no sons between them, no one was to be left in any doubt that Henry's eldest daughter, the Lady Mary, was no longer the heir apparent:

> that then the said imperial Crown and other the premises shall be to the issue female between your Majesty and your said most dear and entirely beloved wife Queen Anne begotten; That is [to] say first to the eldest issue female, which is the Lady Elizabeth now princess.[2]

What the act did not do – and Henry may or may not have been aware of this – was legally bastardise Mary. In fact, the act did not mention Mary's status at all. The general assumption may have been that if her parents' marriage was invalid Mary was illegitimate and therefore automatically excluded. Certainly Anne's aunt, Lady Shelton, took the position that 'by statute she was declared a bastard and incapable'. In fact Henry could still argue that she was born in good faith. If the succession, or her marriage, or any other cause required it, Henry could still pass her off as his legitimate daughter.[3] The act also included a proviso that 'all the nobles of your Realm' as well as every other subject must swear to uphold its provisions. Whether this was supposed to include Richmond is not clear. Henry's other subjects were allowed to wait until they 'shall be at their full ages', but if they were fourteen they would have been in wardship, not attending parliament or pursuing their own legal disputes through the king's courts more eagerly than many adults. The political advantage of Richmond's public endorsement of Elizabeth's position as heir apparent may have outweighed any legal niceties.

The Act of Succession made it quite clear that only the king's legitimate issue, those 'lawfully begotten', could succeed to the throne. However, if the king was once more disappointed in his hopes for a prince, the teenage youth might increasingly seem a rather better prospect for the throne than Elizabeth. The dire warning included in the statute against breaking the provisions of the act stressed that 'every such person and persons of what estate degree or condition they be of' would be guilty of high treason and condemned to death. The sentiment was obviously designed to check the enduring loyalty and popularity still enjoyed by Mary, whom many in their hearts still saw as the king's rightful heir. But it was equally relevant to Richmond and any of the nobility, many of whom had little love for Anne Boleyn, who might be prepared to support his claim to the throne.

Even as Anne became more visibly pregnant, displaying 'a goodly belly', Richmond took on further responsibilities at court. He was in regular attendance at parliament. Of the forty-six sessions where attendance was recorded from January 1534, Richmond was absent on just thirteen occasions. When the Order of the Garter celebrated the Feast of St George at Windsor that year it was decided that 'the noble Youth, the most deserving, Duke of Richmond should supply the Sovereign's place'. Richmond was assisted by a select group of nobles, including the Duke of Norfolk and the king's cousin, the Marquess of Exeter, who duly observed the solemn feast on 17 May 1534. In their letters to Arthur, Viscount Lisle, both John Husse and Sir Francis Bryan picked up on the fact that Richmond had deputised for the king.

Once his duties were discharged, Richmond did not rejoin the court as it moved to Richmond Palace. Instead, he headed straight from Windsor Castle into Dorset. There is no indication that he was in any disgrace. It was common to spend the summer away from the heat and dust of London. Richmond also made a similar progress to another of his manors at Sheffield. If Richmond was to be accepted as a landed magnate, it was expected that he would occasionally spend some time on his estates. Although, just as he had been kept out of the way in September 1533, it was perhaps thought best by all concerned that he should remain quietly in the country until the king's legitimate son was safely born.

Richmond had now developed into a well-respected figure. As he travelled towards his Manor of Canford in Dorset he was greeted outside the town of Salisbury by a number of local dignitaries who 'received his grace very lovingly in offering themselves to be at his commandment'. As he came to Salisbury itself the mayor and aldermen of the town came out to meet him bearing gifts. Once he was settled at Canford he was sent 'divers and costly presents', in exactly the sort of token of esteem that would be shown to any established lord.

While he was at Canford Richmond received some news which prompted him to write to Thomas Cromwell. He had been told 'by my friends in these parts' that the king 'is fully purposed within short while to take his voyage into France'. The duke was perhaps keen to reaffirm those friendships which he had made during the previous year while he was living at the French court. He hinted rather broadly 'I would have been very glad to have given attendance upon his said highness if it had been his grace's pleasure'. In the end Richmond did not go to France, but then neither did the king. Anne was now in the latter stages of pregnancy and, as in 1533, these last few months seem to have been difficult. When Henry postponed the French meeting 'on account of her condition' he may well have had real reason for concern.

Richmond also had reason to be worried. Ironically, he had more to fear from another daughter than the longed-for prince. Henry's first-born son could expect to retain his lands, offices and a unique place in his father's affections, even if there was an heir. Another daughter was more dangerous. Anne Boleyn's overtures of friendship towards Mary were more political than personal. If she could be persuaded to recognise Anne as queen, Elizabeth's position as heir apparent was assured.[4] With Richmond there was no such incentive for good relations. If Anne were to bear yet another girl her desire to protect the claims of her children, especially in the face of any moves from the king's only male issue, might become ever more desperate.

In the event, it was Anne's fortunes, rather than Richmond's, that faltered. At about eight months she miscarried, and hindsight suggests that the baby was a son. The whole matter was quickly swept aside. Henry and Anne set off on the court's summer progress as if the pregnancy had never happened. In normal circumstances a miscarriage, especially after Anne had had a successful pregnancy, would not be serious cause for concern. But these were not normal circumstances.

For Henry's subjects the question of the succession had become a thinly spun thread 'upon which dependeth all our joy and wealth'. Anne's confidence was shaken and when she objected to her husband amusing himself with the ladies of the court, as he had always been accustomed to do before she became his sole interest, Henry was bitter in his disappointment and rebuked her that 'she should remember where she came from'. Henry's own confidence was also rocked by this echo of Katherine of Aragon's misfortunes. As with the shock of his infant son's death in 1511, this latest crisis seems to have affected his virility. His romantic dalliances might serve to convince the world he was indeed, 'a man like other men'. Yet, while Henry could play the gallant lover, it would be more than a year before he could actually make his wife pregnant again.

The events of recent years had done nothing to settle the uncertainty of the succession. Even Henry's policy of ennobling his relations had rebounded upon him. The king's cousin Henry Courtenay, Marquess of Exeter, seems to have enjoyed a good relationship with Richmond. When the duke was eleven he gave him 'a bay ambling gelding for his own saddle'. Yet Exeter found himself in prison when his servants were caught claiming that if anything happened to Henry VIII 'My Lord Marquis would be King, and they lords'. The death of Henry's nephew, Henry Brandon, who had been honoured as Earl of Lincoln at Richmond's elevation, can only have added to the general mood of uncertainty. Despite years of much upheaval the king was still no closer to securing his legitimate male heir.

When Henry returned from his summer progress, Richmond

was recalled to court. In November 1534, he played host at a St Andrew's Day feast in honour of the visiting French Admiral, Philippe de Chabot. In January 1535, he was also at court for the New Year celebrations. Henry gave him the now traditional silver gilt, weighing in at 55 ounces. Anne also gave him a piece of silver gilt, a cruse with a cover, which in a rather back-handed compliment, the duke sent to his sister Mary for her New Year's gift. Known for her good eye for clothes Anne did rather better with 'a bonnet, finished with buttons and a little brooch', which Richmond added to his wardrobe. In the New Year he was still with the king at Westminster, adding his vote (in accordance with the King's wishes), for James V's election to the Order of the Garter.

Now aged fifteen, he began to assume duties for his father on a more regular basis, although sometimes it was his very youth and inexperience that made him useful. When Chapuys paid a visit in February 1535, to find 'all the Lords were in Council', he was not insulted because 'the Duke of Richmond . . . remained to entertain me'. However, Richmond's usefulness could also have a political edge. His presence at Tyburn in May 1535 at the execution of three Carthusian monks was a clear signal of Henry VIII's tacit approval of their punishment for flouting the king's new laws on religion. The Imperial ambassador wrote with shocked disbelief that Richmond and 'several other lords, and gentlemen courtiers, were present at the execution, openly and quite close to the victims'. Chapuys believed that the king himself had wanted to be present 'to witness the butchery'. Instead, his son's attendance was perhaps the next best thing and a public indication of the king's mind.

Richmond also continued to spend some of his time away from court. In general he does not seem to have followed the king on his summer progresses, instead preferring to use the time to visit his own estates. On one occasion he travelled as far as his Sheffield manor, although he did not find the area very much to his liking. Unlike Canford, which boasted two parks, he complained rather petulantly to Thomas Cromwell that

Sheffield offered little to amuse him as 'here in this country [county] where I lie I have no park nor game to show sport nor pleasure to my friends'. Obviously hoping that Cromwell would help him out, he enclosed a list of the nearby parks belonging to the king and others, which he had had his eye on.

As the months passed and Anne still failed to conceive, speculation grew that some other solution to the succession crisis would be necessary. For the first time since his elevation in 1525, Richmond featured in the gossip. However, it was not the dutiful son himself who had attracted attention, but the ambition of Thomas Howard, Duke of Norfolk, who was described as:

> being one of the greatest men in the kingdom, and having sons and the Duke of Richmond for his son-in-law, might . . . if disorders ensued to get the rule into his own hands.[5]

Having a niece as Queen of England had not brought Norfolk all the benefits he felt were his due. Richmond's marriage was intended at least as much for Anne's benefit as his own. Now it appeared that she could not ensure that a son with Howard blood would sit upon the throne. Relations between him and Anne became increasingly tense and his loyalty to her grew correspondingly thin. When Anne lost her temper and 'heaped more injuries on the Duke of Norfolk than on a dog', he stormed out and vented his spleen on the first person he met, calling his queen and sovereign lady every possible name under the sun.

In the circumstances the idea of his own daughter as a more dutiful and benevolent queen, with the ultimate prize of his grandchild as a future king, must have seemed a more tempting prospect. Although Chapuys might believe that Anne 'now rules over and governs the nation' so that even Henry dared not contradict her, Norfolk was astute enough to realise that her long- term security depended on the safe delivery of a prince. Richmond was a route to continued power and influence that did not rely on the fortunes of his niece.[6] Outwardly, Richmond was every inch the king's loyal and obedient son. Yet backed by the power and ambition of the Duke of Norfolk, Anne would be foolish not to see him as a threat. Matters did not immediately come to a head, but Norfolk increasingly had little reason to support Anne and her offspring, and every reason to promote the fortunes of his royal son-in-law.

Richmond's links to Norfolk and his interests went beyond his marriage to Mary or his friendship with Surrey. Norfolk had replaced Lisle as Vice-Admiral to the Duke of Richmond. He had replaced Wolsey as the chief custodian of the lands and person of the lunatic George, Lord Tailbois. He held the wardship of Richmond's uncle, George Blount, and he also assumed an increasingly active role in Richmond's own affairs, over and above his concerns that the duke should maintain an appropriately splendid household. This was facilitated by the fact that a number of Richmond's servants, notably John Uvedale and William Brereton, already had established links with the Howard family.[7] By March 1535, John Husse, who acted for Lisle, knew that any business with Richmond's household would be decided, not by the duke's governor, George Cotton, but 'the conclusion of the same shall depend much upon my lord of Norfolk's goodwill and pleasure'.

In some respects Norfolk's involvement reflected Wolsey's earlier role, in directing and overseeing daily business. While the duke was still in fact a child it was only sensible to have someone keeping an eye on his officers and lands. Yet as Richmond grew older, rather than simply directing matters, Norfolk actively sought to work with his son-in-law. When problems arose in Richmond's landholdings in the Welsh Marches in 1535, Norfolk accompanied Richmond on a stately progress to Holt to address the problem.[8] The idea was plain. Rather than imposing his will, so that Richmond grew to resent his interference, Norfolk was keen to ensure that the young duke came to reflect his own sympathies and prejudices.

As he approached his sixteenth birthday the Duke of Richmond was developing into a most promising candidate for the throne. Not only was he still the king's only son, but the praises heaped upon his mental and martial abilities were entirely reminiscent of the adulation showered upon his father at his accession in 1509. He was 'a goodly young lord, and a toward, in many qualities and feats'. On the very verge of manhood, the danger of a minority could be argued to be past. For political reasons, Henry's nephew, James V of Scotland, had been declared of age when he was fourteen. If anything untoward happened to Henry, a similar policy could easily be adopted towards Richmond.

There were still a number of factors stacked against him, not least that according to the law, Elizabeth was the heir apparent. Moreover, under the terms of the 1534 Act of Succession, the stigma of his illegitimacy was still an effective block to any consideration of his accession. Even if Richmond mounted a claim against Elizabeth he would still have to contend with the popularity enjoyed by Mary. Support for 'the Princess', as she continued to be called by the Imperial ambassador, endured. The feeling was not sufficiently strong to convince Charles V to back his support for his cousin with action, although John Snappe cannot have been the only Englishman willing to give his life and all he had 'upon my Lady Mary's title against the issue that should come of the Queen'.[9] The strength of feeling for Richmond was unlikely to be tested while the king or his subjects held out any hope of a prince, and by October 1535 Anne Boleyn finally fell pregnant again.

At the New Year in 1536, things seemed, on the surface at least, to be much as they had been two years earlier. Having successfully given birth to a thriving baby daughter, Anne was now expected to produce her brother. The court enjoyed its customary revels and Henry produced his usual parcel of silver gilt for his son. This year the present was particularly impressive. A bowl with a star in the bottom was engraved with Richmond's arms. A jug, with its handles made to look like two serpents, was decorated with the initials 'H' and 'A' beneath a crown, and another 'standing bowl' was capped with the figure of a small boy bearing a shield and spear with an engraved inscription in French. Some evidence, perhaps, that Richmond, at least, had accrued some benefit from his time in France.

Yet things were not the same. The optimism engendered by Elizabeth's birth had been sorely damaged by Anne's subsequent miscarriage. Anne was dismayed and her enemies were encouraged to find that she was no longer the sole object of her ardent lover's attentions. As was his custom when his wife was pregnant, Henry had developed a roving eye and this time the subject of his affections was a young woman named Jane Seymour.

It is easy, with hindsight, to read too much into the many storms and tempests of Anne and Henry's marital relationship. Yet Anne was all too aware that she had created a dangerous precedent. Her concerns about the propriety of her ladies demonstrates her concern that she should be seen to act as befitted a Queen of England, presiding over a well-ordered household as her predecessor had done. Her insistence that their necklines should be demurely filled with 'chests' – material inserts which covered any cleavage – was perhaps less a question of fashion than a natural jealousy that a rival might rise from their ranks. Many of those qualities which had made her an enticing mistress ensured she was unsuited to the role of the patient wife, not least because she loved Henry with a passion and could not 'shut her eyes and endure, just like others who were worthier than she', when Henry as much as looked elsewhere.

For the moment this was all it was. Indeed, Anne was getting off lightly. Henry's relationship with Jane was chaste, in the true tradition of courtly love, something that cannot be said of many of Henry's liaisons during Katherine of Aragon's numerous pregnancies. It was Anne's fear that what she had done others might now emulate, and the circling of her enemies made this something more than a romantic diversion.

Anne was notoriously unpopular. Neither her shirts nor her smocks for the poor, nor her traditional gifts of Maundy money, (even though she increased the amount to considerably more than Katherine had been accustomed to bestow) was enough to redress her reputation. In the eyes of many she was a 'goggle-eyed whore', a she-devil who had stolen the king from his true and rightful wife. She was the architect of all Mary's misfortunes and she bore the brunt of public criticism regarding many of the most unpopular measures of the Reformation, not just the changes in religion, but the accompanying draconian measures against treason in word or deed. As good men like Sir Thomas More and John Fisher went to the scaffold and the country endured the perils of famine and the threat of hostilities with the emperor, it begged the question whether the new regime was actually the will of God after all. When Henry VIII's own fool, Will Somers, was bold enough to gauge the mood of the country and call Anne a 'ribald' and her daughter a bastard, the queen's only real security was Henry's affection, the child she carried and the king's first wife.

When Katherine of Aragon died on 7 January 1536 Henry's immediate reaction was joy and deliverance, declaring 'God be praised that we are free from all suspicion of war'. All now seemed set fair for the birth of his prince, whose mother would be indisputably the only queen in England. The prospect of invasion was converted into the possibility of reconciliation with Charles V. Ever willing to believe that God espoused all his causes, Henry no doubt took this timely blessing as a sign that all would, at last, be well. Anne's public reaction was equally joyous. 'Now I am indeed a Queen' she declared. But even as she and Henry went to mass in great state and Elizabeth was shown off to the court by her proud father, she must have realised that she might be the victim of her own success. Now no one could require Henry to return to Katherine. If he ever chose to put her aside, he would be free to marry again and it would be much easier a second time.

On 24 January 1536, there was a further crisis. Henry was jousting in the tiltyard at Greenwich when he fell from his horse. Unlike the incident in 1524, this accident was gravely serious. The king did not recover consciousness for over two hours. It was an anxious time. Were Henry to die, the question of the succession, so long pondered, considered, but avoided, would be drawn dramatically into focus. If Anne's unborn child were the long desired male heir, England would have its king, only to be plunged into a long minority which would endanger the realm. If the pregnancy failed or the child was a girl, Elizabeth would be queen. However, even Anne's most ardent supporters cannot have viewed the accession of a two-year-old girl with any real enthusiasm.

Henry's other daughter was now a woman of nineteen. Her supposed illegitimacy was the least of her problems. It had not yet been enshrined in law and it would be a simple thing to argue that she had been born in good faith. She was popular with the English people and would be accepted across Europe as Henry's rightful successor. Except that all the dangers of a ruling queen, which had concerned men in 1525, still stood between her and the throne.

Richmond might seem to hold all the cards. The king's only son could ascend the throne without any danger of a minority and rule in succession to the father whom he so closely resembled, apart from the fact that he had no legal title to the throne. The law of the land still clearly stated that that the king's bastard issue had no rights in regard to the succession. Even if Henry revived sufficiently to murmur his consent, the problem of Richmond's illegitimacy would remain. With no clear candidate from among Henry's own children and a host of cousins and other nobles, such as Henry VIII's nephew James V, who might decide to try their luck, there was the all too real prospect of war and perhaps years of disorder. Luckily, Henry survived – this time. However, the incident was a worrying reminder, if any were needed, that Henry was not immortal. If the question of his successor could not be decisively settled, then England's future would be very bleak.

However, only days later, on 29 January 1536, Anne Boleyn miscarried for the second time. To make matters worse, the child would have been a son.[10] Already badly scared by his recent brush with death, this time Henry's reaction bordered on hysterical. The king feared that his second marriage was no more blessed than his first. His anxiety swept him onwards:

> he had been seduced and forced into this second marriage
> by means of sortileges and charms . . . owing to that he held
> it as nul. God . . . had well shown his displeasure at it by
> denying him male children.[11]

Tellingly, Anne is said to have blamed Norfolk for her misfortune, claiming that he had broken the news of the king's accident too abruptly. With more passion than prudence, she also blamed the king, allegedly upbraiding him for his part in this tragedy by casting in his face how his attentions to Jane Seymour had distressed her. Emotions were clearly running high. Whether this episode would have been enough to seal Anne's fate, had the king been left to his own devices, is impossible to say. Her enemies regarded the high drama with glee. They had all the ammunition they needed and battle was joined.

The events of January 1536 set the tone for the months to follow. Henry's panic-stricken concerns about his second marriage were nurtured and fuelled. The tempting prospect of Jane Seymour was set before him as a viable, nubile and altogether more compliant alternative. With Katherine now dead his next union would be free of any impediment or doubt. Surely then there would be no reason for sons not to follow. By March 1536, Jane's elder brother, Sir Edward Seymour, was a member of the King's privy chamber, a sure sign that Henry's interest had been stirred. Since a new marriage would also allow Mary to be acknowledged as having been born in good faith, her supporters threw in their lot with the Seymours. However, Richmond's position was rather less clear cut.

His personal relationship with Anne may on occasion have been rather strained, with Anne making efforts to observe propriety through gritted teeth, but he had little to gain by her removal. With the king's freedom to marry again came the prospect of further issue. Although Edward Seymour had been

Richmond's Master of the Horse at Sheriff Hutton, that appointment had come from the crown. Equally, when Richmond had appointed Seymour as steward of his Manor of Canford in Dorset, in 1528, it was at the king's command. Richmond may even have felt resentful, since he had intended to give the stewardship of all his lands in Dorset to his chamberlain, Sir William Parr. Since Richmond's interests were far more intimately associated with the Duke of Norfolk, who had little love for the ambitious Seymours, neither of them were likely to view this new development with any particular pleasure.

Unlike Norfolk, Richmond could at least rest assured that he was safe from any repercussions, should the Seymours succeed in securing Anne's downfall. Despite his links to the Howards, and thus by implication the Boleyns, he was no ordinary magnate. He remained close to his father and in March 1536, his particular usefulness to the king was demonstrated once again. During negotiations for a meeting between Henry VIII and James V at York, it was proposed that 'the Duke of Richmond and the eldest son of the Duke of Norfolk and of the Marquis [probably Exeter] shall be made hostages for the security of the King of Scots'.[12] While Mary and Elizabeth's supporters nailed their colours to the mast, Richmond's activities give little clue to his feelings. At a chapter of the Order of the Garter held in April 1536, he voted both for Anne's brother, Lord Rochford and for Sir Nicholas Carew, who was no supporter of the Boleyns. His actions probably reflected the mood of much of the court as they waited to see which way the die would fall.

Yet Richmond's own interests were too extensive for him to be completely unaffected by the events that now raged around him. As the net closed around Anne Boleyn, one of those arrested under suspicion of being her lover was William Brereton, who was Richmond's steward in the Marches of Wales. Since the self-confessed architect of Anne Boleyn's downfall was Thomas Cromwell, the selection of Brereton is unlikely to have been made at random. Brereton's activities in Wales had made him something of a thorn in Cromwell's side as he attempted to reform local government, so the downfall of Anne Boleyn provided a tailor-made opportunity to pluck him out.¹³ If the young duke was in any way concerned at these moves against one of his servants, he was cautious enough to keep his own counsel. Whatever his own feelings, Brereton's death presented no danger to him and he was wise enough not to intercede for his servant against the wishes of the king.

Richmond was not among the twenty-six peers who were summoned to give judgment at Anne Boleyn's trial. It was perhaps considered a little indelicate to allow a young man, who had not yet consummated his own marriage, to sit in judgment on his stepmother's sexual crimes. However, he would not have been ignorant of the proceedings. Norfolk, who had no intention of being dragged down by his niece, presided over the court as Lord High Steward and Henry Howard, Earl of Surrey, deputised for his father as Earl Marshal. However, Richmond was present at her execution. It was said that 'a malign smile seemed to pass over the features of the young Duke of Richmond', but this report was not contemporary. Richmond's attendance was almost certainly the will of the king and intended, as at Tyburn in 1535, to make a political point. Richmond's personal feelings were not at issue.

The loss of Anne was probably no great blow to Richmond. If nothing else she was a rival for his father's time and affection. When the king decided he wanted Anne to have Margaret Beaufort's former Manor of Collyweston in Northamptonshire, which Richmond had enjoyed since 1525, the duke had written to Cromwell with perhaps a hint of disgruntled petulance 'the which manor as I understand the king's Highness' pleasure is that the queen's grace shall have'. Indeed, the Imperial ambassador eagerly seized upon a rumour that Anne had intended to murder Richmond. With a certain gory enjoyment he recounted how on the evening of Anne's arrest, Richmond had gone to ask his father's blessing, before retiring for the night. At the sight of his son the king had been moved to tears and said:

that he and his sister, owed God a great debt for having escaped from the hands of that cursed and poisoning whore who had planned to poison them.[14]

Others, including the chronicler Charles Wriothesley, also picked up on this allegation. In fact, it seems to have been nothing but a ploy of the Seymour faction to manipulate Henry's ability to feel hard done by and play on his affection for his children to insure against any sudden changes of heart.

While Anne's anger and frustration against Mary sometimes spilled over into wild threats, there is nothing to suggest that Richmond was a particular target, although Anne may well have been fearful of the strength of Henry's feelings for his only son. Any satisfaction Richmond might have taken in Anne's demise would have been tempered by the knowledge that Henry and Jane Seymour were immediately betrothed. On 30 May they were married and once more there was the possibility of a legitimate heir to the English throne.

However, there were further repercussions of Anne's downfall; a move that could only be to Richmond's benefit. On 17 May 1536, Thomas Cranmer, in his capacity as Archbishop of Canterbury, declared the king's marriage to Anne Boleyn to be unlawful. In an echo of Henry's separation from Katherine, the grounds were confidently declared to be 'entirely just, true, and lawful impediments', which had been unknown at the time of their marriage. The small detail that if Anne had never been Henry's lawful wife, she could hardly have committed adultery, was conveniently overlooked. This measure was directed at Elizabeth. With her parent's marriage decreed unlawful, she, like Mary before her, was now reduced from the state of Princess of England and heir apparent, to the Lady Elizabeth and the king's natural daughter.

A man who believed his wife had committed adultery would naturally have reason to be suspicious regarding the paternity of his children. Sir Thomas Burgh had secured an Act of Parliament to bastardise his offspring when he divorced his wife for this offence.[15] However, as Henry never gave any indication that he doubted Elizabeth's paternity he must have had another reason to take such a drastic step. Whatever Anne had done or not done, the good faith of only one of the parents was sufficient to salvage the legitimacy of a child. Henry had obviously married Anne in good faith, yet now he was left with three illegitimate children and no legitimate issue at all.[16]

If this was simply intended to tie up loose ends and prepare the ground for the host of children that Jane was to produce, it was an extremely high-risk policy. On the other hand, the repercussions were not entirely negative. All other things being equal, as the king's only male child Richmond automatically took precedence over his sisters. Eleven years after his elevation to the peerage, the prospects of Henry VIII's bastard son once more became the focus of gossip and speculation.

With hindsight, the greatest obstacle to his succession was Edward, the son Henry would have from his marriage to Jane Seymour. However, in the summer of 1536 this prospect may not have seemed so certain. One of the accusations levied at Anne was that she had gossiped about Henry's virility, or rather lack of it. If questions about the king's potency could be raised in such an official forum, who could blame his subjects if they harboured similar doubts? Unlike Anne, Jane was not pregnant when Henry married her, and although Henry quickly began to boast that a prince could be expected 'in due season', there was in fact no guarantee that his new queen was capable of bearing a child. Conversely, recent events had proved beyond a shadow of a doubt that one accident, one illness or a single stroke of misfortune, could take the king at any time. In this atmosphere, Richmond's friends had reason to believe that the situation could be turned to their advantage.

Certainly Norfolk's conduct towards Mary Tudor was not the most prudent line to take if he truly believed she would be ever be queen. Mary was not alone in imagining that Anne's downfall would be sufficient to restore her to her father's favour. Instead, Norfolk was dispatched to know if she was now prepared to renounce the authority of the Pope and acknowledge that her parents' marriage had been unlawful. Shocked and disbelieving, Mary vehemently refused. In the drama which followed Norfolk reportedly railed at her that:

> since she was such an unnatural daughter as to disobey completely the King's injunctions, he could hardly believe . . . that she was the King's own bastard daughter. Were she his, or any other man's daughter, he would beat her to death, or strike her head against the wall, until it was as soft as a boiled apple.[17]

At first Mary continued to refuse, but quickly found herself under greater pressure than she had ever experienced while her mother was alive. The judges agreed that her action was treasonous and the punishment for that was death. Whatever Henry's true intentions, since Mary was still his daughter, not to mention a useful political tool, she was led to believe that if she insisted on being a martyr to her cause then the king would oblige her. Even the Imperial ambassador now advised her that she would achieve more by her submission. On 22 June 1536, Mary capitulated and put her signature to a document that acceded to all the king's demands.

That Henry chose this point in time to insist upon her obedience is evidence of the insecurity over the succession. Should he and Jane have no issue, or worse still yet another girl, Mary's exact status would be crucial. Alone among Henry's children, she had been accepted by the world as his legitimate child for most of her life and this belief could not be allowed to fester. The Imperial ambassador had no doubt that Henry was trying to clear the way to nominate Richmond as his heir, 'that being no doubt the King's chief reason for insisting so much on the Princess [Mary] subscribing to the statute which declared her to be a bastard.' The timing cannot be coincidence. After all, Mary had maintained her obstinacy over the last three years and Henry had been positively lenient to her in the face of what was a very dangerous example to others. Perhaps he had expected that the arrival of his legitimate prince would silence all dispute, only to be persuaded, in the light of recent events, that it was sensible to have a contingency plan. Given Norfolk's close association with Richmond it is interesting that he was sent to require Mary's obedience.

Despite Henry's affection for his daughter, it would not have been difficult to persuade him of the folly of allowing her to continue in her disobedience. As long as Mary was allowed to flout her father's laws and dispute his arguments, she was an encouragement to all those who believed that the English Reformation was only a temporary inconvenience. As a father, Henry was angry and embarrassed at his daughter's conduct. As a king, to allow her to continue to question his laws was a licence for others to do likewise. Those of Mary's friends who dared speculate on her prospects of accession were arrested and interrogated and Norfolk's reports of Mary's wilful obstinacy were hardly likely to soften Henry's attitude towards his daughter. One way or another, the threat Mary represented had to be negated.

The idea that Norfolk encouraged Henry's ire cannot be discounted. In 1533, Mary had told Henry, 'I doubt not that your grace does take me for your lawful daughter, born in true matrimony'. And after so many years even the most obedient subjects, Norfolk included, occasionally slipped back into old habits when dealing with 'the Princess'. The Imperial ambassador caught wind of some gossip or proposal which suggested naming Mary as the heir-apparent (without restoring her title of princess), with the proviso that if Jane and Henry had a child their claim would take precedence. If Richmond were to take precedence over her, there could be no doubt that she was only the king's natural daughter.

On 6 June 1536, the Imperial ambassador reported an interesting exchange at court:

Already no less a person than the Earl of Sussex, stated the other day in the Privy Council, in the King's presence, that considering that the Princess was a bastard, as well as the Duke of Richmond, it was advisable to prefer the male to the female, for the succession to the Crown. This opinion of the Earl not having been contradicted by the King, might hereafter gain ground and have adherents.[18]

This is unlikely to have been a sudden notion. The possibility had been in the back of everyone's mind since 1525. Until now it had been mere speculation, the kind of subject which might be spoken of in asides, but was dangerous to voice openly and even more risky to commit to paper. To actually broach the subject to the king's face and get away with it was a significant development. The Earl of Sussex, Robert Radcliffe, was a long-term friend and supporter of the Duke of Norfolk. Even so, he was unlikely to have taken such a risk unless someone, probably Norfolk, had already sounded out the king. His comment was perhaps intended to test the waters. If Jane did not produce a son, would the country be prepared to accept the king's bastard son as the heir apparent?

In the wake of Anne Boleyn's downfall, Norfolk can have taken little comfort in the king's marriage to Jane Seymour. Her brother Edward had already looked set for a promising court career, now the world was at his feet. Norfolk's best hope of maintaining power and influence was through Richmond, his daughter and, hopefully, their children. Now was the time for the association which he had been nurturing for the last seven years to come into its own. If Jane did produce an heir, then the Howards close links to the king's illegitimate son would be their insurance against isolation on the fringes of political affairs. If she did not give birth to a prince then Richmond was developing into a most promising candidate for king.

Since all of the king's children were now (one way or another) declared to be illegitimate, none of them were eligible to inherit the throne, which meant that the heir-apparent was Margaret Douglas, the daughter of Henry VIII's elder sister Margaret, by her second husband Archibald Douglas. Widely reputed to be one of the most beautiful women of her generation, she had been living at the English court since 1530 and Henry treated her almost as if she was his own daughter. While her claim was not as strong as Mary's, Norfolk would need to be sure that any threat she represented to Richmond's position was also safely neutralised. Norfolk may simply have hoped to see her safely married off or he may have had some inkling that she was up to no good. Since Henry had demonstrated himself to be positively prudish about Mary's morals and manners it would not have taken a very grave indiscretion to convince the king that Margaret's conduct was unbecoming to a royal heiress. However, nothing can have prepared him for what now emerged.

It was discovered that Margaret Douglas had been secretly married to the duke's half-brother, Lord Thomas Howard, since Easter 1536. Worse, Norfolk's own daughter Mary, Duchess of Richmond, was suspected of having known about the match and it emerged that 'divers times' she had been their only chaperone. If the poems inscribed by Margaret and Thomas in the anthology known as the *Devonshire Manuscript*, which belonged to the Duchess of Richmond, are any indication, this was a love match, albeit a very risky one. For any member of the nobility to contract a marriage without the king's permission was courting danger. In the present circumstances, to secretly marry one of the possible claimants to the throne was sheer madness.

Henry reacted with predictable anger. On 8 June 1536 both Margaret and Thomas were sent to the Tower. Chapuys reported that Henry VIII was 'very much annoyed by his niece's marriage'. By seeking to ally himself with one of royal blood Thomas was accused of 'maliciously and traitorously minding and imagining to put division in the realm': a clear reference to Henry's anxiety over the prospect of a disputed succession. It is entirely probable that Norfolk was self-serving enough to betray his half-brother to the king. Not only would Margaret's arrest and imprisonment make Richmond's position stronger, but also it was the only way to ensure that neither Norfolk, nor indeed his daughter, were implicated in the couple's guilt. The Duchess of Richmond in particular was fortunate that her role was not more strictly examined. Both Thomas and Margaret maintained that she had not been told of their marriage, but she was clearly a close friend and confidante. It was probably only her father's fancy footwork and her marriage to Richmond which saved her from more stringent enquiries.

Instead, moves were afoot to set Richmond up with his own residence on the banks of the River Thames. With Coldharbour Mansion still unavailable, Richmond had hitherto been forced to find other lodgings when he was in the capital. In October 1534 he had been using the London home of the Bishop of Norwich. Now such arrangements were no longer thought to be suitable and the king decided 'for certain causes moving his Highness, of his most noble and abundant grace' to give Baynards Castle over to his son. The king's grant (in the Statute 28 Henry VIII c34) of the London town house that had formerly belonged to Richard III's mother, Cecily, Duchess of York, was perhaps the final sign of Richmond's emergence into full adult life and an indication that a decision had been made, as Richmond approached his seventeenth birthday, to allow him to co-habit with his bride of three years, Mary Howard.[19]

Baynards Castle was the house where Henry VII had spent the first few weeks of his reign in 1485 and Henry VIII had used it as an offical residence for his queens: Katherine, Anne and later Anne of Cleves. Despite its two impressive towers, topped by French-style turrets, it was more a gracious residence than an actual castle. In 1501 it had been described as 'beautiful and commodious for the entertainment of any Prince or great Estate'.[20] When Richmond and his wife took up residence in their new home, a tangible signal would be sent to all that he had left his childhood behind him. Once Richmond was living with his wife there would also be the reassuring prospect that sons would shortly follow.

It all looked fairly promising. For the good of the realm and the survival of the Tudor dynasty, even Mary's supporters might well be persuaded that Margaret Beaufort's prudence in 1485 had created a precedent. Just as she had allowed her claim to be overlooked in favour of her son, they could perhaps be convinced to throw in their lot with the male heir, especially since they could take comfort in the fact that Norfolk's religious beliefs placed him firmly among the ranks of the conservatives. Of the new learning he was once famously heard to remark:

I have never read the Scripture, nor never will read it. It was merry in England afore the new learning came up; yea, I would all things were as hath been in times past.[21]

Even Mary herself might not be that difficult to convince that she should allow her brother to take precedence over her.

From her earliest childhood Mary had understood that the throne was the birthright of the male heir. Her insistence on her rightful title as princess should not be taken as evidence of political ambition. The rumours that now circulated that Mary was to be created Duchess of York, or otherwise similarly recognised, were perhaps part of a larger scheme to ensure Richmond's place in the succession, which may have been enough to satisfy her. Katherine of Aragon had raised her daughter to believe that certain aspects of government were outside a woman's competence. Having just endured a salutary lesson in obedience to her father's will, if Henry had chosen to name Richmond as heir-apparent, there is every likelihood that Mary would have accepted his decision.

From among the ranks of the nobility Norfolk was, without doubt, Richmond's greatest ally. Richmond's stepfather Edward, Lord Clinton, was only seven years older than Richmond himself and still at the very beginning of his promising career. His attempts to prove his loyalty during the Pilgrimage of Grace (the rebellion in the north) when he raised a company of five hundred men only to watch them desert to the rebel side, leaving him to flee with a single servant, aptly demonstrate how fragile his power base presently was. Still some distance from the Elizabethan Earl of Lincoln he would become, he simply did not have the resources to make a significant contribution to any plot. In the first part of the 1536 subsidy he paid just £5.

While the king's relationship with Elizabeth Blount remained good, she was no Margaret Beaufort to rally support for her son. Richmond's relations with his maternal kin were warm and affectionate. He had provided a glowing testimony for William Gresley, of Drakelow in Derbyshire, the husband of his mother's younger sister Rose. When Richmond went to Shrewsbury in 1535 his uncle, George Blount, neglected other business to come and pay his respects. His other uncle, William Blount, was a servant in Richmond's household at the time of his death in 1536. However, the Blounts had not made any real political capital out of their relationship with Richmond and never rose above their customary gentry status. Indeed, sometimes their relationship to the duke was a positive disadvantage. When George Blount wanted to purchase a former abbey, Henry, Lord Stafford objected that he was already well provided for, being 'my lord of Richmond's servant and hath a fair house of his own to dwell in or two'. Instead, the property went to Stafford for his large brood of children.

Nothing could be taken for granted. If Norfolk was a powerful ally he was also something of a liability. Charles Brandon, Duke of Suffolk, was not the only English nobleman who would not welcome a grandson of the Duke of Norfolk on the throne, especially when he might feel that that his own daughters, from his marriage to Henry's sister, also had a claim. Then there was the question of how the news might be received abroad. Even if Mary would agree to step aside the country still had to look nervously to the possible reaction of Charles V or even the ambitions of Henry's nephew, James V of Scotland, who, legal niceties aside, might be able to rally French support to back his claim. Even so, if Henry were to name Richmond as heir-apparent, who knew how the picture might change before Henry actually died?

The 1536 Succession Act did little to clarify the king's intentions. For the first time it did not confine the succession to the legitimate line. Instead Henry was granted the authority to designate whomever he liked as his successor, either by letters patent or by his last will 'at your only pleasure'. What the act did not do was give the remotest hint of whom Henry had in mind. Rather it recited the dangers of designating an heir apparent:

> such person that should be so named, might happen to take great heart and courage, and by presumption fall into inobedience and rebellion.[22]

There were dire warnings should any of Henry's possible heirs usurp the rights of any of the others. To attempt to do so would forfeit their claim to the throne and to ensure obedience the grounds and punishments for treason were also increased.

The message was clear. The decision was the king's alone and he would make his choice in due course. The Act of Succession went some way to calm the mood of speculation and debate that had occupied recent months. To the great comfort and relief of the realm it also put in place a legal framework which would allow Henry to designate a successor on the grounds of their suitability, rather than be constricted by the fallout of his matrimonial difficulties. Yet it is difficult to escape the feeling that Henry had been persuaded to this course of action by the anxious lobbying of his courtiers. For his part, as long as he had breath in his body and the leisure to wait, Henry VIII seems to have had no intention of relinquishing his long held conviction that God would grant him a prince.

While the act allowed the king to name Richmond as his heir, it was not exactly a statement of intent. It also recited the traditional formula, which ensured that any sons born to Henry and Jane were first in line for the succession. Even more tellingly, if there were no sons then the crown would pass 'to the issue female between your Majesty and your said most dear and entirely beloved Wife Queen Jane begotten'. As a further reassurance to everyone (with the possible exception of the queen) there was similar provision for legitimate issue by any subsequent wives.

Even so, many observers were convinced that Henry was on the brink of naming his son as heir apparent. The Imperial ambassador, Chapuys, reported that Richmond 'was certainly intended to be his heir and successor.' He was not alone in his conviction. Others also believed:

In case of there being no sons at all of this last marriage, it is believed the King's determination was, that the succession should go to his bastard son the Duke of Richmont [sic].[23]

Their confidence should not obscure how far removed from the throne Richmond remained in 1536. Henry would not easily abandon his dreams of a legitimate male heir. Also, he was no longer confined to a straight choice between his three children. Henry Courtenay, Marquess of Exeter, or any other suitable noble might now be chosen over the king's bastard son. Yet for the first time there was also no reason why Henry should not name Richmond as his successor – if he wished to do so.

The idea that Henry was about to name Richmond as heir apparent, only to receive the devastating news of his illness and death, is dramatic but untenable. With the benefit of hindsight, on 23 July 1536 Chapuys confidently declared that 'had he not fallen ill' Henry was planning to have his son proclaimed as his successor by parliament. Yet on 8 June 1536, Richmond was still well enough to appear in public for the opening session of parliament without his health provoking any cause for concern. Richmond had a very public role in the proceedings – being placed just ahead of his father as he carried the king's 'cap of maintenance'. He would have attracted a good deal of attention as the lords went in solemn procession from York Place to Westminster. Then there was a mass and a speech before the lords 'put off their robes and so rode to York Place to dinner'. Yet through the whole of that business no one thought to mention that Richmond was looking a bit peaky.

The idea that Richmond's health had been in visible decline

for some time is based on the account of the chronicler, Charles Wriothesley who said 'he pined inwardly in his body long before he died'. Yet Richmond's presence about the court, not to mention the plan to send him up to Scotland, does not indicate that his health was failing. In all outward respects it was business as usual. In April 1536, the Venetian ambassador had to calm the fears of his French counterpart that the project to give Richmond the Duchy of Milan had been revived. In May he was appointed chamberlain of Chester and North Wales, an office formerly held by one of Anne Boleyn's supposed lovers, Henry Norris. A few days later he was among those to whom Charles V addressed letters of credence for his new ambassador.

Far from contemplating his own demise, Richmond was eager to secure another one of Norris's offices for his servant Giles Forster. Even before Norris was condemned, Richmond wrote to the Bishop of Lincoln about 'the trouble and business that Mr Norris is now in, the which I think is not to you unknown' and blithely requested the office on the grounds that 'it is presupposed with many men that there is no way but one with him'. Unfortunately for Richmond, the good bishop was of much the same mind regarding Norris's fate and had already offered that office, the stewardship of Banbury, to Thomas Cromwell. Richmond was more successful after the execution of Anne's brother, Lord Rochford, when he obtained the offices of Warden of the Cinque Ports and Constable of Dover Castle.

If Henry had truly intended to proclaim Richmond as his heir during this session of parliament it might have been prudent to give some tangible hint, to test possible reactions if nothing else. However, when the Lord Chancellor, Lord Audley, gave his opening speech, he concentrated instead on the idea of legitimate heirs and stressed Jane's fertility. In truth there was no reason to make any such announcement. The act itself was all the insurance policy the king needed and he had no intention of dying just yet. In the meantime, why invite difficulties by declaring your hand? With Richmond present and apparently in good health, there is no reason to think this was a last minute change of plan or indeed that Henry had any idea that Richmond would not live long.

The first report of his illness did not leak out until a month later on 8 July 1536,[24] when, predictably, Chapuys was the first with the news:

> There is however no fear for the present of the Princess losing her right to the throne of England, for the King's bastard son, I mean the Duke of Richmond, cannot according to the prognostication of his physicians live many months, having been pronounced to be in a state of rapid consumption.[25]

Although we do not have the lurid reports of swollen limbs, scabby skin and foul stenches that accompanied the death throes of Edward VI, contemporary observers were convinced that the young king's illness was 'the same as that which killed the late Earl [sic] of Richmond'. Modern medical opinion has suggested that this was not actually tuberculosis but 'a suppurating pulmonary infection', which without recourse to antibiotics led to fatal complications.[26]

At the time of his death Richmond was at St James's Palace in London. Later to become the residence of several royal princes, including his half-brother, Prince Edward, this has prompted certain authors to assume it was also earmarked as a residence for the duke. In fact, in July 1536 Richmond's household was at Tonge in Kent, where it had been based since October 1535. The accounts of his kitchen show the ducal household moving from Lewes to Sheffield, through Godstone to Tonge from where Richmond and several carts of his belongings had come to London in appropriate ducal state for the parliament. Until quite recently he had been lodging with the king at court. However, when Henry moved on to Sittingbourne in Kent, Richmond was obviously not well enough to accompany him and remained behind in London. Yet the fact that he died at St James's is not evidence that he was ever intended to live there.

As his sickness became apparent and his condition grew more serious, it would clearly have been unwise for Richmond to remain with the court. Aside from the obvious risk of infection, there was also the danger of rumour and gossip. The anxiety of recent months would not be calmed by the news that the king's only son was seriously ill. However, to expose Richmond to a journey of any length could also be dangerous. St James's Palace was close at hand – in addition, the transformation of the former monastic hospital into a royal residence was not yet fully complete – Richmond and his entourage could be installed there without attracting a great deal of attention. Perhaps the peace and quiet of the former religious house would work its own miracle.

Instead, the duke now fell into a rapid decline. By 18 July 1536, news of his illness was more widely known. When John Husse wrote to Viscount Lisle, 'My Lord of Richmond [is] very sick. Jesu be his comfort,' he clearly believed the situation was quite serious. His condition now quickly deteriorated and, if anything, the opinion of his doctors was to prove optimistic. On 23 July 1536, Chapuys sent off a quickly scribbled note, 'I have just this moment heard that the Duke of Richmond died this morning, which is not a bad thing for the interests of the Princess'. The date of his demise has also been recorded as the 24th or even the 25th, but Chapuys is unlikely to have been mistaken. Once more Henry was blessed with nothing but daughters and some unfortunate messenger was dispatched to inform the King of England that his only son was dead.

Henry's immediate reaction to the news has not survived, although judging from subsequent events it seems to have been close to the emotional hysteria produced by Anne Boleyn's second miscarriage. Beside himself with grief, all of Henry's familiar fears and anxieties resurfaced. If Jane had been pregnant he might have had the courage to take the news more stoically. As it was, the timing could not have been worse. For eight days nothing happened. Henry's first instinct seems to have been that the news should be kept quiet and the body quickly disposed of. The king cannot rationally have expected to keep the news of his son's death a secret for very long, but perhaps he was not in any condition to be rational. According to his own account, Thomas Howard now took the initiative and asked that he might be allowed to take his son-in-law to be buried among his ancestors in Norfolk.

This, at least, was some distance from the capital. Henry agreed to his request, but there were certain conditions. Norfolk was afterwards plain about what had been expected. 'The King's pleasure was that his body should be conveyed secretly in a closed cart'. Richmond's corpse was wrapped in lead according to the custom of the time and placed in a simple wooden coffin, which was covered over with straw. In stark contrast to his magnificent progress northwards in 1525; there would be no impressive entourage, no accompanying procession. The only attendants allowed were Richmond's governor, George Cotton, and his brother Richard, who served as comptroller of the duke's household. Even they were not allowed to wear Richmond's livery. Norfolk afterwards admitted that there was no closed cart provided, nor in fact had anything been done with any great secrecy. Within days Chapuys was relaying all the details, even down to the 'two persons clothed in green who followed at a distance'. Still, it can hardly have seemed to matter. Nothing could change the fact that Richmond was dead.

The Duke of Richmond was originally buried in the Howard family vault at Thetford Priory in Norfolk. If the superstition that a whole host of mourners was required to ensure that the departed was wrested from the clutches of the devil was correct, Richmond did not fair terribly well. At his death one of the memorandums for his household had asked what lengths of black cloth would be given to his various officers, counsellors and servants to wear at his funeral. In the event, it does not seem that any were needed. Norfolk was there and Surrey also came to honour his friend. Four of Richmond's geldings were delivered to Mary, Duchess of Richmond, to bring her home for the ceremony, but George and Richard Cotton seem to be the only ones of Richmond's servants who were allowed to be present.

The Prince Henry born in 1511 to Henry VIII and Katharine, who lived for just over seven weeks, had been accorded a solemn funeral. In a blaze of torchlight, a whole host of English nobility and 160 poor men, dressed in black cloth provided at the king's expense, walked in solemn observance alongside the tiny coffin and the choristers of the Chapel Royal sang him to his rest. However, the seventeen-year-old Duke of Richmond departed this world with the minimum of ceremony. Yet when Norfolk heard reports that the king was displeased with the manner of Richmond's funeral, he initially assumed it had not been done secretly enough.

He had good reason to be confused. In the face of Henry's grief and panic-stricken desire to sweep the whole matter under the carpet, Norfolk had apparently done what he could to provide Richmond with some semblance of a decent funeral. Now that the king had recovered from his initial shock and dismay, Norfolk found he was being berated for disposing of the body without the pomp and ceremony usually accorded to a duke at his funeral. As Henry began to regret his impetuous decision, Norfolk became a convenient scapegoat. Norfolk plaintively requested 'I trust the King will not blame me undeservedly'. However, while he was mourning in discreet retirement in the country, he was not well-placed to defend himself at court. It was all too easy for enemies like Thomas Cromwell to encourage the king's dissatisfaction and convince Henry that the whole mess was in fact Norfolk's doing. The duke had good reason to be upset, especially since he had been left to bear all the expense.

Richmond's eternal well-being was not entirely neglected. Under the regulations of the Order of the Garter, Richmond's fellow knights were obliged to pay for masses for his soul.[27] At no small inconvenience to himself, Arthur, Viscount Lisle, paid for services by the Greyfriars in Reading and the Friars of Calais. His passing was also commemorated as part of ceremonies of

the Order of the Garter in May 1538, when a procession of
nobility, led by the Earls of Sussex and Cumberland, bearing
Richmond's banner, marked his death in the traditional
procession of the offering of the hatchments.

But provision of a suitable tomb was apparently left entirely
to the efforts and coffers of the Duke of Norfolk. In 1539, when
Henry intended to dissolve Thetford Priory as part of the
ongoing Reformation, Norfolk protested that he was in the
process of providing two tombs for himself and Richmond,
'which have already and will cost him ere they can be fully set up
and finished, £400 at the least'.

Henry did not react to Richmond's death with lack of
affection. To be occupied with the business of his son's burial
and memorial was to remind himself and those around him that
he no longer had a son. Richmond's loss was always going to be
a bitter blow. Richmond was everything Henry could have
wanted in a son and there is no doubt that he loved him. If after
seventeen years he had also come to view the duke as an ever-
present insurance policy for the succession, then his death must
have been even harder to bear.

The birth of Prince Edward in October 1537 gave Henry less
reason to dwell on the loss of his bastard prince. Yet seventeen
years of pride and affection were perhaps not so easily erased.
The king's fondness for Henry Howard, Earl of Surrey, which
resulted in a surprising degree of tolerance toward him in the
face of concerted efforts by the Seymour family to blacken his
name, was perhaps due to his close relationship with Richmond.
However, if his sister, Mary, Duchess of Richmond, expected
Henry would extend to her the same regard out of respect for his
son's memory, she was to be sorely disappointed.

6

Landed Magnate

The Duke of Richmond had been no ordinary magnate. If a child of Richmond's age had acquired his title by inheritance, he would have become a ward of the crown. His wardship and marriage would have been granted with more thought to the financial or political benefit to the king than the care and husbandry of his estates. An heir in wardship had the legal status of a child and responsibility for his lands and welfare was entirely at the discretion of his guardian. When men purchased a wardship in order to marry their own offspring to the heir or heiress, they at least had a vested interest in maintaining him and his property. Otherwise, it was not unknown for lands to be plundered and assets stripped as the guardian sought to accrue the maximum profit from his investment while the heir was in his power. Not until Richmond was granted licence from the king to enter into his estates, once he was considered of full age, usually twenty-one, would he have gained any legal control over his own interests.

Yet from 18 June 1525, the six-year-old Duke of Richmond was treated as if he was an adult. He was not financially supported by his father, but instead expected to provide for himself from his own estates. He attended the king's parliament like any other peer of the realm and he paid taxes like any other subject, parting with the sum of £90 on one occasion in 1536. When his rights were challenged he defended his title in the king's law courts. Although both Thomas Wolsey and the Duke of Norfolk assumed a supervisory role over his lands and officers, Richmond was not in any legal sense their ward, not least because his own father was still alive. While it was not unusual for a royal prince to be granted a degree of autonomy at an early age, by rights Richmond's experience should have been more like his uncle, George Blount, the ward of the Duke of Norfolk, or his half-brother George, Lord Tailbois, in wardship to William Fitzwilliam, Earl of Southampton, rather than that of an independent magnate.

At his creation as Duke of Richmond and Somerset and Earl of Nottingham he was granted extensive lands and possessions. His estates would include over 120 manors in more than twenty counties across England and the Welsh Marches, granted in tail male to him and his legitimate heirs. Intended primarily to provide an income sufficient to support the new duke in a manner appropriate to his rank, Richmond could now expect to enjoy all the traditional rights of the lord of the manor. They were not simply rents and revenues. Leet and manor courts held in his name brought in additional fees. He was also entitled to other privileges such as the goods of felons and the appointment of preachers to his clerical benefices.

His lands would also provide a range of other perks and income. Poole, in Dorset, was a source of alum, used for making paper and fixing dye. The Isle of Purbeck was famous for its stone, which was much in demand as a building material. In 1533 the oaks felled in Cheshunt in Hertfordshire over the previous five years had produced 1,200 cartloads of timber. Leases of both wind and water-mills provided another steady means for a lord to realise the value of his holdings. Bourne in Lincolnshire held three fairs every year. Parks were also a valuable means of patronage, both for the pleasure of the hunt and their supply of game. The gift of a side of venison was such a prized commodity that recipients often noted whether the compliment extended to a buck (which was larger) or a doe. Even rabbit warrens and fishponds were valued as much or their opportunities for sport as for their ever present supply of fresh food.

The lands earmarked for Richmond were set out in letters patent dated 11 August 1525. With a stroke of the king's pen he found himself the lord of numerous honours, lordships, manors and tenements which had formerly belonged to Margaret, late Countess of Richmond, her father John, late Duke of Somerset and their ancestors. It might seem that Margaret Beaufort's death in 1509 had left a convenient vacuum, and there is some truth in this. Even the resources of the crown were not infinite and putting together an estate of this size was no easy task. Forty-three provisos and exceptions were required to protect the interests of those affected by Richmond's grant, including the king's own interests in the Duchy of Lancaster. Even so, the errors made in the statute supposed to confirm the endowment, where several manors were actually thought to be in the wrong county, reflect just how complicated the undertaking was.

Nevertheless, Richmond was not simply given Margaret's lands en bloc. He did not receive any of her estates in Leicestershire, Surrey or Wiltshire. He was also granted other property, most extensively his lordships in north Wales, which had not been part of her holdings. Nor had the possessions now granted to Richmond simply languished in the hands of the crown for the past sixteen years. In particular, Margaret, Countess of Salisbury, would actively challenge his right to the Manor of Canford in Dorset. As recently as March 1525, Sir William Courtenay had been granted the reversion of Coldharbour Mansion, a right he was now required to relinquish in favour of the duke. Even so, the mansion itself still remained in the hands of George Talbot, Earl of Shrewsbury, at no small inconvenience to the duke. Seen in this light the composition of Richmond's lands was obviously as much a matter of policy as practicalities.

The management of such extensive holdings was a major responsibility. Stewards, bailiffs and farmers were required to oversee the lands. Secretaries, receivers, lawyers and other officials were needed to deal with general administration. A landowner also had a duty to take care of his tenants. Manorial courts were designed to dispense law and keep order, while the lord's right of presentation of clerical livings touched their very souls. At the apex of all this activity stood the ducal household itself with its opportunities for advancement and employment.

The direction and control of such widespread interests was no simple task for any established magnate and it was all the more complicated when that magnate was only six.

The intention to treat the child as if he was an established peer would not always fit in with the realities of the situation. Richmond was surrounded with the officers and servants thought necessary to reflect the prestige of a duke. Most of these men had won their places by some connection to Thomas Wolsey or through prior service to the crown. A few, like James Morice, who acted as Richmond's general receiver, came naturally to his service from his prior association with Margaret Beaufort. Several stewards and bailiffs appointed by Henry VIII simply continued in their posts. In no sense was this an affinity in the traditional sense. The selection of these men did not stem from, or even consider, the wishes of the duke.

Until June 1529 there was also further tension. Richmond's household was not simply his private concern. It was the king's Council of the North. The legal and executive business of his officers was a matter of government concern. In theory, the supervision of his lands, the rewards bestowed on his servants and the patronage exercised by the duke was his private business. Yet Wolsey's role as his godfather and a minister of the crown meant that this line was rarely observed. That Richmond's officers would report to Wolsey over the progress of the assizes at Newcastle or York was normal and expected. But it is hard to imagine the Duke of Norfolk's or Earl of Northumberland's officers approaching the cardinal for advice on what manner and form their Christmas and New Year celebrations should take.

Some areas of Richmond's affairs were naturally controlled by the crown. The appointment of a Nottingham pursuivant-at-arms, 'attending on the Duke of Richmond and Somerset' was firmly the prerogative of the king.[1] The appointment of George Lawson, the duke's cofferer, as joint auditor of the three lordships of Middleham, Richmond and Sheriff Hutton in Yorkshire, was made by Henry VIII under letters patent.

Richmond's authority was not sovereign and both he and all his servants were still Henry's dutiful subjects.

Sometimes this could work to Richmond's advantage. In July 1528 his father decided that Richmond's schoolmaster Dr Richard Croke should be rewarded for his good service with a benefice valued at £24 per annum, which was presently in Wolsey's hands. However, the cardinal had his own ideas as to who should benefit. Now the king summarily informed him that 'it is too small a value to give to Master Wilson, or any other his chaplains, and this man had never anything'. Wolsey was plainly reluctant. In August Henry sent another message to 'put you in rememberance' that the benefice was to go to Richard Croke. Even when Richmond was older the king might also decide to be generous. In February 1531 he rewarded Richmond's servant, Ambrose Skelton, with a grant of the land and rights to a 'ferry and passage' on the River Severn out of the king's possessions in Gloucestershire.[2]

The king was also the greatest source of power and protection. When even the most just title might be challenged, that Richmond looked to the crown to protect his and his servants' interests was nothing out of the ordinary. In April 1528, when it appeared that his former chaplain William Swallow might lose the benefice in Devon which Richmond had recently bestowed on him, the duke had no hesitation in asking the king to intervene on his servant's behalf, sending 'this my writing penned with mine own hand' to add weight to his request. Unfortunately for Richmond, his father also often chose to interfere in matters, which by right or courtesy should have been left to the duke.

One such example took place in April 1527 when Richmond was seven years old. John Stackhouse, the bailiff of Richmond's Manor of Cottingham in Yorkshire, died. The office was 'in my Lord's gift'. Not only did Richmond have every right to grant it as he saw fit, it was expected of a duke to demonstrate good lordship by rewarding his servants. His council wrote hopefully to Wolsey asking to be allowed to appoint George Hartwell to the post, adding the rather pointed request that in future any such vacancies 'for the better encouraging of his said servants and chaplain to take pains in his service' should be given to Richmond's own officers. Yet in this case, as in many other instances, his council's wishes were not respected. The post, which was worth £6 a year, went to Edward Vaux whom Henry VIII had also appointed as bailiff of another of Richmond's manors in the area at Longton.

Richmond's own correspondence makes it clear that he had been told he could exercise his own patronage. The statute 22 Henry VIII c.17, which confirmed the lands entailed upon him, stressed that despite his tender years his authority was equal to any adult's:

Albeit the said Duke at the time of the making of any such gift grant or patent were and yet is within the age of 21 years in like manner and effect as if the same Duke at the time of the making of the same gifts grants leases and by him made had been of the full age of 21 years.[3]

In reality, it was absurd that everything should be given over to the whims and wishes of such a young child. In theory Richmond's council would exercise the guardianship of his interests in his name, gradually drawing the duke into the decision-making process as he grew older. In practice, these lawyers and clerics were painfully aware that the diminutive duke outranked them.

The Tudor age contained no absolute rites of passage. A child of seven could contract a marriage, hold down a job and be held morally responsible for its actions. However, none of these made it an adult. Those who remained financially dependant, either on their master or a parent, could be classed as children well into maturity. A statute on apprenticeships dismissed any man under twenty-four as 'without self judgment and not of sufficient experience to govern himself'. Medical and educational texts, the sort of work they were employed to do and the parameters of the law, all made some concessions to the fact that a child was not the same as an adult. Yet to society in general, the distinction between the two states was not simply a stage of life, but a reflection of perceived position in society.

The respect due to authority took no account of age. It was widely accepted that children lacked the skills and experience to function effectively in the adult world. A child was taught 'to submit [itself] lowly and reverently to all [its] betters'. However, a child of rank, whether he was a gentleman, an earl, a duke or a king, commanded exactly the same 'reverence' from his servants and inferiors as any adult counterpart. None of Richmond's council would have been permitted to appear in his presence without removing their hats and observing the appropriate obeisance. The little duke might be persuaded, cajoled or completely circumvented, but his direct will could not be disobeyed by his councillors.

To be fair, many of Richmond's officers were genuinely concerned to see that his lands were well cared for and his household well run, in a manner befitting his status as the foremost peer of the realm. Unfortunately, neither the king nor Wolsey felt any compulsion to fall in with their wishes.

Since none of Richmond's council had any rank of their own to support their 'requests', conflicts did arise. John Uvedale, a former protégé of the Howards, had served as Richmond's secretary since 1525. With the rise of Anne Boleyn, Uvedale found himself ever more in her service at court and away from the north. At his request, and with the agreement of Richmond's council, John Bretton was appointed to act as his deputy in his absence. Then Uvedale was promoted and the king decided that Thomas Derby should take his place as secretary to the duke. In anticipation of Derby's arrival, Bretton found himself another position in the south of England and effectively handed in his resignation to Richmond's council.

The council refused to accept it. They had no idea when Derby was supposed to arrive and 'being desolate of any other person able to exercise the said room' asked Bretton to stay on. To keep him there they promised that he might have all the profits arising from the position. It was a good deal for Bretton. As deputy he had been accustomed to paying all the 'issues and profits remaining and growing of the same' to Uvedale in return for a set fee. Now his income would be significantly increased. Needless to say, he stayed. However, neither Uvedale, nor indeed the king, was best pleased with this turn of events. Even though Uvedale was no longer Richmond's secretary, Bretton was accused of stealing his rightful income and on 31 January 1528 he was ordered to be imprisoned in York Castle.

At first Richmond's council complied with the king's order. However, on 9 March 1528 they advised Wolsey that 'as the matter in transit between him and John Uvedale be of no great weight or importance' they had gone ahead and released him. Amid lurid descriptions of the 'sore and contagious' diseases, which had swept through the jail and sent fourteen of the prisoners to their death, they stressed Bretton's frailty. Although they recited the measures they had taken to keep Bretton at York until the whole business was cleared up, they also offered a solution of their own. If the king insisted on giving the profits to Uvedale, which they believed Bretton had earned and genuinely deserved, then 'we at our own cost and charge shall pay and sustain the same as we in performance of our promise be bound of good conscience to do'.

Significantly, they were anxious that neither Wolsey nor the king should 'think that ever we presumed to allocate any person to that room or office' (surely exactly the sort of thing the duke's council should have been doing). In reality, however earnestly they spoke of the trust and judgment that had been placed in them, these servants of the crown could not expect to command the level of consideration and autonomy which would be allowed to a duke. Perhaps because of this, even at this early stage, Richmond regularly wrote to the king on behalf of his officers in his own hand. Realising that the bailiff of his Manor of Torpell in Northamptonshire, John Brede, was 'a man far in age' the young duke asked 'in my most humble and most lowly wise' that the yeoman usher of his chamber, Robert Markham, might jointly hold the post, presumably with an eye to stepping into Brede's shoes as his infirmity advanced.

The extent of Henry's involvement in Richmond's affairs does seem to have exceeded normal bounds. In 1528 the duke again reminded his father that:

> My lord Legate's grace of late signified unto me it was your high pleasure that when any like offices or benefices appertaining to my gift should chance to be voided that I by the advice of my council should dispose and give the same at my liberty.[4]

At first sight, Richmond seemed in no position to make demands. He was the king's dutiful son as well as his obedient subject. He owed everything he was to his father's good will and he was still only nine years old. However, not even the king or Wolsey could blatantly ignore the express wishes of the duke.

Things came to a head with the death of Sir William Compton in May 1528. When he succumbed to the sweating-sickness which swept across the land, his demise left the stewardship of two of Richmond's manors, one in Somerset and the other in Dorset, vacant. Since the king had appointed Compton, he clearly felt he had every right to appoint his successors. He earmarked Sir Giles Strangeways and Sir Edward Seymour for the posts. Admittedly, these lands were now in Richmond's hands and technically the right of patronage belonged to the duke. Since both men had links with Richmond's household, Henry might feel that appearances were being observed. On 10 July 1528 the king's instructions were duly sent to the duke, only to discover that Richmond had already granted the office in Somerset to his 'trusty and diligent servant' Sir George Cotton and the post in Dorset to his chamberlain, Sir William Parr.

The conflict presented all involved with a dilemma. The decision, albeit made 'by the advice of my council' was undeniably Richmond's. Even Wolsey had to be apprised of events by Sir Thomas Magnus. The duke explained his action as if it was the most natural thing in the world. He had a great number of servants who had not yet received any reward, Wolsey had assured him that he should fill any vacancies and so he had. Although Richmond was careful to stress that the posts were not that important, one being worth only 100s a year, and was anxious to assure Henry that 'the same are and shall be at your most gracious commandment' he did not actually revoke his grants. For its part, his council took refuge in confusion, claiming Henry's exact wishes were unclear. It is tempting to assume that this decisive action had been intended to catch the king on the hop. Now they had succeeded in granting the offices, the ball was in Henry's court.

As long as those areas in which the king expressed an interest remained vacant, Richmond and his council had scant grounds to refuse him. However, if Henry seriously expected Richmond to serve as an effective representative of the crown, the duke's own authority must also be seen to be respected. While Henry might appropriate some of the duke's patronage to his own use, by couching his requirement in the nature of a request, any move to overturn a decision already made could set a dangerous precedent. Since Richmond's jurisdiction, as both a bastard and a minor, was limited by what was allowed to him by the crown, it was especially important that Henry should acknowledge and defer to his son's personal prerogative. Although Henry was doubtless not best pleased at having his intentions blocked by his nine-year-old son and his council of clerks and lawyers, he could not afford to ignore the potential damage to the duke's carefully crafted, but still fragile, political persona if he decided to overturn his appointments.

In the end it seems a compromise of sorts was reached. Like most compromises it was far from ideal. For the moment, Sir Giles Strangeways was to be disappointed.[5] Sir Edward Seymour was more fortunate. On 25 August 1528, in a document impressively adorned with Richmond's own seal, the duke granted Seymour the stewardship of the Manor of Canford and the other premises in Dorset. By these means the dignity of both the king and the duke was preserved.

As Henry's representative at Sheriff Hutton, the duke's role was clearly defined. As a private magnate Richmond's authority depended more on his personal reputation. Many of Richmond's officers served on local government commissions. Several of his council also had their own links with areas, in particular the city of York. Richmond's cofferer, Sir George Lawson, served as an alderman for the city and was subsequently to represent York as both a Member of Parliament and as mayor. Sir Richard Page, the duke's vice-chamberlain, was recorder of York from 1527 until 1533. However, when Richmond wanted to secure the post of 'sword bearer' for his servant Alan Ary in January 1528, the response of the city council was distinctly lukewarm. They told Richmond that they wished to wait 'unto such time as the King's grace and the lord Cardinal's grace pleasure might be further known'.

Given Richmond's age and circumstances they may have been genuinely concerned not to offend the king. However, the referral to a higher authority also provided them with a convenient excuse to defer making any answer. Relations between the city of York and Richmond's council were not always good. In August 1528, the town was called to account in a dispute over taxes. Also the city had already had Wolsey's servant, Robert Fournes, foisted upon them. His appointment had proved most unpopular and the mayor had apparently reproached Fournes to his face:

> Master Fournes what do you here? There is not one in this hall that hereafter will company with you or anything will do for you. There is not one in this city that loveth my lord Cardinal or you or any other that longeth to my lord Cardinal.[6]

Despite Richmond's request, the office went to Henry Fawkes, a merchant who had enjoyed the freedom of the city since 1504. The personal authority of the duke was clearly not sufficient to counter the resentment of the city. Although to be fair no magnate, with the possible exception of the king, could realistically expect that his will would always to be granted.

Conversely, perhaps with an eye on his possible future prospects, many people were keen to gain entry into Richmond's service. William Eure was 'very desirous to have my lord of Richmond's fee'. Although the fee itself was only £10, he declared it was worth more to him than 'a thing of far greater value'. When Sir William Bulmer's age and infirmity weighed too heavily upon him for him to be able to continue in his duties as the steward of Richmond's household and other offices, he was quick to offer his sons as convenient replacements. A third generation of his family, Matthew Boynton, the husband of Bulmer's granddaughter Anne, was also found in Richmond's service.

A large number of Richmond's own servants were keen to use their influence to secure places in his household for their friends and relations. Nicholas Throckmorton, who with three older brothers lamented the fact that he had little chance of inheriting his fortune, probably owed his position as a page to his uncle, Sir William Parr, who served as the duke's chamberlain. Henry Partridge, one of the young, unmarried gentlemen of the chamber, was possibly the son or younger brother of Richmond's former nurse, Anne Partridge. The 'master Skeffington' who was a groom of the privy chamber in September 1531, was probably a relation of William Skeffington, by that point serving as Richmond's deputy lieutenant in Ireland. Robert Johns, one of the yeoman of the chamber, may well have been a relation of the yeoman of the wardrobe, Hugh Johns.

Perhaps this was nothing more than the general scramble for offices and advancement, an age-old desire to get on in the world. When Sir Jason Laybourne expressed his wish to serve the Duke of Richmond, he was equally interested in any other preferment that might supplement his income. Philip Morice, the brother of the young duke's general receiver, went to considerable lengths to be received into Richmond's employment. He used his brother's connection as a valued servant of Thomas Cranmer, so that

Cranmer would presume on George Boleyn's obligation to him, in order that Boleyn might approach his uncle, the Duke of Norfolk, to grant Morice a place in Richmond's service. The young duke's household does seem to have been a useful link into royal service. Thomas Eynns from Shropshire was not alone in finding that his time with Richmond would lead on to a position in Prince Edward's household. Even though Richmond's prospects of the crown were never exactly spoken of, many in his service must have hoped to profit by association with him. At the very least he was the king's son and a duke in his own right. Any man would be pleased to serve such a master and there were increasingly rewards to be had.

Richmond was clearly anxious to live up to his position and did the best he could with numerous gifts and grants from his personal possessions. George Cotton received a horse with a flaxen mane and tail that had been a present to the duke from Sir William Skeffington. Even the 'sore worn' gift of a doublet of cloth of silver, which Richmond gave to Nicholas Throckmorton, was still a valuable present. Throckmorton also received a crimson riding coat, a gown of black velvet and a riding coat 'of new coloured cloth' from the young duke. Nor was he the only beneficiary. John Jenny, one of the unmarried gentlemen of the chamber, received a doublet of purple velvet embroidered with gold chains and lined with black and Hugh Johns, the yeoman of the wardrobe, was given a black velvet riding bonnet, trimmed with gold. Henry Partridge, who was perhaps rather more Richmond's own size, found himself the proud owner of seven pairs of former ducal hose in various colours, as well as a black bonnet with twenty-seven solid gold buttons.

If Richmond might seem to be a gullible target from whom benefits and rewards could be easily extracted by flattery, then the same could sometimes be said of his father. If getting what you wanted meant pleasing your patron, then such practice was not foul means, but good business practice. Gifts and tokens were a customary and expected part of good lordship. Richmond's pointed reminder in 1527 that 'it hath not been my chance as yet hitherto to prefer any one of my servants to any manner of promotion either spiritual or temporal' was not the complaint of a child, but the concern of a duke who cannot repay the good service of his officers in an appropriate manner. Sometimes the monetary fees were little recompense for the trouble and expense of the office. It was the fringe benefits, which could be goods, prestige or opportunities for personal gain, which were the real attraction.

Richmond's half-brother, King Edward VI, would voice a similar concern when he declared 'my Uncle of Somerset dealeth very hardly with me and keepeth me so straight I cannot have money at my will'. This was not exactly pocket money, but intended to reward those supplicants and players who came before their king. Wolsey acknowledged that one of the aspects of Richmond's affairs that needed to be redressed was the arrangements for personal expenses 'for giving of rewards, for playing money unto my lord's grace [and] for his apparel' which obviously needed to be replaced more frequently than for an adult. This problem, at least, does seem to have been amended. At his death in 1536 Richmond's almoner handed over about £490 in ready money which he had been holding for the duke.

Despite all the difficulties, examples of Richmond exercising his own patronage are easy to find. When the parsonage of Dimby fell vacant in 1529, Richmond overrode the customary rights of Margaret Pole, Countess of Salisbury, in order to bestow it on his tutor Richard Croke. Giles Forster, who served as master of the horse after the departure of Sir Edward Seymour, earned £3 6s 8d per annum as the steward of Merton in Westmorland. Even lesser servants could benefit from Richmond's generosity: Robert Metcalf, a clerk of the kitchen received 2d a day as bailiff of Cottingham in Yorkshire. At his death several of Richmond's servants held offices within his lordships. If George and Richard Cotton seem to have done exceptionally well, with a clutch of such posts between them, they repaid Richmond with eleven years of loyal service. Since they were the only servants allowed to accompany his body into Norfolk, they were perhaps particularly close to the duke.

An unusual aspect of Richmond's patronage, given Richmond's lack of years, was his connection with Haltemprice Priory in Yorkshire. In February 1528 Brian Higdon advised Wolsey that the prior at Haltemprice was dead and that two of the brethren were coming up to London to ask for a replacement. He described the priory as being well built, with lands worth about 200 marks, and added 'the Duke of Richmond and Somerset is founder'. Since Higdon was both Richmond's chancellor and Dean of York he is unlikely to have been mistaken. A founder's responsibilities might include sponsoring an establishment's business in the royal courts or protecting the financial interests of the monks. In return the founder was assured of the grateful services of the monks in praying for them and their family, they had a right to lodgings in the priory during their lifetime and a place of burial after their death.

The claim that Richmond was indeed their founder was reiterated in the visitation of the monasteries in 1536, when the priory was also found to possess the relics of the arms of St George, a part of the true Holy Cross and the girdle of St Mary 'which is thought to be helpful in childbirth'. However, the sense in which Richmond was the founder is questionable. The priory did draw some of its income from lands in his possession, but that would not give him founder's rights since Sir John de Meaux had founded a religious house at Haltemprice in 1406 so it was not a new foundation. On the other hand, a re-foundation would have enhanced Richmond's status. Richmond already maintained a chapel in his household. Adorned with tapestries of the passion of Christ, staffed by clerics in vestments of cloth of gold and crimson velvet embroidered with Richmond's arms, and a choir, it was as much a matter of prestige as religion. Although being the benefactor of a religious house had obvious benefits for the next world, it was probably hoped this move would enhance Richmond's image on earth.

In general, Richmond's age was not a serious handicap when it came to the administration of his lands. It could even be a positive benefit. When Charles Brandon, Duke of Suffolk, had formerly held the lordship of Bromfield and Yale, he had used its income to raise credit and the revenues sharply decreased.[7] Instead, Richmond could count on experienced officers like his surveyor and general receiver James Morice who had faithfully served both Henry VIII and Margaret Beaufort. It was his duty to collect rents and fees from the various stewards and bailiffs and handle the practical details of grants and leases. Things did not always run smoothly. Wolsey suggested that the repairs of houses in Boston harbour in Lincolnshire should be arranged before they fell into the sea and in 1534 bad weather in the north meant the harvest failed and Richmond's tenants claimed they were too poor to pay him any rent.[8]

Examples of Richmond's own involvement in the care or exploitation of his lands are not easy to find. While no magnate of his status would have overseen day-to-day business, many took an active interest in what was, in essence, their power base. A number of Richmond's estates, like Maidcroft in Kent, were let out to farmers. When Richmond bought the Lordship of Arwystli and Cyfeiliog in Montgomeryshire from Sir John Dudley, the manor court was told 'that the said estate be kept in my lord Ferrers' name as farmer and not in my lord of Richmond's name'. In other cases, parts of his estates were leased to various monastic houses. Syon Monastery in Kent, and St Mary's Chantry in Lincolnshire both held lands from the duke. In 1535 a vicar in Kingsbury Hundred was paying just over 7s in rent to Richmond in his capacity as Lord of Langport in Somerset. This was not the most productive way of realising the value of property, since the possibility for development and improvement was lost in return for a fixed fee. Parcels of land let out to farm or lease were a standard form of land use for those with extensive properties and not in themselves a reflection of Richmond's youth. However, it did provide the duke with a steady income and relieved his officers of some responsibilities.

Unlike an actual minority, where the ward might grow to find his assets stripped and his lands despoiled, Richmond's holdings do not appear to have suffered unduly in the hands of his officers. When Richmond took possession of the Manors of Wrestlingworth in Cambridgeshire and Bassingbourn and Orwell in Bedfordshire in 1525, they yielded a sum total of £45 10s 10½d. After his death that sum total was £45 10s 10d exactly. It was not the place of Richmond's council to make innovative (and possibly risky) developments. They had to answer to the king. Richmond's occasional purchases did not compare with the policy of acquisition in Lincolnshire undertaken by Edward, Lord Clinton. The modest improvements made to his residences, including some building work at Sheffield, were insignificant beside the magnificent works commissioned by the king. The policy of maintenance and repair was nothing like Margaret Beaufort's extensive programme, which included an ambitious scheme at Boston in Lincolnshire to prevent flooding.

Although Richmond would take a keen interest in many aspects of his responsibilities, his personal involvement in the care or exploitation of his lands seems to have been at best sporadic and at worst non-existent. In a rare example, in 1534 the duke was taken to view a breach in the sea defences at Poole in Dorset. He solemnly reported that the damage was likely to hinder the collection of custom dues and also be to 'the great annoyance and decay of my said town . . . unless some good remedy be shortly had in that behalf'. Time and again in numerous counties the period of Richmond's tenure coincides with a significant gap in even the basic records, like manor court rolls. This perhaps explains how Richmond's lordship has sometimes been completely overlooked, with local histories often omitting any connection with Richmond at all.

Significantly, this apparent lack of interest did not extend to the question of his title. Any attacks on his rights were vigorously defended in the king's courts like any adult magnate. When Thomasyn Andrews of Fremington in Devon committed suicide, all her goods and cattle 'to the value of £20 and above' were forfeit to the duke, as lord of the manor. Instead, Elizabeth Chicester, and four accomplices conspired to keep her possessions for themselves. Casting himself as 'your son and faithful subject' Richmond complained to the king through his Court of Star Chamber. When thieves broke into his park at Bedhampton to slaughter and steal his deer, Richmond again sought to obtain a subpoena. The bill pointed out that their actions were in violation of the king's laws and lack of suitable punishment would set a perilous example to other like-minded offenders.

Richmond's eagerness to assert his rights could also result in a less welcome use of the courts. In 1531 Randall Lloyd, Richmond's deputy steward in his new lordship of Bromfield and Yale, refused to allow the customary general pardon at a change of lord or lady, where all rents, debts and other due monies would be waived in return for a single fee of six marks, so the tenants took their case to the Star Chamber. The king was asked 'of your most noble and abundant grace, to admit the said tenants and inhabitants to their said old ancient customs'. Regrettably, the verdict does not survive. While it is probably safe to assume that Richmond had certain advantages in securing a favourable verdict, it is to be hoped that his officer was not allowed to use the good name of the duke to perpetrate such an unjust practice.

It is, of course, hard to say exactly how personally involved Richmond was in preparing the cases. In a sense, that did not matter. If Richmond was to operate effectively as a magnate, then it was important that he was being seen to act like one. In 1533 when a dispute broke out over John Sidney's rights to certain lands of the Manor of Lamarsh in Essex, Sidney professed himself to be 'very loath to contend with the said Duke'. However, this did not prevent him from defending the lands in question from Richmond's officers 'with force and arms in riotous manner'. When Richmond applied to the king for a subpoena to enforce his lawful entry, John Sidney stood his ground and submitted a rebuttal to refute the duke's arguments.

Such issues were part and parcel of landholding in the sixteenth century, as men increasingly used litigation for all manner of ends. That Richmond sought redress from the crown, was not an indication of any lack of authority, but helped to underscore his position as the rightful lord.

Nowhere was this more apparent than in a long-running legal wrangle over the rightful ownership of a single manor in Dorset. When Richmond was granted the Manor of Canford in 1525, the dispute had already been running for eight years. In simple terms, the king claimed the manor as parcel of the dukedom of Somerset, while Margaret, Countess of Salisbury, alleged it was hers as sister and heiress of Edward, Earl of Warwick. Margaret had actually been granted Canford, along with other manors, in 1513 as part of the earldom of Salisbury only to have the king's favourite, Sir William Compton, cast doubt on the proper descent of some of her lands. Margaret firmly believed he was motivated more by malice than by justice, because 'he obtained not his purpose of her in marriage'. When she refused to take him as her husband he took revenge on her by suggesting to Henry that Canford and certain other lands did not belong to the earldom of Salisbury after all.

Most likely, William Compton would not have been as eager to pursue the case if his marriage proposal had been accepted. However, as steward of Canford, he had access to the title deeds and other documents. If something in those documents called Margaret's title into question, he had a duty to tell the king. Wolsey mounted an investigation on behalf of the crown and, by October 1518, the manor was back in Henry's hands. The king clearly believed the matter was concluded by June 1519 when he appointed Robert Bingham as bailiff and keeper of Canford, but Margaret was less willing to let the matter drop.[9] It was not so much Richmond's acquisition of the manor in 1525 which encouraged her to revive her claim, as the death of Sir William Compton in 1528.

The Countess of Salisbury was quite certain that she was the rightful owner of Canford. In her suit she told the king:

it is thought and advertised clearly by her council that she
hath as good right there unto as she hath to any other lands
of the said Earldom, not doubting that if his grace were
informed thereof according unto her right and title but his
grace would suffer her to enjoy them.[10]

In response to her charges the duke's council set about attempting
to prove his clear title to the lands. The challenge was taken very
seriously. Thomas Magnus advised Wolsey that all the duke's
receivers and auditors in the south of England had begun 'to search
and inquire in every place of their circuit, for all such evidence'.
Margaret, who, after all, had had plenty of time to marshal her
arguments, was keen for the case to be heard. Magnus was determined to stall until the results of the searches were known.

His caution was fully justified. Richmond had had his own
problems in asserting his title to the manor. Even armed with
the king's letters patent, the duke had been unable to take
possession of all the relevant deeds and documents. Resorting to
a bill in the king's Court of Chancery, it was alleged that one
John Incent 'refused, and yet doth refuse, contrary to all right
and good conscience' to deliver up the documents. Given that
Compton had allegedly found something in those papers that
had refuted Margaret's title, Incent's action was more than
simply inconvenient.

John Incent was the Master of St Cross Hospital, Winchester
and 'a clerk of both laws'. Since the lands had originally been
purchased by Cardinal Beaufort specifically to endow St Cross
Hospital he probably had a better claim to the manor than
either Margaret or Richmond. Yet in his answer to Richmond's
bill of complaint Incent slanted his evidence to Margaret's
benefit. He claimed that John, Earl of Salisbury, had owned the
manor, only to forfeit it to the crown in the reign of Henry IV
when he was found guilty of high treason. In fact, the lands had
legally reverted to the king. Incent also asserted Margaret's
superior title and asked that she should be called before the
court in order to set out her own case in person.

Richmond retorted that the manor was his because of the king's grant by letters patent. Margaret responded to this by claiming that it had only passed to the crown because of the minority of Edward, the late Earl of Warwick which meant that she, rather than the king, was the true heir and Henry had no right to grant her manor to his son.

Margaret obviously believed that she had the better claim to Canford. She did not dispute Richmond's ownership of Deeping in Lincolnshire, which was also granted to her in 1513 and subsequently repossessed by the crown. However, Margaret's argument did not take account of the fact that both Henry VII and Margaret Beaufort had held Canford in their right as Beaufort heirs, before Edward's attainder. While the true heir was St Cross Hospital, the king's title to the manor was better than Margaret's and as such he could give it to whomsoever he wished.

In spite of this the dispute continued. In September 1531, Cromwell approached Margaret's eldest son, Lord Montague, to try and bring the matter to an end. However, in 1533 his desk was still littered with various legal papers relating to ownership of Canford. Richmond's residence at Canford in the summer of 1534 may either have been a final salvo in the attack to emphasise his ownership or a signal of the conclusion of the dispute. Either way the arguments seem to have run their course. After nine years Richmond was finally able to enjoy Canford's parks and amenities in peace.

When a different sort of conflict broke out in Richmond's lands in Kendal, it was again not in itself a reaction to having a child as their lord. Rather it reflected a deeper resentment already brewing within the locality over the issue of control. Richmond had held part of the barony of Kendal since 1525. The first indication that things were getting out of hand came in April 1532. William Parr, nephew to Richmond's chamberlain, complained to Thomas Cromwell that Robert Tarne 'a very insolent and light person' had repeatedly broken into his park at Kendal to kill and steal his game and deer. There had been trouble on previous occasions when Tarne had verbally abused his keeper, William Redman. This time Redman responded with a few choice words of his own. A fight broke out and Tarne was injured. According to Parr, the villain now intended to turn the situation to his own advantage by suing not only Redman, but Parr's cousin, Sir Jason Laybourne, who served as Richmond's steward in the area. Tellingly, Tarne had acquired some powerful supporters, such as Sir Thomas Clifford and the Earl of Cumberland, who served as sheriff there, and Parr had no doubt that the true motive behind the case was their resentment of Parr's and Richmond's authority.

According to Parr it was customary for disputes within the barony of Kendal to be settled locally by the steward. However, he claimed Laybourne's efforts to do so were being hampered by men like Cumberland and Clifford, 'intending for ill will and malice that they bear unto my said lord of Richmond and me, to infringe the said laudable custom' by using the king's courts. Parr was being inundated with complaints from poor men who were being forced to make costly trips to London to try to seek justice. He begged Cromwell that any such cases should be referred straight back to the barony of Kendal. In an Act of Parliament passed in 1532 Richmond acquired further interest in the barony after an exchange of lands with John, Lord Lumley. The arrangement seems to have been in Richmond's favour, and and the unfortunate Lumley was asked to relinquish a parcel of five manors in return for an annuity of £50. In the circumstances it was obviously intended to increase Richmond's profile and authority as lord of the barony. It also had the added advantage of discreetly bringing the area more firmly under royal control.

The effectiveness of the new arrangements was almost immediately put to the test. In blatant disregard of Richmond's authority, Sir John Lowther, the under-sheriff to the Earl of Cumberland, and other men, including Sir Thomas Clifford, decided to hold the sheriff's court in Kendal. When challenged in the name of the king and Richmond not to hold any such assembly within the duke's liberties, they openly questioned Richmond's title. As Parr reported with some indignation:

I answered and said that my said lord of Richmond's
authority was openly proclaimed and rehearsed in the
King's market in Kendal under the King's broad seal and
they answered again and said that they knew none such.[11]

Since everyone was well aware that Sir Thomas Clifford had
been present when Richmond was publicly proclaimed, this was
obviously a lie. It did not bode well for their respect for
Richmond's authority, but it did set the tone for the disputes
and disagreements that followed.

Although it might seem that Richmond's youth was a licence
to flout his authority, the duke's interests were vigorously
protected and continuously asserted by his steward and other
officers. Then Henry himself wrote to the Earl of Cumberland,
commanding him to cease his interference in the Duke of
Richmond's liberties. No one could deny the might and power of
the king, yet even his letters had little effect and Cumberland's
men continued to harass Richmond's tenants. In fact, for a time
things got worse. Jason Laybourne sent up a list which set out
all the ways in which Cumberland was using his position as
sheriff to the detriment of Richmond's legal rights as lord of the
barony, including his efforts to indict Richmond's officers
simply for attempting to perform their designated duties.

Their actions were more an attack on the authority that
Richmond represented than an affront to the personal power
and authority of the duke himself. If Cumberland and his
friends could ignore the directives of the king, any magnate
would surely have encountered similar problems. As such,
Cumberland and Clifford's activities were a direct challenge to
the security of the realm and therefore the crown, one that
Henry could not allow to stand. With the combined power of the
king, the Duke of Norfolk, Thomas Cromwell and his own
officers ranged behind him, it seems the balance of control
finally tipped in Richmond's favour, although the duke's
problems within the barony did not entirely cease. In March
1534 a band of marauders broke into Richmond's lands at New

Hutton to despoil his corn and wine and the duke took his complaint to the King's Court of Star Chamber. However, there were no further reports of difficulties on any scale regarding Richmond's authority as lord of the barony.

As the Duke of Richmond grew older his own involvement in such matters began to increase. However, even in June 1534, when the fifteen-year-old duke might reasonably look for some leeway to make and execute his own decisions, the king's wrath might suddenly descend. After Richmond had returned south in 1529, his cofferer, Sir George Lawson, was one of those officers who remained in the north, but he still expected to receive his usual fee as a member of Richmond's household. Richmond decided to discharge him from his post as cofferer, presumably to appoint someone who would actually reside in his household. As soon as he heard the news Henry wrote in astonishment that the duke had discharged an officer who had given such good service 'whereof we cannot a little marvel'. Although he stopped just short of overriding the duke's authority entirely by requiring him to reinstate Lawson, Richmond was told in no uncertain terms to continue paying his fee.[12]

Richmond was obviously keen to exercise the authority that his father had given him and he was happy to presume on their relationship when this was to his advantage. Matthew Boynton was only one of several of Richmond's servants who carried a testimonial from the duke when seeking some preferment at court. Sometimes Richmond's requests capitalised on other personal relationships. In February 1534 he persuaded Arthur, Viscount Lisle, to take on a certain James Bellingham 'and for my sake to further and prefer him into such room of retinue as should then next immediately happen'. Sometimes the arrangement was more businesslike: the monks of Bindon in Dorset offered to take care of Richmond's deer park, if he got them a licence to elect their own abbot. However, on at least one occasion, Richmond was to let his enthusiasm for a cause carry him forward, when prudence and mature judgment might have stayed his hand.

In June 1534, John Cooke, the registrar to Stephen Gardiner, Bishop of Winchester, took advantage of Gardiner's absence from court to unburden himself of numerous resentments against his employer, including the non-payment of his stipend. Since Cooke was also commissary of the Admiralty in Hampshire, one of those he chose to approach was the fifteen-year-old Duke of Richmond.[13] The duke was sufficiently convinced of the justice of his case to write to Gardiner in Cooke's favour, requiring him to redress these wrongs. Gardiner flatly denied all the charges and added a veiled rebuke that Richmond should leap to such conclusions and that 'I should, following your Grace's request made upon such a ground, give courage to Master Cooke in the exercise of his untrue reports'.

Casting his bread as wide as possible upon the water, Cooke had also complained to Thomas Audley the Lord Chancellor, Thomas Cromwell and the king. No doubt to Cooke's dismay, Cromwell's response was far less impetuous than the high-handed tone adopted by Richmond. Gardiner was to be given the opportunity to clear his name. With the matter thus referred to the authority of the crown, Richmond's own involvement came to an end. Gardiner's meticulous response to Richmond's intervention was in a way an acknowledgement of the duke as a political force. However, Gardiner was also at pains to point out to the young and as yet inexperienced duke just how far he was deceived in his assessment of Cooke's character, not only in this matter, but also 'in the use of his office of the Admiralty under your Grace, wherein they talk of his demeanour otherwise here than I think your Grace hath heard there'.

Richmond's judgment was also called into question the following year when the sixteen-year-old was implicated in worrying disorder in the Welsh Marches. Although the king's preoccupation with Anne Boleyn might seem reason and excuse for Henry to curb Richmond's fortunes, instead, in 1531, the twelve-year-old duke's extensive holdings had been increased even further with the acquisition of a number of lordships in the Marches of Wales. In October 1531 his officers took possession of the lordships of Bromfield and Yale, Ruthin, Clirk and Holt and these holdings were augmented in 1532 when he acquired the former Dudley lordship of Arwystli and Cyfeiliog.

This was, in part, a reflection of a broader pattern to bring the Marches of Wales under closer crown control. Wales had technically been part of the realm since the Statute of Rhuddlan in the thirteenth century. However, there were a number of administrative anomalies, not least its division into a number of independent lordships which were ruled by powerful individuals like Rhys ap Griffith. This was not Thomas Cromwell's idea of a well-ordered kingdom. In the light of Henry's ongoing changes in religion, it was important to assert the authority of the king. A concerted programme of reforms, which culminated in the Act of Union in 1536, was already well in hand. In 1534, the appointment of Roland Lee, Bishop of Coventry and Lichfield, as President of the Council of Wales signalled a new determination to reduce the Welsh Marches to order.

Even as Cromwell organised a series of legislation and a goodwill visit by the king, Lee began an enthusiastic policy of change. He travelled tirelessly around the Marches, encouraging the law-abiding and striking terror into the hearts of villains, boasting that he had executed 'four of the best blood in Shropshire' as he left a trail of death and imprisonment in his wake. In 1534 Richmond's tenants in Arwystli and Cyfeiliog, objected to the arrest of Sir Richard Herbert for the murder of Hugh ap David Vaughan. Protesting his innocence they declared they 'would not keep court, nor pay the duke of Richmond money, as long as he was in ward'. By 1536, Lee was commending the same tenants for the taking of two outlaws, although he was convinced they were motivated more by fear and hope of gain than any love of justice. However, despite their best efforts Lee and Cromwell found that their labours were being hampered by the powers of the remaining marcher lords and chief among these, according to an estimation taken before December 1531, was Richmond himself.

In October 1535, Lee became concerned that 'letters directed from my lord of Richmond's grace' were being used to ensure that certain murderers held at Holt Castle were being 'respited or delayed of their trial and not put to execution'. The Duke of Norfolk flatly denied it. To his knowledge Richmond had not had a hand in any such letters. Lee knew differently, advising Cromwell 'yet of truth it is otherwise as the said letters directed to the Steward there do testify by their subscriptions'. In the same letter he worried that Richmond should not be encouraged to support such causes, adding 'it is not for his honour to see his badge and livery, as is by the parties alleged, worn upon strong thieves' backs'. Lee was almost certainly thinking of the influence of William Brereton. The duke's servant wielded no small measure of power in the marcher area as Richmond's steward of Holt, Chirk and Bromfield and Yale and his conduct positively invited suspicion.

In 1534, Brereton had been part of an investigation into alleged irregularities under Abbot Robert Salisbury at the Abbey of Valle Crucis within the lordship of Bromfield and Yale. Far from being an impartial observer, Brereton seems to have been in the thick of things. The abbot of Cymer Abbey in Gwynedd offered him £40 if he could secure his transfer to Valle Crucis, which would necessitate Salisbury's removal. It is entirely possible that the whole investigation was Brereton's idea in order to achieve this end.[14] In 1536 Brereton's acquisition of certain tithes also looks suspiciously like a bribe. Such activities, especially when coupled with Brereton's numerous offices, were inevitably going to attract Cromwell's unwelcome attention.

Richmond's relations with Thomas Cromwell were generally good. When there was a problem with a grant to one of his gentleman waiters, John Travers, in respect of fishing in the River Bann in Ireland, the Lord Lieutenant of Ireland wrote to Cromwell to ask that he be allowed to enjoy it. When Henry VIII decided to grant Collyweston to Anne Boleyn, Richmond turned to Cromwell to ensure that the grant he had made to his gentleman usher, Anthony Drillard, to be bailiff and keeper there, would be honoured, advising the secretary 'I being very loath he should be excluded'. When the exchange was effected (in the statute 27 Henry VIII c.21), a proviso was duly included to protect Drillard's interests. He was still serving as bailiff there, earning 7*d* a day, when Richmond died in 1536. Although if this was an example of Richmond's influence with Cromwell, it is also illustrative of Cromwell's relationship with the duke. Some years earlier Drillard had secured his place in Richmond's household by letters of recommendation from his patron Thomas Cromwell.

As the king's son, Richmond was in a unique position to require Cromwell's assistance. Yet Richmond's relationship with Cromwell was rather different from that with the king's previous first minister. Thomas Wolsey's indiscriminate interference in Richmond's affairs had been done under colour of being both Richmond's godfather and the minister responsible for the king's Council of the North. Cromwell had no such excuse. Now that Richmond's household was, in all practical senses, independent from the government of the north, there was no real reason for him to involve himself directly in the duke's business. Also Richmond was no longer a child in the schoolroom. Accordingly, when the duke's interests clashed with Cromwell's envisaged programme of government reform, it was the minister who was required to tread carefully.

On the surface, Brereton's relations with Cromwell seem to have been reasonable. As late as May 1536, hearing a rumour that some religious establishments in Cheshire were to be suppressed, Brereton saw nothing wrong in hopefully lobbying Cromwell in expectation of even greater spoils. Brereton could count on some powerful supporters: not only was he Richmond's steward, he also enjoyed the favour of the Duke of Norfolk, who acted as the overseer of his father's will. If this was not enough, he was also a groom of the privy chamber and apparently well-liked by the king. It did not give Cromwell a lot of room for manoeuvre.

In response to this latest development, plans now suddenly emerged for the Duke of Richmond, accompanied by the Duke of Norfolk, to make a progress up to Holt. The official reason was Richmond's investiture as Lord of Holt. However the idea, which was probably Norfolk's, would also allow the young duke to address the state of his affairs in person. Coming two weeks after Lee's complaints, the timing was no coincidence. Ralph Broke was amazed that the dukes would make such a journey 'now in the time of winter'. On one level it was obviously desirable that Richmond should redress problems within his jurisdiction in person. It was an effective way to rebuff Lee's criticisms of mismanagement in his name and, to be fair, the problem of justice was not completely neglected. An agreement was reached for an exchange of prisoners between Powis and Chirk. However, the manner in which the progress was conducted and received suggests that the visit was also something of a political statement. Richmond was asserting his authority as an independent magnate and as such might have been perceived as striking a blow for the other marcher lords.

As Cromwell intensified his efforts to eradicate the power of the marcher lordships, it is only natural that some of the lords began to look to the king's son as their best hope for survival. As long as Richmond enjoyed his traditional rights and privileges, there was hope for them all. Despite the unseasonable time of year, his visit attracted attention. Ralph Broke was probably not the only man who put off other business to pay his respects. The people of Shrewsbury were particularly determined to make a good impression. The town bailiffs agreed to provide food and drink. The main street and both the bridges were scrubbed clean and Richard Clarke, a barber, was paid the princely sum of 2s 4d to ride out and give a warning when Richmond and Norfolk entered the county. As the two dukes entered the town they were greeted with a host of presents, including swans, calves, oxen and capons at a cost of £5 18s 2d.

The townspeople were clearly prepared to spend a significant amount of time and money to secure Richmond's goodwill. The extent to which Richmond's influence would have been effective in blocking reform is less certain. On the one hand, the Act of

Union in April 1536 was a measure of Cromwell's resolve to effect change. On the other hand the minister's determination to remove Brereton is an indication of how seriously he took the issue of Richmond's authority in the Marches. It is entirely probable that the combined power of Richmond and Norfolk, together with the threat of Brereton in the privy chamber and close to the ear of the king, convinced Cromwell that no fundamental solution to the problem of the Marches would be possible as long as this status quo remained. Unfortunately, this conviction probably helped Brereton to the block.

Not all historians are convinced that the extent of Brereton's influence supports a conspiracy theory. Retha Warnicke makes the valid point that Brereton 'was not the only powerful courtier in the region'. Others have dismissed him as a man who 'carried little political weight'. Certainly he was not a major court player like Rochford. Even his removal from the Marches would not clear the way for political reform. However, perhaps it was a well-timed signal that resistance was not only useless, but dangerous. If Cromwell wanted to make an example to underline this point, then Brereton had certainly been annoying enough to be a prime candidate. One instance that must have particularly rankled occurred in 1534, when Brereton had used his influence to block Cromwell's efforts to save the Flintshire gentleman John ap Gryffith Eyton from the gallows. Instead, the steward had had Eyton arrested in London and returned to Wales for execution. In the end it was not Brereton's conduct as steward that provided Cromwell with the means to dispose of him. Indeed, if Brereton's hope of patronage in May 1536 is any indication, he was totally unaware of what was about to happen.

By this point the musician Mark Smeaton was already under arrest, accused of committing adultery with the queen. His arrest on 30 April was quickly followed by that of the courtier Henry Norris on 2 May. At this point Anne herself was dispatched to the Tower, having been informed that she was believed to have had adulterous relations with Smeaton, Norris and one other. In the event, Smeaton, Norris and three others were accused. These were Anne's brother, George Boleyn, Lord Rochford, the courtier Francis Weston and William Brereton.

The cloud of suspicion which blew up around Anne Boleyn gave the secretary the excuse he had previously lacked to move against Brereton. The evidence against all the supposed paramours of the queen is uniformly weak. This was a political coup, not a crime of passion. Indeed, Cromwell seems to have toyed with removing other members of the court. Both Sir Richard Page and Sir Thomas Wyatt made it as far as the Tower. Outside, several others waited anxiously to see if they would be the next to be implicated.

A man who uses and abuses his power as Brereton did, was bound to make enemies. When cast as a man with a voracious sexual appetite, who had had several lovers as well as the queen, many were eager to believe his guilt. To his credit, Brereton did not claim to be an innocent pawn. But he knew that he did not die for any of the reasons that had been rehearsed. On the scaffold he admitted 'I have deserved to die if it were a thousand deaths. But the cause whereof I die judge not'. Cromwell no doubt rubbed his hands with glee. Far from protecting him, Brereton's established links with the Howards could now only drag him down. To be accused of having cuckolded him was a sure way of removing any hope of assistance from the king and Brereton was left vulnerable and exposed, an easy target for the minister.

It is impossible to measure how far Brereton's loss would have affected the balance of power in the Welsh Marches. The rush of applications for his offices gives some indication of the vacuum he left. But Richmond's own death shortly afterwards changed the picture so dramatically that the fate of the marcher lords seems to have been sealed. The duke's loss was keenly felt. The steward of Ruthin was convinced that it was the 'utter undoing of me and all the other Marches'. He was probably right. Richmond had not particularly striven to identify himself with the rights and causes of the government of the Marches. Yet while he lived, some degree of autonomy for the lordships seemed assured. In the climate of 1536 the reassurance this gave may well have been more apparent than real. However, after Richmond's death there was little to stand in the way of even greater reform. Now the greatest marcher lord was the king.

Any measure of the extent of the influence that Richmond was able to command is always inextricably bound up with his relationship to the king. Yet like any 'good lord' Richmond was keen to champion his officers in matters not directly related to his own affairs. When his gentleman usher, Thomas Delaryver, was accused of killing a stag on land belonging to the Abbot of Byland in 1534, Richmond was quick to defend him, claiming not only that his servant had been wrongfully accused, but also that the steward had gone ahead and indicted him against the wishes of the abbot. When another member of his household was having trouble securing his rightful inheritance, Richmond pointedly intervened expressing his wish for a speedy and successful conclusion. The duke may even have been instrumental in securing William Biddlecombe's return to parliament as the Member for Poole. Certainly, Richmond subsequently wrote to Cromwell asking him to 'give credence' to the burgess.[15] Until Richmond had greater control over the selection of his officers this cannot be seen as an affinity in the traditional sense, but it was clearly a role he aspired to.

Richmond was also called on to fulfil other duties of a nobleman. He exchanged New Year gifts with several members of the court. On one occasion a standing cup with a cover, which Richmond had received from the king as part of his New Year gift, was sent to Elizabeth Stafford, Duchess of Norfolk, as her New Year gift. In 1534, probably as a favour to his servant, John Jenny, Richmond stood as a godfather. To mark the occasion Mistress Jenny's infant was presented with the little silver salt that had been part of Anne Boleyn's present to him at the New Year. When Mistress Amy got married in 1536, Richmond gave her another silver salt, this time part of the king's New Year gift to him. When the Countess of Westmorland had a baby Richmond gave the noble child an appropriately more ostentatious gift of a silver gilt layer.

The division between the actions of the duke and those acting in his name are sometimes difficult to discern. In theory this was not important, as long as the authority represented by the duke was respected. In practice, the decision to establish Richmond as an independent marcher lord raised questions of authority and control which seem more relevant to a minority government than a child in wardship. On the whole Richmond's rank and status were respected. To any career-minded noble the importance attached to Richmond as a member of the peerage and the king's son made his age somewhat irrelevant. Even the king was always careful never to deliberately override his actions, although, on several occasions Henry might well have required the intervention of his ministers to persuade him this was the prudent course.

For his part, Richmond was obviously eager to be seen to be acting like a proper adult magnate – and it cannot be denied that his servants and officers were keen to encourage him to support their causes. It would be easy to blame his youth or 'evil councilors' for his rasher actions and occasional lapses in judgment. However, Richmond's arrogance was also a factor and even in the later part of his life men like Cooke were able to exploit his desire to be seen to be exercising his authority. Maturity might have brought him better judgment, but it is unlikely to have tempered his ambition. Even at this age Richmond was more than willing to swim among the sharks of Tudor politics to further his affairs. As the stakes increased, that game had ever greater rewards.

7

Legacy

The seventeen-year-old Duke of Richmond departed this world as he had entered it, in quiet obscurity. His life had been spent in pursuit of the model renaissance education. He had been schooled in the manners of a courtier and tutored in the arts of war. He was reported to favour the magnificence of his father in both looks and character and Henry's affection for his son was widely known. Yet Richmond did not live to be a great general or statesman, he did not even enjoy the dubious notoriety of dying nobly on the scaffold, nor could he be revered for his martyrdom at the stake. Finally, and perhaps most importantly, he left no progeny to recommend him to posterity.

It is difficult to find any enduring legacy. The only real portrait of Richmond is a miniature attributed to the Flemish artist Lucas Hornebolte. Even this shows the duke somewhat *déshabillé*, in just his shirt with the neck open and his hair covered with a finely decorated skullcap. Although this might easily be taken as a depiction of Richmond on his deathbed, it is more likely that this was intended as an *aide-mémoire* for the only other surviving image of the duke, in the illustrations included in the new register of the Order of the Garter produced in 1534. Richmond, with his red hair, is clearly visible in both the procession of the knights and on the left-hand side of the king in the grouping around the throne. While no such assembly, which included Francis I of France and James V of Scotland, ever actually took place, it is thought to be a good likeness of the English knights.[1] This would explain his unusual attire. Since Richmond was to be portrayed in his Garter robes in the finished portrait, his features were all that were required.

The fact that neither possessions nor portraits of the duke have survived can partly be explained by the normal economy of the Royal Household. Richmond's clothes and furnishings were by and large reabsorbed into the king's wardrobe. The expensive fur trimmings and gold laces from his robes were removed for use in other garments and the bedding, tapestries and other furnishings were recycled for use in some other household. Even those items which were spent and worn would be kept. Such pieces could be used to furnish the apartments of disgraced nobles in the Tower. Richmond's gold and other valuables would have gone to the king's jewel house, and there was a significant amount of this. His plate alone – pieces of gold, silver and silver gilt – filled four coffers and even that did not include 'certain parcels which remain in the hands of the Duchess of Richmond'. There were also four blocks of gold and others of silver, as well as other jewels which remained with George Cotton. Much of this would have been lost as the pieces were melted down or broken up to be placed in new settings.

Part of his goods were immediately granted away. If Richmond had been an adult magnate, he would have been expected to reward and remember his friends in his last will. It was customary to provide his servants with lengths of black cloth for funeral clothing and wages commensurate with their years of loyal service. The few gifts made out of Richmond's goods did not really compare, but they may not necessarily have reflected the wishes of the duke. Two days after his death John Gostwyk began an extensive inventory of the duke's goods. Even as he was taking the inventory Gostwyk asked that he might be allowed to buy a mule 'which I have already in my custody . . . for she is too little for the King's Highness'.

It was probably the king's decision to deliver several parcels of silver gilt to 'my Lady's Grace', probably Mary Tudor. Richmond would no doubt have approved of his half-brother, Lord Tailbois, having his green taffeta and velvet coat. The horse with its saddle and harness of black velvet, which was given to Surrey, was most likely Richmond's own. His widow, Mary Howard, was allocated a few bits and pieces, including two solid silver spoons and one silver gilt spoon, but how Viscount Lisle came by one of Richmond's chairs is less clear.

Richmond did not leave the sort of grand building enterprises that proclaimed the power and wealth of his elders to the world. He displayed no real delight in scholarship. Indeed, according to the inventory of his goods, all the books in his household were strictly for religious services, so it is hardly fair to expect any examples of poetry or polemic. If he inherited his father's love of music, it was as a performer rather than a composer. If he had loved art with the same passion that he reserved for sport and hunting, then the relics he left behind him might have been more numerous.

The extent of Richmond's influence is perhaps more easily weighed in the void left by his death. The most immediate and pressing problem was the redistribution of his offices. Any hopes that Norfolk harboured of regaining his former position as Lord Admiral were quickly dashed. That post went to a rising privy councillor, Sir William Fitzwilliam. Instead, Norfolk was sent to Sheriff Hutton to quell the mounting disorder in the north. Another star in the ascendant, Sir Edward Seymour, was given the office of chancellor and chamberlain of north Wales, which Richmond had recently acquired from the condemned Henry Norris. Sometimes the solution was simple and straightforward. The former deputy-captain at Berwick, Sir Thomas Clifford, slipped seamlessly into Richmond's office as captain of the town and castle. However, not all the vacancies were so easily filled.

Despite Richmond's apparent lack of involvement in the mechanics of government in Ireland, his sudden death caused immediate repercussions. The Irish parliament had been in the midst of a session, called under his authority as Lord Lieutenant. Now that he was dead, the concern was expressed that his authority was no longer valid and 'the authority of the Parliament was extincted and all acts in the same Parliament ensuing . . . [were] faint and void in law'. Since the Parliament had dealt with a number of important matters relating to church and state, it was suggested a new commission should be sent over to ensure the acts were fully ratified in law. After some deliberation, Cromwell decided the statutes were perfectly valid. However, the decision not to appoint another Lord Lieutenant of Ireland is evidence that Richmond's particular usefulness to his father was not easily replicated in other men.

As a landed magnate Richmond's loss also caused other problems. Since there was no possibility that his wife might be pregnant, all his property immediately reverted to the king. Even so, it was not exactly a seamless transition. When the steward of Ruthin wrote to commiserate with the Duke of Norfolk on his loss, he pointed out that the deputy receiver there intended to take advantage of Richmond's death by keeping all the revenues, rents and profits which he had collected. In Yorkshire, Richmond's former tenants in Masham and Nidderdale reacted with dismay at the demand for 'the God's penny and a gressom due on the change of lord' on top of a year's rent, tithes and other payments which now all fell due at the same time.[2] Their reaction contributed to the worrying anarchy in the north. Not only did they refuse to pay their rents, but they added their voices to the protests against the suppression of the monasteries.

Henry soon moved to reassert his authority over Richmond's former holdings. Within weeks, William Orrell, a page of the king's chamber, had been appointed bailiff of the Richmond fee in Norfolk. The king's officers were charged with collecting outstanding debts and fees, although it would be more than two years before the bailiff of Richmond's Manor of Droitwich in Worcestershire paid up the £10 19s which was owing. It took Henry even longer to turn his attention to the Welsh Marches. Not until October 1537 were the Earl of Worcester and others sent to investigate Richmond's holdings there; and it was not until March 1538 that Robert Wingfield was made auditor of the possessions of the Countess of Richmond, including those back in the king's hands because of Richmond's unexpected death.

A number of large grants helped to minimise the disruption caused by Richmond's death. Henry's long-time friend and former brother-in-law, Charles Brandon, Duke of Suffolk, was particularly fortunate with a significant spread of lands in the Midlands. The king's cousin, Henry Courtenay, Marquess of Exeter, was given the disputed Manor of Canford and other lands in Dorset. In order to support his new dignity as Lord Admiral, Sir William Fitzwilliam was allowed land in Devon and elsewhere.

These large grants were followed by a trickle of smaller grants. Men and woman from all levels of court society, from Henry's final queen, Katherine Parr, who received the lordship and Manor of Thorpe Achurch in Northamptonshire, to John Cocke, one of the king's footmen, who received a lease of lands in Overstone in Northampton, benefited from Richmond's death. The Manor of Kingsbury, in Somerset, went to Roger Amyce, whose father-in-law had been Richmond's cofferer. However, the Manor of Boston, in Lincolnshire, was perhaps a special case. In 1545 it paid £646 15s 4d for the right to become a corporate borough. Significantly, even though Jane's pregnancy was known only months after Richmond's death, there was no attempt to reserve any of his holdings for an expected prince, an indication that Henry did not envisage Richmond as his heir.

With the dismantling of Richmond's estates came the break up of his household. Among Cromwell's papers is a note 'to know what the King will do with the Duke of Richmond's servants'. Many of the duke's officers had been with him since his creation in 1525. Now they found themselves scrambling to find other positions. The £528 purse which Henry allowed them 'at the defraying of that household' would not go far, and as Henry was due to receive a year's worth of rent and revenues from Richmond's lands and had already taken £490 in ready money from the duke's almoner it was only a token gesture, rather than a serious attempt to defray their hardship.

The most fortunate stayed in royal service. Richard Cotton found himself serving his king in another role when he was called to help combat the Pilgrimage of Grace. Hugh Johns, Richmond's yeoman of the wardrobe, was lucky enough to find alternative employment with the king. Some looked hopefully towards the household of the duke's half-sister Mary, which the rumours had it 'shall be shortly advanced and the number of persons thereof augmented'. Others were subsequently accepted into the household formed for the new Prince Edward, although it took Thomas Eynns three years to secure his position there and in the meantime he complained of his 'great costs and charges . . . whereby I am more than half undone'. A few men looked to their friends and relations to secure continuing employment. Sir Thomas Darcy, a former gentleman waiter, was particularly fortunate when he moved effortlessly into the service of his rising relation, Edward Seymour.

One of the most interesting choices of patron for Richmond's servants after their lord's death was Thomas Cromwell. Being old and infirm, Thomas Holland did not feel able to accept Cromwell's offer of a post, but rather than waste the opportunity, he was quick to send up his son and heir instead. When the Duchess of Norfolk was looking to aid a brewer named Arnold, who obviously secured his place in Richmond's household through his connections with the Howards, she confidently approached Cromwell for his help, as it was evidently common knowledge that he had taken on several of Richmond's former servants. The fact that the Blount's youngest son, Henry, was accepted into Cromwell's service might reasonably have arisen out of an association with Richmond. Thomas Eynns spoke of Cromwell's fondness for the duke as 'doth plainly appear in the bounty and goodness that you did after his death most charitably extend for his sake only to divers and sundry his servants'.

Those who had no powerful patron to assist them were not quite as fortunate. One of the most wretched was William Wood, sometime servant to the duke. Having been employed in

Richmond's stables at Sheriff Hutton on the basis of food and drink only, he had, by his own admission, loitered on in the duke's household without any master. On Richmond's return south he had followed the establishment to Wolsey's residence of the More in Hertfordshire and then on to Windsor, surviving by attaching himself to anyone in Richmond's service who would accept him. By July 1538, he was in trouble with the Council of the North for using seditious words and his career remained firmly in the doldrums.

One of those most intimately affected by Richmond's death was his widow, Mary Howard. Whereas before she could have looked forward to presenting the King of England with a grandson, now her future was uncertain. At first sight her prospects seemed promising. At seventeen she was still younger than many girls at their first marriage. She now had not only her father's wealth and her mother's royal connections to recommend her, but her rank and status as Duchess of Richmond and Somerset and her expected income as a widow, making her a most attractive prospect.

Although the young couple had never lived together, decorum did require a decent period of mourning. The young Duchess of Richmond retired from the court to her father's house at Kenninghall in Norfolk. In November 1536 the duke assured Cromwell, 'it is not possible for a young woman to handle herself more discreetly than she hath done since her husband's death'. As well as the three geldings with their bridles, saddles 'and all other things belonging to them' which brought her back to Norfolk, she had an unspecified amount of her husband's plate and jewels. While these things were not without value, there could be no serious question of her remarriage until the question of her jointure had been settled.

However, almost as soon as Richmond was in his grave, Henry began to express doubts about the validity of his son's marriage to Mary Howard. Everyone was happy to agree that their union had never been consummated. What the king now began to question was whether sexual intercourse was a requirement in contracting a binding and lawful marriage. Rather than granting Mary's jointure, Henry decided to refer the matter to the judges and lawyers. Anxious at both the possibility of doubt and the delay, Norfolk expressed his hope that a favourable decision would quickly be secured. The duke's anxiety was increased by the knowledge that he was about to make an imminent departure to Sheriff Hutton in Yorkshire on the king's business. Since this meant leaving his rather headstrong daughter to her own devices he was keen to see the matter settled before he left.

If Norfolk hoped that mention of his good service would force a speedy resolution, he was to be sorely disappointed. Despite a stream of letters he was unable to secure any sort of a decision. Cromwell replied with promises and platitudes, but little sign of any action. In May 1537, almost a year after Richmond's death, Norfolk wrote somewhat testily from Sheriff Hutton: 'good my lord make an end for my daughter's cause, all learned men do say that I spoke with there is no doubt of her right'. Mary also believed that her marriage had been entirely valid. As such, her first instinct was to blame her father. Obviously, he had not presented her case properly to the king. In fact the duke's many letters, several written in his own hand, makes it clear that his daughter's suit was never far from his thoughts. Mary dismissed her father's undoubted efforts as nothing but words. She was convinced the king could not know the true facts for 'so just a Prince' would never deny his son's widow the justice that was allowed to the 'worst gentlewoman in this realm'.

To her father's horror Mary suggested that she should go to London to press her suit in person. When that request was denied she did the next best thing and wrote to Cromwell pleading for him to intercede on her behalf. According to her father she had been 'put in such comfort by learned men that her right is clearly good', that she could not see any reason for the delay. What she blatantly failed to appreciate, and what her father was all too painfully aware of, was that the delay had little to do with the vagaries of matrimonial law and everything to do with the mood of the king.

All the evidence supports the view that Mary was legally entitled to her jointure. When Cromwell asked the Archbishop of Canterbury for his opinion, Thomas Cranmer was embarrassingly direct:

> I assure your lordship that without further convocation of doctors I am fully persuaded that such marriages as be in lawful age, contracted per verba de presenti, are matrimony before God, and the same cause is (as I remember) plainly opined and declared in the king's grace's book of his own cause of matrimony.[3]

Although even a contract made in the present tense could be dissolved by mutual consent, strictly speaking this was illegal. The Church courts strongly disapproved of such actions, preferring to back the validity of the marriage. In the eyes of both the law and the Church Mary and Richmond had been husband and wife. Ironically, it was probably the justice of Mary's position that was causing the delay. The judges were reluctant to deliver a verdict that would upset the king, who was not happy to hear any decision which would require him to honour his financial obligation.

As Cranmer had rather pointedly observed, Henry was no stranger to matrimonial law. This was no naïve misunderstanding. According to her mother, Mary was supposed to receive £1,000 a year from the king as her widow's jointure.[4] Henry can hardly have viewed the prospect of bestowing such a significant sum of money with very good grace. Not only was there no hope of grandchildren, but to add insult to injury Norfolk had been allowed to forgo the substantial dowry that the king could normally have expected for the marriage of his son. Also, while Mary and her father were always careful to stress the role of the king in arranging the marriage, it is evident that his treacherous queen, Anne Boleyn, had persuaded him into it. In the circumstances, he had every reason to want to be rid of the whole matter.

If Mary's marriage was invalid, she would lose more than her jointure. As Richmond's widow 'the right high and noble princess Mary Duchess of Richmond and Somerset and Countess of Nottingham', was ranked next to Henry's own niece, Margaret Douglas, and above her own mother, Elizabeth Stafford, Duchess of Norfolk. Any irregularity in the marriage would automatically return her to her former rank as 'the Lady Mary Howard', daughter to the Duke of Norfolk. Much as Henry clearly wanted to save himself unpleasant expense, he is unlikely to have been aware of this. If he succeeded in his challenge, the Howards would lose every right and benefit from what had once seemed such a prestigious match.

In recent months Norfolk had worked hard to distance himself from the disgrace of his half-brother, Lord Thomas Howard, which was rapidly followed by the downfall of his niece, Anne Boleyn. Yet despite his sterling service during the Pilgrimage of Grace, when his need for Norfolk's military experience had helped the king to put aside his resentment over Richmond's funeral, the fortunes of the Howards remained at a decidedly low ebb. Norfolk's duties in the north, albeit as the king's lieutenant, effectively kept him from court. In his absence, men like Thomas Cromwell and Edward Seymour, now the king's brother-in-law, had Henry's ear. When Norfolk learnt that matters relating to Scotland were to be discussed, he begged to be allowed to return so that he might share the benefit of his experience. At the bottom of his letter he scrawled in his own hand 'the loss of one of my fingers should not be so much to my sorrow as to be in fear not to see my master at this time'. However, even that did not work and he continued to be kept from the king. Until Norfolk could engineer his own return to favour, he was hardly in a strong position to push his daughter's case.

In the circumstances, David Starkey's claim that Norfolk 'gave [Mary] no backing in her efforts to get adequate maintenance from the King', is perhaps a little harsh. It is never wise to lose sight of the fact that Norfolk was notoriously self-serving. He was certainly not going to risk anything which might prejudice his own return to favour. Yet, within those parameters, he made concerted efforts to bring the case to the king's attention. On his return from the north, Norfolk wrote from Kenninghall asking permission to come to London with his daughter and a small entourage. When Cromwell fobbed him off with a vague answer Norfolk did not give up, but pressed Cromwell 'to advertise me whether you thought I should displease his majesty with bringing her up or not'. Unfortunately, his efforts were frustrated when sickness swept across East Anglia. Kept at home by the risk of infection, he was reduced to sending up the treasurer of his household to speak to Cromwell on his daughter's behalf.

Despite his undoubted efforts and the justice of her case, Mary would not receive her jointure until the king decided to permit it. Regardless of appearances, Norfolk did have some advantages. As one of only two remaining dukes in England, he had a usefulness that could not easily be dispensed with. Thomas Cromwell could manoeuvre to keep him from the court, but he could not block his attendance when the king wished to consult him. His role as Earl Marshal at the funeral of Queen Jane or his selection as one of Prince Edward's godfathers, had nothing to do with his personal relationship with the Seymours, but was a reflection of his rank and status as one of the greatest peers in the realm. Sooner or later his patience and good service would surely be rewarded.

Norfolk's efforts to restore the Howards to favour were not helped by his own dysfunctional family. His son and heir, Henry Howard, Earl of Surrey, found the meteoric rise of a gentry family like the Seymours impossible to bear. In the summer of 1537, the tension between the Earl of Surrey and Edward Seymour (created Earl of Hertford at his nephew's christening in October 1537) erupted into open violence. Surrey tried to strike the king's brother-in-law within the precepts of the court. The due punishment for such a crime was the loss of his right hand. Fortunately for Surrey, the king was indulgent enough towards the Duke of Richmond's childhood friend to commute his sentence to a few months comfortable, but embarrassing, confinement at Windsor Castle.[5] On his release the duke tried to keep his son more quietly in the country, but Surrey's volatile temper would not be so easily contained.

Then there were the Duchess of Norfolk's attempts to tie her own financial difficulties to the question of her daughter's jointure. After an acrimonious marriage, the Duke and Duchess of Norfolk had formally separated in 1534. Cromwell's attempts to reunite the couple were hampered by her allegations of a history of maltreatment and abuse. Among other instances of violence Norfolk had, she claimed, had her bound 'till blood came out of my finger ends' and beaten 'till I sp[a]t blood'. Norfolk refuted her claims as wilful slander, but his determination to keep his mistress of eleven years, Bess Holland, whom the duchess described as 'that harlot which has put me to all this trouble', at Kenninghall and parade her openly at court enraged his estranged wife. The duchess also protested vehemently at the reduced circumstances in which her husband expected her to live. A gentlewoman could not live on £50 a quarter 'and the one quarter and half the other is spent before it commeth in'. Hearing that Mary's jointure had not yet been paid, she asked Cromwell to ensure that the king did not grant Mary her settlement until she first received hers.

The Duchess of Norfolk might have believed that her marriage, purchased by her father at a cost of two thousand marks, which had endured for twenty-two years and produced five children, gave her case precedence over her daughter's brief, childless union, which had come at no cost to the family, but society would not condone her behaviour. Convention expected a woman to turn a blind eye to a husband's infidelity. Instead, the duchess was mortified that her children tolerated Bess Holland's presence and was particularly distressed that Mary went about in her company. Her bitterness was perhaps all the sharper because they did not support her in her battles with their father. She roundly declared there was 'never woman that bare so ungracious an eldest son, and so ungracious a daughter, and unnatural'. Yet the issue was rather more complicated than such high emotion allowed. Mary's reliance on her father's bounty made it difficult for her to side with a mother whose own behaviour was not above reproach.

The duke also had his hands full ensuring that his wilful daughter, who was justly convinced of her lawful right, did not assert her claim more forcefully than was politic. Like her mother, and rather too like her cousin Anne Boleyn, Mary was a woman of strong opinions. Norfolk admitted that 'in all my life I never commoned with her in any serious cause ere now' and he had not been entirely comforted to discover her grasp of the legal niceties. Henry would not take kindly to being lectured on his duties and responsibilities by his former daughter-in-law. Thankfully, Mary seems to have reserved her more tempestuous outbursts for her long-suffering father. To Cromwell she wrote in grateful thanks for 'how painfully you daily . . . labour . . . to the king's majesty for my matter', humbly assuring him that she would accept whatever arrears that Henry might deign to give her.

Instead, it seems another solution was initially considered. As early as November 1536 Norfolk had been expressing a desire to see Mary safely married again, except that he believed:

> at this time there is neither lord, nor lord's son, nor other good inheritor of this realm, that I can remember, of convenient age to marry her so that in manner I reckon herself undone; for if she should marry, and her children not to inherit some good portion, they were undone.[6]

Norfolk's concern that Mary might be persuaded into an unsuitable match proved groundless. Suitors were not exactly beating a path to her door. As well as the exacting standards of her father, it would be a very poor bargain indeed to have agreed terms on the basis of a marriage to the dowager Duchess of Richmond, widow of the king's son, only to find that marriage ultimately declared invalid and your wife stripped of all rank and royal connection.

Now, after almost two years of dispute and delay, Norfolk had apparently reconsidered his position. Now he 'knew but 2 persons upon whom he thought meet or could resolve in his heart to bestow his said daughter'. However, the king was so unimpressed with the second gentleman that he could not even remember his name. The other, whom Norfolk admitted was the one 'to whom his heart is most inclined', was Sir Thomas Seymour.

The sudden death of Queen Jane had not markedly affected the rising fortunes of the Seymours. Their relationship to the future king seemed to assure their ascendancy for decades to come. Whatever Norfolk's personal feelings towards the family, he knew Edward Seymour, in particular, was a man of ambition, bolstered by ability and military skill. Already Earl of Hertford and a privy councillor, it was clear that he was a rising force and a man to contend with. His praise of Thomas 'for his towardness and other his commendable merits' was perhaps slightly more tongue-in-cheek. However, while Edward was already married, Thomas was not. Ever the astute politician, Norfolk was naturally reluctant to allow such a valuable asset as an unmarried daughter to remain unrealised. A union between the two families would be more than a diplomatic *rapprochement*, it was an attempt to safeguard the Howards' own role at the heart of English politics.

Scenting an opportunity to sweep this whole unpleasant business of Mary's jointure under the carpet, Henry was keen to endorse the match, declaring 'one of such lust and youth . . . should be able to please her well at all points'. Not unreasonably rather taken aback at an overture of marriage from such a quarter, Sir Thomas Seymour was rather more cautious and asked Cromwell to sound out the Duke of Norfolk's intentions. Despite the Seymours' royal connections, a union between a duchess and a knight was by no means an equal match and the history of difficulties between them had hardly fostered good relations. However, the Seymours were painfully conscious of their gentry roots and marriage into one of the two remaining ducal families would enhance their dignity and assuage such criticisms. To reject such an auspicious union, especially when the king heartily approved, would not be entirely wise.

Everything seemed in order. Even Cromwell had his own reasons to support the marriage. The conservative Duke of Norfolk's disapproval of the increasingly protestant line being taken in religion would hopefully be tempered by closer links with the reforming Seymours. Yet suddenly the negotiations stalled, as it seems Mary was not at all happy to hear she was to marry again.

Mary Howard has sometimes been painted as something of a coquette, a flighty young thing who loved nothing more than the spectacle of the court. Resentful at being left to moulder at Kenninghall, she would be eager for any excuse to return; she was not the sort of girl to reject anyone as charming and handsome as Sir Thomas Seymour. Yet Mary's own letters make it very clear that she was not easily swayed by anyone. The doubts over her marriage to Richmond had left Mary sensitive about her status. As the wife of Sir Thomas Seymour courtesy might allow her to retain the title Duchess of Richmond, but there would be no formal acknowledgement that she had been the duke's true and lawful wife. If she married now she might never receive her jointure.

If Mary had hoped to force the king's hand by refusing to countenance the marriage until the question of her jointure was settled, she was to be disappointed. If she was to succeed, it was to be on Henry's terms. In October 1538, Henry once again had his eye on the prize of the Duchy of Milan, this time through the marriage of his elder daughter, Mary, to Charles V's cousin, the Infante Dom Luis of Portugal. In his eagerness to secure such a trophy, the king considered throwing in the hands of all his other available female relations, including his younger daughter Elizabeth, his niece Margaret Douglas and Mary (whom in this context he presumably accepted as his true daughter-in-law) for whatever Italian princes the emperor 'thought most convenient and meet to be retained in alliance'. In the end sanity prevailed and this particular initiative was not even included in the proposals. Yet Mary was still no closer to obtaining her goal.

In the end it was, perhaps predictably, her father's martial service which turned the tide. When Henry was badly frightened by the threat of war in the winter of 1538 the Howards were restored to favour.[7] Shortly afterwards, on 11 March 1539, Mary received the first of a series of grants. The king did not exactly cast this first payment as a capitulation. It stressed that Mary had been unable to recover her dower from the law and specifically recorded that the union had never been consummated. Nor was it particularly generous, providing an income of £12 per annum, although Mary could perhaps take some comfort in the fact that these lands, as part of the honour of Richmond in Norfolk, were a tacit acknowledgement of her position as dowager Duchess of Richmond.

Subsequent grants to augment her income were not made out of her late husband's estates at all, but drawn from Henry's newly acquired stock of monastic properties. Recent events, which had seen England excommunicated by the pope, the recall of the French and Spanish ambassadors and the very real threat of invasion, meant that the conservative Duke of Norfolk was operating from a much stronger position. Many people believed that the passing of the Act of Six Articles, which affirmed the king's (and therefore his country's) belief in the seven sacraments, meant the tide of reformation was on the wane. At last, finding himself back in Henry's favour, Norfolk was finally well placed to plead his daughter's suit. By 1540 Mary had been granted a range of former Church properties, which gave her an income in excess of £744 a year.

Given the delay in recognising Mary's entitlement, it may have been difficult to provide for her out of Richmond's former lands. In the four years since Richmond's death, large parts of his holdings had already been re-granted, although it is difficult to avoid the other conclusion: that possessing of such a convenient wealth of land allowed the king to appear to be bountiful, without actually feeling the pinch. Certainly, the lump sum of £90 that she was given 'in reward' in February 1539 probably represented all that he deigned to give her as arrears.

Even though the question of her jointure, and by association her status, appeared to have been settled, Mary's life did not immediately fall into place. She was, no doubt, gratified to be included in the reception for the king's fourth wife, Anne of Cleves. In all the accounts of the preparations and at the reception itself she was ranked next in honour to the king's niece, Margaret Douglas. However, plans afoot to include her in the household came to nothing when Anne arrived in England with a clutch of her own attendants.

Despite the unspecified amount of plate and jewels from her husband's household, these lean years had been difficult for Mary, nor is it certain how generous her father had been. To take on the burden of Mary's expenses might be seen as an acknowledgement that she was his responsibility as his daughter, rather than the king's charge as dowager Duchess of Richmond and a relict of the Crown. In April 1537 Norfolk wrote to Cromwell about 'the defraying of my daughters charges' and thanked him for his 'pains taken therein', but whether this resulted in any hard cash is less certain. It was later reported that Mary's 'coffers and chambers [are] so bare as your Majesty would hardly think. Her jewels, such as she had, sold, or lent to gage [pawned], to pay her debts'. The prospect of a bright new future at court, when her cousin Catherine Howard became the king's fifth wife, must have seemed her salvation.

The king's distaste for Anne of Cleves, who 'had breasts so slack and other parts of her body in such sort that [he] somewhat suspected her virginity', is well documented, as is his growing attraction for Catherine Howard, his 'rose without a thorn', whom he believed to be innocent and pure. Whatever Anne of Cleves' apparent faults, Henry can hardly have chosen a more unsuitable replacement. Even if Norfolk was unaware of the full extent of his niece's sexual experience, he would have known of her giddy temperament, rather too much like her feckless father to do him any political good.[8] This in itself tends to suggest that it was Henry, rather than Norfolk, who first looked on Catherine as a suitable bride. Catherine's step-grandmother, the dowager Duchess of Norfolk, later confirmed that Henry had taken a fancy to her 'the first time that ever he saw her'.

Whatever the possible pitfalls ahead – and no one could have expected that Catherine would be stupid enough to continue her wanton behaviour once she was queen – the opportunity was too good to waste, especially since the failure of the Cleves marriage also gave Norfolk the excuse to bring down Thomas Cromwell. Once again Henry needed a scapegoat and the architect of this distasteful union was an obvious choice. Norfolk helped destroy his credit with the king and Henry did the rest. The minister was even denied the right of a trial and was sentenced to death by Act of Attainder, a novel form of control that he himself had recently suggested to the king. At last it seemed that the Howards were firmly back in the ascendant. Yet even as Mary enjoyed her time in the new queen's household, perhaps rather to the chagrin of the Earl of Rutland, who lost to her at cards, one wonders how many of the Howards knew that their new ascendancy was a gamble.

When Catherine's infidelity came to light after only eighteen months of marriage, the queen's household was immediately broken up. Largely thanks to Norfolk's fancy footwork, reminding Henry that 'a great part of this matter is come to light by my declaration to your Majesty, according to my bounden duty', he and his immediate family emerged unscathed. In November 1541, when Margaret Douglas, who had been residing in disgrace at the former convent of Syon after her romance with Sir Charles Howard, brother of the queen, was summarily ordered to remove to Kenninghall in order to make room for the erstwhile queen, Mary was politely requested to accompany her 'if my lord her father and she be so contented'. As she returned to Norfolk, Mary must have taken some pleasure in having the company and society of her friend. Yet as she reached her twenty-fourth birthday, the dowager duchess must have wondered if her prospects would ever live up to the glittering promise of her girlhood.

Glimpses of Mary's life at Kenninghall do not show her living in obscurity or isolation. Correspondence from court passed to and fro, she continued to send the king his New Year gift and he in his turn did not completely forget her. In 1544, when he was anxious to raise funds to further his military successes in France, Mary was one of those dowager ladies earmarked to be applied to for a loan. Henry's sixth wife, Katherine Parr, was rather more gracious in her remembrance, sending a present of a stag from Woking Park. That Mary entertained company is evident in February 1545, when she sought a dispensation for herself and her guests to eat meat during Lent and at other prohibited times. She was also occasionally to be found back at court. In 1546, for example, she was present for the visit of the French ambassadors. But this was a far cry from the sort of life that a young woman of her age and status might feel she had a right to expect. Most significantly, she still did not have a husband, a household or children of her own.

Now that Mary had been granted what was, to all intents and purposes, her jointure, Norfolk made another attempt to marry her off to Sir Thomas Seymour. This time Norfolk also planned to marry his grandchildren, the offspring of Henry Howard, Earl of Surrey and his brother Thomas Howard, to Edward Seymour's sons and daughter, with the idea that the connection between the two families would grow alongside the future King Edward. It was a shrewd political move. Yet, as in the summer of 1538, it seems that the Duke of Norfolk's carefully constructed designs to further the family fortunes were once more destined to fall foul of his own children.

That Surrey allowed his pride to override political good sense and openly objected to his children being matched with a Seymour is not exactly surprising. For Mary to let a chance of matrimony slip through her fingers for a second time demands more explanation. It is easy to lay the blame at Surrey's feet, providing a convenient excuse for her later conduct. Yet it was unusual for a woman to remain unmarried, when all her hopes of wealth, security and status were bound up in the prospect of husband and children. Thomas Seymour was distinctly eligible, with excellent prospects of advancement, and many women in Mary's circumstances might have been grateful for such a catch.

Instead, Mary was no keener to marry Thomas Seymour now than she had been in 1538. Sir Garwen Carew, a courtier and contemporary, confirmed 'her fantasy [fancy] would not serve to marry with him'. Perhaps she felt she was marrying beneath her. Perhaps she saw through the charming and handsome exterior to the man whose ambition was rather greater than his abilities. Whatever her reasons, although Mary acknowledged that her father was keen to promote the alliance, she was clear about her own sentiments and would not have him. As a result, the proposal was cause for a furious argument between Mary and her brother. In a heated exchange Surrey suggested she should not refuse the marriage straight away, but use this opportunity to get closer to the king. If Henry spent enough time with her perhaps he 'should take such a fantasy unto you that you shall be able to govern like unto Madame d'Éstampes'. Since the Duchess d'Étampes was the mistress of Francis I, Mary was predictably outraged. Because of her marriage to Richmond, in the eyes of the law and the Church, that would have been like sleeping with her own father. Even for the sake of her family she would not stoop to that, rather she wished 'all they should perish, and she would cut her own throat rather than she would consent to such a villainy'.

The idea that a man of Surrey's proud bearing seriously intended such a thing is plainly ludicrous. Also, if the exchange had been conducted in the full view of onlookers then it is amazing that such a gossip-worthy event was not more widely reported at the time. When Hugh Ellis, a servant of the Howards, was later asked whether he was aware of Surrey's plan to install his sister as the king's mistress, he had heard nothing about it.

Mary herself certainly did not intend the episode to become public knowledge when she confided in Sir Garwen Carew.[9] This does not mean that the incident did not take place; simply that Surrey did not expose his sister to public humiliation. Unfortunately, if the row was conducted in private, Surrey may well have allowed his disgust at the whole concept of an alliance with the Seymours to be expressed rather more graphically than was prudent and Mary was perhaps too upset and indignant to see his disgust and sarcasm for what it was.

Whatever Surrey's intentions, his words and actions were ammunition for his enemies. In 1544 the king had made it clear that in the case of a minority, membership of Edward's Regency Council would be dictated by his last will. If those who were keen for greater reforms in religion were to triumph, then religious conservatives like Norfolk had to go. Another leading conservative, Stephen Gardiner, Bishop of Winchester, was easily discredited when he compounded a string of mistakes, including a failed attempt to secure the downfall of Katherine Parr, by demurring over an exchange of lands with the king. The need to move against Norfolk was more pressing, but proved more difficult. The Earl of Surrey was an easier target. The son's proud bearing and outspoken attitude would be the ideal means by which to drag down his father.

At first it seemed all would go well. Some slanderous words and an unsuccessful military offensive in Boulogne were slender but sufficient grounds for Surrey's arrest. Norfolk was summoned to London and promptly arrested in his turn. With both men securely in the Tower the ground shifted. Now all the rumours agreed that the two men were being detained under the far more serious charge that during the king's recent illness they had conspired to seize control of Prince Edward. This was widely reported and it was even said that Surrey had already confessed. The ground was prepared for a joint execution, even as far as sounding out the likely reaction of the King of France. Yet Surrey did not die for this, nor for the rumours that the Howards had attempted to restore the pope. Surrey did not even die for the reasons rehearsed at his trial. Surrey died because his enemies willed it.

Mary's actions helped seal her brother's fate. Not only would she seem prepared to cooperate in Surrey's downfall, but she would seem willing, even eager, to provide details which would send him to the scaffold. A bitter woman, who had her mother's vindictive temper and her father's sense of self-preservation to encourage her to betray and destroy her own family, has long been the historically accepted face of the Duchess of Richmond. Yet this same woman would tirelessly petition for her father's comfort, innocence and release and raise her brother's children as if they were her own, at considerable personal expense. Also, if she was supposed to be the willing accomplice of her family's enemies then someone had not tutored her very well.

As soon as Norfolk and Surrey were safely under arrest, the king's commissioners sped at once to Kenninghall. They arrived at daybreak to find Mary had only just risen and was not ready to receive them. They broke the news of her father's and brother's confinement to a woman 'sore perplexed, trembling, and like to fall down'. On her knees Mary declared that she would conceal nothing and this has often been taken as evidence of complicity. Yet since she knew her father to be a true and faithful subject of the king, what did she have to hide? As the commissioners went about their business, cataloguing the family goods in preparation for their seizure by the crown, Mary must have seen how grave the danger was. It seems that she hoped to follow her father's example that obedience and submission was the best route to being graciously forgiven. From the outset the king's own officers were of the opinion that her 'frank disposition' was in the hope of obtaining the king's mercy.

The evidence Mary gave was not an outpouring of bile, but her responses to a series of questions put to her by the king's commissioners. However, as Norfolk's opponents scrabbled to find something that would embroil him in his son's misfortunes, Mary had an entirely different agenda. Rather wearily her interrogators reported:

Some passionate words of her brother she likewise repeated, as also some circumstantial speeches little for his advantage, yet so as they seemed to clear her Father.[10]

Admittedly, in her desire to help her father, Mary risked her brother's liberty and perhaps even his reputation, but not his life. Surrey's dislike of the new nobility, and in particular the Seymours, was well known. Not even Norfolk's enemies could find a way to use her complaints that Surrey had dissuaded her from going too far in reading the scriptures. Many of her other points descended into reports of Surrey's posturing and name-calling. There was nothing here to bring her brother to the block.

The idea that Surrey had encouraged his sister to become the king's mistress initially seemed more promising. To seek such influence hinted at dangerous ambition. The possibilities were spelt out with certain passages marked in Henry's own hand, with an unwitting Norfolk, who had not even been present at the time of the argument, being implicated in his son's designs:

If a man compassing *with himself to govern the realm do actually go about to rule the King* and should for that purpose advise his daughter or sister to become his harlot *thinking thereby to bring it to pass and so would rule both father and son as by this next article doth more appear what this importeth.*[11]

Even this was not Mary's fault. Rather than having been volunteered by her, the exchange had already been reported to the king's commissioners by her supposed confidant, Sir Garwen Carew. In any case, this also proved to be a dead end. First the article was watered down to ask whether Surrey had ever tried to use 'any person' to influence the king. Then, when it seemed Norfolk could not be linked to this particular ploy, this line of investigation was quietly abandoned.

However, in the midst of Mary's deposition, the king's officers touched on the question of Surrey's coat-of-arms. Evidence given by a former Howard retainer, Sir Robert Southwell, had suggested that Surrey had made changes which indicated a right to bear the arms of England. Tantamount to asserting a claim to the throne, Surrey's actions appeared to encourage comparison with his maternal grandfather, the Duke of Buckingham, who had been executed for his dynastic ambition in 1521. With fairly blatant foolishness Surrey insisted on including the Stafford arms in his shield, which in his father's case were more prudently represented by a blank quarter. It was dangerous territory. As other witnesses eagerly 'substantiatcd' the claims,[12] it seems that there was a growing conspiracy to bring Surrey down on this point, in the face of a dearth of other usable evidence.

When the king's commissioners eagerly addressed this issue with the Duchess of Richmond, they were obviously hoping for something of substance. Instead, Mary's answers were either vague – 'she thought her brother had more than seven rolls' – or easily proven to be mistaken. For example, the crown 'to her judgment much like a close crown' was not the crown of England at all, but the crown of Scotland, which had been included in the Howard's arms to mark her paternal grandfather's victory over James IV of Scotland at the battle of Flodden in 1513.[13] The daughter of a duke, especially one as jealous of her status as Mary, might be expected to be more knowledgeable about her own family crests. Mary was not a foolish woman. Unlike Bess Holland, who sought to save herself by reporting what was convenient, Mary successfully managed the semblance of cooperation, without disclosing any evidence that was ultimately fit to be used.

Mary's first objective was not to save herself, but to clear her father, whom she correctly identified as the real target. However, this did not mean she was eager to speed her brother to the scaffold. Two siblings who were close in age, who boasted similar acerbic temperaments but very diverse viewpoints, cannot always be expected to get along. Commenting on Surrey's plot to make Mary the king's mistress, Hugh Ellis had declared he had never seen them 'so great together to wish her so good a turn'. Yet in protesting her father's innocence she had also admitted that 'nature constrained her . . . to desire the well doing of his son, her natural brother'. Certainly, Mary thought well enough of her brother to make him the steward of her lands. Perhaps she expected that if her father was cleared her brother would also be released. If not, she was also well aware that he had been in trouble with king before and had always escaped lightly. Perhaps she hoped Henry's affection would be enough to shield her brother from real harm.

In view of the forces closing about him, it is perhaps a little unkind to judge that if anyone was responsible for his downfall it was Surrey himself. His legal right to bear any sort of arms was less at issue than his possible intentions and his arrogant bearing. Belatedly, Surrey seems to have realised that it might be wise to rein in his regal pretensions. A hastily penned note to Hugh Ellis made a significant change to his magnificent portrait of imperial imagery and heraldic designs. The painter was 'to leave out the tablet where my lord of Richmond's picture should stand'. Following his father's more prudent example in displaying the family's blood relationship to Edward III through the Stafford line, the tablet was now to be daubed over with black paint. Yet, in truth it seems nothing now could save the House of Howard.

In the end, despite all the evidence collected against him, Surrey was indicted on the single and decidedly shaky charge of quartering his arms incorrectly. The grounds for the attainder of the Duke of Norfolk were even weaker, lacking any real semblance of treason. However, even Norfolk's well-trusted expedient of throwing himself on the king's mercy and confessing 'my crime no less than high treason and although I do not deserve it, humbly beg his Highness to have pity upon me' was not enough this time to save him or his son from the full rigour of the law. Surrey was duly executed on 21 January 1547. At least one contemporary also believed Norfolk had been secretly beheaded in the Tower. In truth, only Henry's own death saved Norfolk from the block. Yet his attainder and imprisonment was apparently enough. It terms of political influence the House of Howard now seemed a spent force.

Mary herself escaped relatively unscathed, with her lands and most of her personal goods untouched. However, she had faced no charges and, more importantly, she was no threat. Alone among her family she had embraced the new order in religion. Her support for Protestant preachers was enthusiastic, defending men like John Huntingdon as of 'such sort as I dare take upon me to answer that nothing shall pass from him contrary to the King's majesty's proceedings'. Yet she did not forget her family. She, and rather surprisingly her mother, were given permission to visit the duke 'at times and with train convenient'. However, Mary was a lone woman with limited resources and her repeated efforts to secure her father's release were largely ineffective. Her repeated pleas 'for license for her father to write to the King's Majesty for mercy' fell on deaf ears.

While she herself was still welcome at court, in November 1551, being part of the reception for the dowager Queen of Scotland, Mary of Guise, it was plainly on the government's own terms. Mary had to tread carefully. At any time the full force of her father's attainder might be applied. Rumours circulated of his death. Mary's difficulties did not stem from lack of interest or effort. She simply did not have the leverage to back up her requests.

In the circumstances, it is particularly surprising that Mary did not remarry. With her father imprisoned in the Tower and her younger brother Thomas too inexperienced to take his place as head of the family, a husband would have been a useful asset. That she did not, may not have been entirely of her own choice. With her brother executed and her father still liable to be so, her prospects were not entirely good. Far from being an auspicious alliance, even to show interest might invite suspicion. Norfolk would be somewhat handicapped in arranging a match from the confines of the Tower, and in the light of all his previous concerns about suitors, finding a fitting candidate may have been difficult. That Mary herself eschewed marriage is also possible. The idea that she still grieved for Richmond seems improbable, in the light of their limited acquaintance. However, other factors, such as the dangers of childbirth or the loss of her personal freedom, may have influenced her choice. Any one of these reasons would be sufficient to forestall serious negotiations, but none of them represented Mary's greatest disadvantage.

For a duchess, Mary was not a particularly wealthy woman. In the subsidies of Edward VI's reign her goods were valued at £200. At the same time a baroness was also assessed at £200 in goods.[14] Kenninghall and other accustomed residences had been lost to her because of her father's attainder. Much of the Howard property had already been re-granted to loyal councillors and Kenninghall, Framlingham and other interests in East Anglia were passed to Mary Tudor. Out of her own lands the Duchess of Richmond had to find the money to pay her debts. The annuity of £20 she granted to Bess Holland was perhaps intended to repay money lent during her time of trouble.

Mary does seem to have struggled to make ends meet. In the last subsidy of Henry VIII her lands were assessed at £626 13s 4d, almost £120 less than the settlement allowed to her by Henry in 1540. Several properties in London and elsewhere were sold off. In July 1546, the Goat Inn in the Strand fetched £80. Other properties were leased or rented out. In the circumstances, the lands worth £5 6s 8d, which Edward VI granted to her in August 1552, seem little more than a gesture. Worst of all, Mary's interest in her lands were strictly for the term of her life only. Any fortune-hunting husband would quickly appreciate that she was not a sound matrimonial investment.

To add to her financial burden, Mary's costs and charges now had to cover her nieces and nephews as well. When it had first been decided to remove Surrey's children from their mother's care, the eldest son, Thomas Howard, had been placed with Sir John Williams, the treasurer of the Court of Augmentations, and his brother and sisters with Lord Wentworth. However, this arrangement did not last long and soon all five children, two sons and three daughters and their cousin Charles Howard, were placed in Mary's care. She took her duties seriously, engaging John Foxe, later the author of the *Book of Martyrs* and already a Protestant preacher of some note, to be their tutor. However, it is difficult to avoid the conclusion that King Edward's satisfaction that he knew 'no better place for their virtuous education' was basically derived from the fact that this was by far the cheapest option.

Finance was clearly an issue; several times Mary applied to the king for some assistance with the children's upkeep. After considerable delay she finally secured an annuity of £100 a year. Although Mary has rather unfairly earned the enmity of Howard biographers by presuming to raise the heirs of the House of Howard in the reformed faith, she did give the children some semblance of a normal life. No longer separated from each other or in the hands of strangers, after much disturbance came stability. The arrangement seems to have been successful. Even when Thomas Howard had succeeded to his grandfather's dukedom of Norfolk and the eldest girl was shortly to be married to Henry, Lord Berkley, the suggestion that the Countess of Surrey might be awarded the custody of her remaining daughters was not acted upon. The girls stayed with Mary.

With the accession of Mary Tudor in July 1553, Norfolk was at once released from the Tower. He recovered his office as Earl Marshal and was appointed president of the new queen's council. Matters were put in hand for the reversal of his attainder and the recovery of his lands. Most of his family shared in the triumph. Even the estranged Duchess of Norfolk, Elizabeth Stafford, was on hand to see her husband released. Mary's nephew, Thomas Howard, assumed his father's title of Earl of Surrey, and his brother, sisters and mother were summoned to court for the celebrations of the new reign. Only Mary, Duchess of Richmond, was not invited.

Unlike Norfolk, who could at least take refuge in his claim that his niece had never liked him, Mary had been close to Anne Boleyn. John Foxe would recall the Duchess of Richmond as being 'one of the chief and principal of her waiting maids about her'. This alone was hardly likely to endear her to Mary Tudor.

For her part, the new queen's recent possession of Kenninghall and many of the Howard treasures might well rankle with the duchess, especially since the queen had also enjoyed several valuable pieces of plate from Richmond's estate which might have eased Mary's path in her penury. Even putting aside the major question of religion (and the queen would not have done that lightly) it is doubtful that these two very different women would ever have been friends. Although the Duchess of Richmond seems to have enjoyed a warm friendship with Margaret Douglas, enough to be her confidante and share tastes in poetry and gossip, the only evidence of any personal contact between Mary and the new queen is a single entry in Mary Tudor's privy purse expenses when the Yeoman of the Cellar to 'my Lady of Richmond' was given 8s in reward, presumably for bringing some message or gift. While Mary continued to prefer the reformed faith, even a semblance of cordiality was impossible.

Perhaps, rather than renounce her religious beliefs, Mary chose to remain in discreet retirement. Her retreat into seclusion was perhaps reinforced by her grief over her father's death just over a year later in August 1554. If her own actions did not demonstrate the level of affection and esteem in which she held her father, then the terms of his will were testament to his fondness and admiration for her as he repaid her family loyalty with the gift of £500:

> as well in consideration that she is my daughter, as that also she hath been at great costs and charges in making suit for my deliverance out of my imprisonment, and also in bringing up of my said son of Surrey's children.[15]

Perhaps her grief also contributed to her own decline. Not long after this her own health must have been giving cause for concern. By 19 January 1556 she was dead, as a grant to William Cordell clearly described her as the late Duchess of Richmond and Somerset.[16]

She was buried alongside her husband in a magnificent white clunch marble tomb. Intricately decorated in the French style, with fluted pillars, ornamented with a frieze of Old Testament scenes and the armorial bearings of the duke and duchess, it stood as a testament to their joint, unfulfilled potential. Despite its evident grandeur, the tomb is unfinished, lacking not only the traditional effigies of the deceased, but any trace of colour. If this was the tomb that Norfolk had originally commissioned to lie in Thetford Priory, its fortunes had been interrupted by far more than the arrival of a legitimate prince.

The dissolution of Thetford Priory in 1540 had prompted Norfolk to seek a more suitable resting-place for his family. He had decided on St Michael's parish church, which still stands in the shadow of Framlingham Castle in Suffolk. However, it was felt that the chancel needed extensive remodelling to accommodate the Howard family tombs in appropriate splendour. Building was duly begun, only to be abruptly curtailed when Norfolk was arrested. His attainder left the churchwardens scrabbling around for funds to make good the work in progress. After his release Norfolk was keen to rehabilitate his family's honour by every possible means. Not only was the building work at Framlingham resurrected, but it seems Norfolk commissioned completely new tombs, for himself, his father, Richmond and Surrey.

Construction of the tomb was again interrupted by Norfolk's death. Unfortunately, the work was still in progress in 1554 when Norfolk directed his executors to bury him 'in such place and order as shall be thought most convenient'. The burden of completing the work would then have fallen to Norfolk's executors. However, funds were limited and Richmond's tomb was, doubtless, not a priority. Only Mary had a vested interest in seeing the tomb completed. The date 1555, engraved on the side of the tomb in a contemporary hand suggests some further investment was made on it before she followed Richmond to the grave.[17] At each corner of the tomb there is still a small figure bearing a trophy of the passion. It is clear that there were originally twelve of these, one to top each of the columns carved into the marble. However, there is no evidence that there was ever any gilt, colour or images of the duke and his duchess to complete the work.

In common with her husband, although Mary's rank as Duchess of Richmond and Somerset entitled her to a lavish and ornate funeral, there is no record that she received any such honours.[18] In view of her religious beliefs, with her death coming at a time when Mary's government was increasingly concerned that the spontaneous reversion to Catholicism they had expected had not materialised, it was probably not such a public spectacle. Although Surrey's youngest son Henry, Earl of Northampton, later arranged for his father's remains to be removed from All Hallows church in London to lie beside his wife, Frances de Vere, in the splendid tomb at Framlingham, he evidently considered the resting place of his former guardian and her husband to be serviceable enough.

Epilogue

Henry the Ninth

The Act of Succession of 1536 raised the possibility that Richmond could have ascended the throne. The bastard status which, for so much of his life, had been a legal obstacle to his accession, was removed. Writing in 1655, Thomas Fuller explored the possibility that neither Mary nor Elizabeth would have sat on the throne of England if Richmond had survived:

> Well it was for them that Henry Fitzroy his natural son, (but one of supernatural and extraordinary endowments,) was dead; otherwise (some suspect) had he survived King Edward the Sixth, we might presently have heard of a King Henry the Ninth, so great was his father's affection and so unlimited his power to prefer him.[1]

Any consideration of what might have been is always a matter of conjecture. However, it can safely be argued that if Richmond had lived on after his father, the history of England would have been very different.

In 1537 the birth of Prince Edward seemed to settle the question of the succession. However, neither the king, nor his subjects, gave up hope of further issue. When Henry decided that Anne of Cleves was not to his liking, there were worries that the king would 'never have any more children for the comfort of the realm'. Equally, the queen's ladies rather boldly pointed out to her that her idea of marital relations – a kiss good morning and a kiss goodnight – was not sufficient to ensure the security of the kingdom. Lady Rutland was blunt 'there must be more than this, or it will be long ere we have a duke of York, which all this realm most desireth'. However, reassuring as it might have been to have more than one 'heir', both Henry VII and Henry VIII had come to the throne as the sole surviving male issue. In theory, there was no pressing reason to assume that Edward could not live to marry and produce children of his own to continue the dynasty.

Contrary to popular belief, Edward was not a particularly sickly child. In 1541 the French ambassador judged him to be 'remarkably tall for his age'. A bout of illness, described as a 'quartan fever' when he was four years old, naturally caused some concern, but generally Edward thrived. Although history often remembers him as a bookish, rather priggish child, he had a lively interest in martial sports. Hunting was a passion, which he pursued with an enthusiasm to equal his father's. He could draw a bow and at fourteen was 'running at the ring', a moderately safer form of jousting where the opponent was a wooden target rather than a flesh and blood challenger. Recounting Edward's exploits in feats of arms, archery, tennis and hunting the Imperial ambassador described him as 'indefatigable'.[2] There was every reason to expect that he would live to emulate his father.

However, amid the relief and jubilation at Edward's birth, many must have wondered if Henry could survive to see Edward grow to adulthood. Those fortunate enough to escape the hazards of plague, warfare, poverty or politics could and did survive to a ripe old age. Elizabeth Blount's second husband, Edward, Lord Clinton, was seventy-three when he died in 1585. If Henry could only survive until he was sixty-three in 1554, Edward would be seventeen years old and England would escape the dangers of a minority. It was always a dubious prospect. However, when Henry VIII died in the early hours of 28 January 1547, Edward was only nine. In theory, Edward was the legitimate heir, the surest route to a peaceful and uncontested accession. In practice, the certain prospect of a minority government brought its own dangers and Henry VIII's personal legacy ensured that the whole question was even more complex.

When government was vested in the personal authority of the king a minority was always a difficult issue. Once it became clear that Henry was going to die, his subjects nervously rehearsed the biblical text 'Woe to thee O land where the King is a child'. Despite the best efforts of his government to bolster his public image as Josiah, the eight-year-old New Testament king who battled against idolatry, and Edward's own assertions of his regal power 'be we of less authority for our age? Be we not your King now as we shall be?', Edward's lack of mature years was a matter of serious concern.

Only those who might hope to profit by the manipulation of the king really stood to gain. Even then, the struggle to control such a prize inevitably led to disorder. Men only had to look at how the Scottish nobility had fought over Henry's nephew, King James V, to realise the dangers. Also, government was invariably weakened when the monarch did not exercise it in person. When Charles V had rebuked Henry for his conduct towards the 'Princess Mary', the king of England had been direct: 'we think it is not meet that any person should proscribe unto us how we should order our own daughter'. Those men who now ruled in Edward's name could not take such liberties with the emperor. While it was argued that a king's authority, exercised through his council, was valid even if 'he were in his cradle,' it was also recognised that 'there is a difference in the judgment of the people'.

Nowhere was this more apparent than over the question of England's religion. In 1547 Edward was heir not merely to the throne, but to the full consequences of his father's reformation. With Edward as Head of the Church in England the concept of authority in a minority government touched not just men's lives, but their souls. It created a wealth of uncertainties. Would England return to the papal fold? Would each change of monarch see a change in religion? The evolution of Royal Supremacy was only recent history and its 'diverse sundry old authentic histories and chronicles' did not provide a sound foundation for the exercise of such ecclesiastical authority by a nine-year-old boy.

The development of Royal Supremacy had relied heavily on Henry VIII's magnificent personality, stressing his high learning and paternalistic guidance. In 1545 Henry had rebuked parliament for taking too much upon themselves in matters of religion 'for in such high causes you may lightly err'. The image of Royal Supremacy was inextricably entwined with the idea that the king's judgment could not err. It was not a role Edward was entirely suited to fill. In 1552 Henry Brabon was indicted by the Privy Council for calling Edward 'a poor child', hardly the proper attitude of respect to the Supreme Head of the Church. Whatever guises Edward's council came up with – and they even resorted to using the practice of king's evil, where the touch of the king would restore the ailing, a ceremony which had far more in common with the Catholic Church they were destroying than the Protestant one they were trying to build – the fact remained that both physically and intellectually, Edward was very young to take on that particular role.

Certainly, his sister Mary chose to take the position that Edward should not make innovations in religion until he was of full age. As religious doctrine in England moved increasingly towards a more Protestant ethos, she openly disputed his government's authority to diverge from religion as Henry had left it. When Edward's council rebuked her for her dangerous example in not observing the law of the land she countered:

I have offended no law unless it be a late law of your own making for the altering of matter in religion which in my conscience is not worthy to have the name of law.[3]

It was a moral rather than a legal standpoint, but she was not alone. Stephen Gardiner also raised the concern that they might be thought to 'fashion God's word after our own fancy'. Until

Edward was adult, it was an argument his council would find very difficult to refute.

At his accession Edward VI had had little opportunity to win the respect and admiration of his subjects. He had not been created Prince of Wales, or even knighted, when he inherited the crown. His public appearances only served to emphasis how young he was. In contrast, Richmond would now have been twenty-seven years old. At this point it is easy to envisage him as an established magnate, whose martial feats and many talents had earned the admiration of all. As he held court at Baynards Castle, perhaps with several fine sons to his credit, men might well have considered that as the senior noble in England, Richmond was a more worthy successor to his father.

At his death Henry VIII had named his nine-year-old son as his heir. His decision to place Mary and Elizabeth next in the line of succession must be seen in light of his hope and expectation that Edward would live to adulthood. Given the stark choice between seeing one of his daughters on the throne and naming a more distant male relative or some suitable nobleman, this was perhaps the lesser of two evils. Safe in the knowledge that it was only an insurance policy against Edward's premature demise, Henry could easily have convinced himself that the measure would not be needed. Since the Act of Succession of 1536 had ensured that their illegitimacy or otherwise was no longer an issue, he did not choose to restore either of them to the rank of princess. In which case, if he had lived, Richmond would still have outranked them. If Henry had chosen to place his bastard son in the line of succession, the correct legal position would have been as heir apparent to the legitimate prince, Edward.

Everything about Henry's policy towards the succession indicates that his first instinct would have been to favour Edward, as his legitimate heir, before Richmond. Despite Richmond's good qualities, to be reduced to assigning his 'Crown Imperial' to a son known by the whole of Europe to be born out of wedlock would sit ill with Henry's tender conscience. Writing in 1958, Charles Ferguson recognised this moral dilemma:

> It would be anomalous at least for the Defender of the Faith to leave his title and his crown to a mongrel, to a child whose parenthood would always be open to question at any moment of crisis. The Defender of the Faith must have what he was entitled to: a legitimate son and heir. His conscience would settle for nothing less.[4]

Such a principled view was all well and good while the king had the leisure to wait for his son to be born and then to grow to maturity. Once the king's health began to fail and Henry was faced with the certain prospect of England under a long minority, could he have been persuaded that Edward's legitimacy was less important than the security of the realm?

If Henry had preferred to recognise what would have been the twenty-seven-year-old Duke of Richmond as his heir, there was a convenient loophole to Edward's prior claim. After the deaths of both Katherine of Aragon and Anne Boleyn, the King of England had been a free man when he married Jane Seymour. Whether he was supposed to be a bachelor (as he believed) or a widower (as both Katherine and Anne's supporters would prefer) there was no doubt that he was at liberty to take a bride. However, the Catholic Church had never recognised Henry and Jane's union, because it had been solemnised after the pope excommunicated Henry. This excommunication meant that he was not permitted to receive the sacrament of marriage. Mary of Hungary expressed the general mood of caution when she said 'We make no mention at present of the young Prince as we are ignorant as yet whether or not he will be recognized as King.' In the eyes of Catholic Europe, Edward was as illegitimate as the Duke of Richmond had been. As news of Henry's death spread, foreign observers watched with interest to see how things would develop.

In reality, Edward's legitimacy (or otherwise) was never seriously challenged in England. The feared prospect of an invasion did not come to pass. Concern about the possible reaction abroad might well have helped to dampen dissent at home. Certainly, the expected uprising in the name of the Princess Mary – expected by the Imperial ambassador at any rate – did not materialise. Once it became clear that Edward was accepted in England, political expediency ensured that even Charles V claimed 'that he had always had a good opinion of [Henry's] last marriage'. In the end only the papal see refused to recognise Edward as King of England.

Unless Henry had chosen to place Richmond in the succession above Edward, it is unlikely that any of these factors would have been sufficient to oust the prince from his throne. Unlike Mary, Edward or Elizabeth, who could all lay claims to have been born within some semblance of matrimony, no one could pretend that the king's eldest son was anything other than a bastard. In the fourteenth and fifteenth centuries the Church had intensified its attitude towards children born out of wedlock. This had resulted in widespread concern regarding the concept of illegitimacy and succession, which was reflected in a rise in the use of bastardy as a political smear. Even if Richmond's illegitimacy had not been a block to his accession, the circumstances of his birth would still have been a liability.

England could have been thrown into a civil war, with Richmond backed by the House of Howard and Edward's claim stoutly supported by the Seymour family. Henry's will had appointed sixteen co-executors to act equally on behalf on his son Edward. Yet within days of his death Edward Seymour had quickly secured his election as Lord Protector. Although it was agreed that he 'should not do any act but with the advice and consent of the rest of the executors' he soon assumed quasi-royal authority. If the mechanics of Tudor government meant it was 'expedient to have one as it were a mouth for the rest to whom all such [who] had to do with the whole body of the Council might resort' then surely Richmond would have been the obvious candidate.

If Richmond had lived it is possible to imagine the politics of Edward's reign taking a different course. Henry might have taken little persuasion to name his beloved eldest son as regent during Edward's minority despite his illegitimacy. He was, after all, his own flesh and blood and showed every promise of being more than capable of shouldering the responsibility. If the policy has unsettling shades of Richard III and his unfortunate nephews, it was perhaps preferable to the alternative of leaving Richmond isolated and possibly increasingly disaffected. Richmond had always been a loyal and faithful son. There is every reason to believe that he would also have been a charming elder brother, whose skill at hunting, hawking and the like was more than sufficient to engender a degree of hero-worship in his younger sibling.

Richmond was certainly intelligent enough to appreciate that there were more subtle ways to ensure a lifetime of influence and satisfaction than risking the usurpation of the crown. Just as John Dudley, then Duke of Northumberland, chose to rule as President of the Council rather than Lord Protector, in the hope of extending his influence over Edward VI into adulthood, so Richmond could have presumed on their blood relationship and common ground to ensure that he remained at the centre of his brother's government. The only question is whether that would have been enough to satisfy the ambition of Henry VIII's eldest son, or the ambitions of the friends around him.

Richmond's survival would also have had further repercussions on the political landscape. In 1536 Richmond's funeral had provided an excuse to isolate Thomas Howard, Duke of Norfolk, from the king's favour. In 1547 Norfolk's enemies had preyed on Henry's concerns about faction and division during a minority. Norfolk's position as one of the greatest nobles in the realm was used against him to suggest that he might seek to overturn Henry's wishes for a Regency Council. Chief among the charges against Surrey was 'if the King should die my lord Prince being of tender age you or your father would have the rule and governance of him'. In the event, it was

Seymour who gained the overall control that Henry was so anxious to guard against and why he was so keen to ensure Norfolk's removal.

The prospect of the king's own son as regent would have provided a far more difficult obstacle. Richmond's continued existence may have been sufficient to save the Earl of Surrey from the block and ensure Norfolk's continued presence on the Regency Council. In this scenario it is hard to see either of the pivotal figures of Edward's reign, Edward Seymour or John Dudley, being able to stand against a settlement laid down in Henry's will which named Richmond as regent and placed Norfolk at his side.

Although Edward's uncle might seem a natural choice as regent or Lord Protector, according to the terms of Henry's will Edward Seymour was ranked fifth in order of precedence. Seymour had relied heavily on the support and assistance of Sir William Paget[5] to achieve his goal. A selection of rather dubious grants (attributed to the wishes of the late king) bribed others to support his elevation as Lord Protector. Even then, it is interesting that he did not presume to declare himself regent. John Dudley, who took up the reins of power after Somerset's execution in 1552, enjoyed a good deal of support from Richmond's former step-father Edward, Lord Clinton. The two men were very close and Clinton married his stepdaughter, Elizabeth, Lady Tailbois, to Dudley's second son, Ambrose. Clinton enjoyed a larger share of gifts and grants during Dudley's tenure than any other councillor and repaid Dudley with his loyalty and military skill. If Richmond had lived, surely that support would have been placed behind his former stepson. After all, Clinton had his own family to consider and as Richmond's half-siblings his own daughters might expect to do well.

With Richmond as regent the history of England from 1553 would need to be entirely rewritten. Once Richmond and Norfolk realised that Edward was dying they would have been well placed to exploit the situation to their advantage. Everything suggests that Richmond and not Mary would have been next in line for the throne. Unlike Mary, Richmond seems to have been quite happy to toe the line of least resistance in religion and this is unlikely to have been an obstacle to his accession. There would have been no 'device for the Succession' which sought to vest the crown of England in the non-existent male heirs of Frances Brandon and her three daughters and no last minute attempt to place Jane Grey on the throne with the express intent of keeping Mary from it. Instead, Edward would have acknowledged his half-brother's position as heir apparent and when Edward finally died on 6 July 1553 England would have faced a very different future, perhaps.

If there had been opposition it would probably not have come from Mary. From an early age she had been taught that the throne of England was the right of the male heir. Her later insistence on her (rightful) title of princess should not be taken as evidence of ambition in this direction. Despite their differences, Mary always maintained her loyalty to Edward as her king and was careful to keep her distance from any sort of plot or political intrigue. This was most noticeable in 1549. During a summer of rebellion the govern-ment's attempts to link Mary with the unrest were not successful. Shortly afterwards, when she was approached to lend her support to a plan to oust the increasingly unpopular Edward Seymour in order to make her regent, she refused to become involved. Katherine of Aragon's daughter was well aware that certain aspects of government were outside the competence of a woman. She expected to be the consort of some foreign prince in a marriage that brought economic and political benefit to her country. The idea that she might rule at all, much less without a husband at her side, would have astonished her.

In 1553 Mary's victory was assured because under the terms of the Act of Succession of 1543 and her father's will she was the legal heir to the throne. However, she and her supporters were in no sense a government-in-waiting. Anyone with any real political ambition had already seen which way the land lay and thrown in their lot with the new regime under Edward. It may be a little cynical to argue that there were perhaps also those who supported Mary, gambling on the fact that she was too middle-aged and too racked by health problems to live long or produce an heir. God willing they need only endure her for a short time before they might have Elizabeth. Perhaps it is rather less cynical to claim that there were those who would prefer any alternative to Jane Grey's new husband Guilford, the youngest son of John Dudley, the unpopular Duke of Northumberland, as king. If Richmond had been the designated heir under the terms of his father's last will, then that support would have flocked to him and he no doubt would have exploited it to its full advantage.

There were, of course, others who might have mounted a claim in reaction to the accession of this bonafide bastard. Elizabeth is an obvious candidate, but in 1553 she was still only twenty and a female to boot. In fact, this was a disability shared by all the near blood claimants. They were either, like Margaret Douglas, female, or, like her seven-year-old son, Henry, Lord Darnley, rather too young to stage a coup on their own behalf. There was also always the possibility that another great lord of the kingdom might choose to stand against Richmond. Although these were rather thinner on the ground than in times past – and the death of Charles Brandon, Duke of Suffolk in 1545 removed one dangerous possibility – the combined ambitions of Edward and Thomas Seymour may well have been sufficient to cause him concern. But they would still have needed to muster sufficient support for a coup and there is no guarantee that this would have been forthcoming.

Any attempt to judge what type of monarch King Henry IX might have become must also be pure speculation. The simple answer is probably very much like his father. If part of the duty of a monarch was to look like a king, Richmond certainly met expectations. His wardrobe was positively splendid. A gown of black velvet embroidered with gold, lined with velvet and satin might be paired with matching doublet and hose and topped off with a bonnet of black velvet with a brooch of gold on the cap set with four rubies. The rings on his fingers, collars around his neck or ornamental garters, were all gold set with diamonds, rubies or pearls. His household glittered with gold and silver plate. A large number of pieces, like the silver salt shaped like a unicorn horn and set with pearls, were gifts from his father and Richmond had amassed enough plate from several years' worth of New Year gifts to set a magnificent table.

Like Henry VIII at his accession Richmond was a fine athlete who loved nothing more than hunting and jousting. It is easy to imagine a sense of *déjà vu* as ambassadors and courtiers attempted to keep the king's mind on business, although it is harder to see him as the patron of learning and scholars that William Blount, Lord Mountjoy, saw in his father. Given Richmond's eager pursuit of the arts of war, it is much more possible to see him pursuing as vigorous a foreign policy as his father, keen to secure his own Flodden or Tournai. However, the direction of his campaigns may have been different. Richmond had a warm relationship with Henri, the former duc d'Orléans who now reigned as King of France, although England's tempestuous relationship with Scotland was perhaps always likely to place more strain on Anglo-French relations than a boyhood friendship could hope to offset.

However, Richmond may also have emulated some of his father's less attractive traits. His pursuit of lands and offices suggests an edge of fairly ruthless ambition. His willingness to promote and defend his officers indicates that he was generous to his loyal friends; however his silence over the downfall of Wolsey and Brereton is a worrying hint towards his readiness to put his own interests before anything else. His conscience in matters of religion appears to have been equally malleable. Although his religious education had more in common with Mary than Edward and Elizabeth, and his chapel was certainly traditional enough, he apparently watched the progress of the reformation without a murmur.

Yet Richmond was also universally remembered as charming, gracious and handsome. There were many who lived to mourn his passing. His mother Elizabeth survived him, living until she was about forty years old. Her growing brood of children was little compensation for the loss of her eldest son. If the Earl of Surrey's poetry is a true reflection of his feelings then he too was deeply affected by the loss of his closest friend. A French poet, Nicholas de Bourbon, who had spent some time teaching in England, also wrote a few lines showing that the whole of England grieved for the loss of Richmond. Men like Richard Croke and the French princes spoke with genuine affection for the duke. That Henry VIII appears to have expunged his son from his memory was perhaps not an indication of any lack of feeling, but rather a sign that his grief was such that he could not bear to be reminded of him.

In historical terms Richmond's memory has been overshadowed by the birth of Prince Edward in October 1537. The achievement of his mother, Elizabeth Blount, in presenting Henry with a son has been obscured by the meteoric rise and spectacular failure of Anne Boleyn. As such, neither have attracted the attention devoted to other aspects of Henry VIII's reign. From the chronicler Hollinshed, who had promised to give an account of Richmond in his history of the dukes of the land only never to complete the work, to the modern accounts of Henry's reign which omit all mention of the duke, Richmond has never been seen as a pivotal figure in Tudor history. Yet for Henry VIII he acquired usefulness almost beyond price.

Often his youth was his greatest asset, allowing a style of government – notably at Sheriff Hutton and with the secret council in Ireland – that would not have been tenable under an established magnate. His dual role as an independent magnate and acknowledged son of the king meant that he could embody royal approval in controversial matters, thus saving the king from muddying his own hands. Without the Duke of Richmond, Wolsey's ploy of attempting to woo the daughter of Portugal from the dauphin of France, so that Mary might one day be Queen of France, could not have been put in hand. Richmond also served his father as a diplomat and courtier. He was also good for the king's image. In simple terms, he allowed

Henry to demonstrate good lordship by giving out extensive lands and offices without risking the danger of an over mighty subject. More significantly, his presence was Henry's tangible assurance that he could have a son – reassurance for his subjects and an insurance policy that Henry took for granted would always be there.

THE BLOUNTS OF KINLET AND THEIR CONNECTIONS

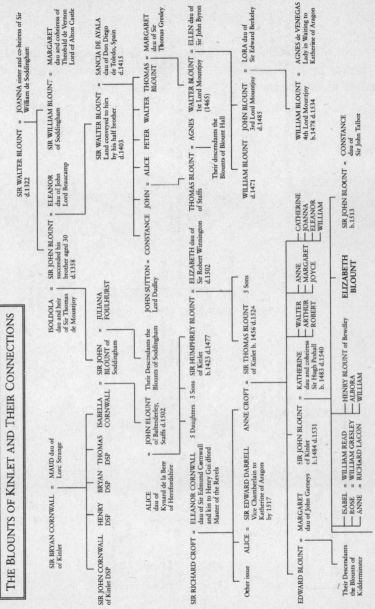

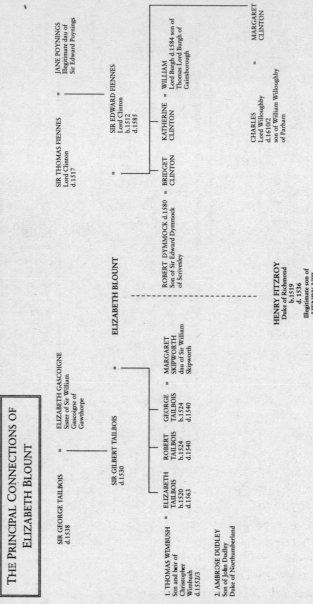

THE PRINCIPAL CONNECTIONS OF ELIZABETH BLOUNT

SIR GEORGE TAILBOIS
d.1538
=
ELIZABETH GASCOIGNE
Sister of Sir William
Gascoigne of
Gawthorpe

SIR THOMAS FIENNES
Lord Clinton
d.1517
=
JANE POYNINGS
Illegitimate dau of
Sir Edward Poynings

SIR GILBERT TAILBOIS
d.1530

SIR EDWARD FIENNES
Lord Clinton
b.1512
d.1585

ELIZABETH BLOUNT

ELIZABETH
TAILBOIS
b.1520
d.1563

ROBERT
TAILBOIS
b.1524
d.1540

GEORGE
TAILBOIS
b.1524
d.1540

MARGARET
SKIPWORTH
dau of Sir William
Skipworth
=

ROBERT DYMMOCK d.1580
Son of Sir Edward Dymmock
of Scrivesley
=
BRIDGET
CLINTON

KATHERINE
CLINTON
=
WILLIAM
Lord Burgh d.1584 son of
Thomas Lord Burgh of
Gainsborough

1. THOMAS WIMBUSH
Son and heir of
Christopher
Wimbush
d.1552/3

2. AMBROSE DUDLEY
Son of John Dudley
Duke of Northumberland

HENRY FITZROY
Duke of Richmond
b.1519
d. 1536
Illegitimate son of
HENRY VIII

CHARLES
Lord Willoughby
d.1610/2
son of William Willoughby
of Parham
=
MARGARET
CLINTON

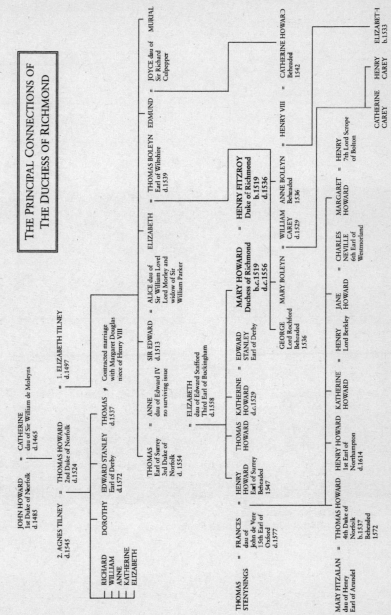

THE PRINCIPAL CONNECTIONS OF
THE DUCHESS OF RICHMOND

Notes

Preface

1. *Inventories of the Wardrobe Plate Chapel Stuff etc. of Henry Fitzroy, Duke of Richmond. . . . Edited with a Memoir and Letters of the Duke of Richmond*, ed. J.G. Nichols.
2. E. Cherbury, Lord Herbert, *Life and Reign of King Henry the Eighth*, p. 165.
3. E. Barnwell, *Perrot Notes, Some Account of the Various Branches of the Perrot Family* (1867), p. 40.
4. D. Edwards, *The Edwardes Legacy* (Baltimore, 1992), p. 22.
5. E. Ives, *Anne Boleyn*, p. 250.
6. Writing in March 1997 Anthony Hoskins put forward a new theory which used revised ages for Henry and Catherine in an attempt to prove beyond any doubt that they were both Henry VIII's children. A. Hoskins, 'Mary Boleyn Carey's Children – Offspring of King Henry VIII', *Genealogist's Magazine*, 25 (1997), n.9.
7. British Library (BL), Harleian MS 252, f. 26.

Chapter One

1. Public Record Office (PRO), E36/215, f. 250.
2. *Letters and Papers, Foreign and Domestic, of the Reign of Henry VIII*, ed. J.S. Brewer et al., p. 395.
3. For a full discussion of the problems Henry VII faced in securing his throne see S.B. Chimes, *Henry VII* (1987), pp. 68–94.
4. *Letters and Papers Illustrative of the Reigns of Richard III and Henry VII*, ed. J. Gairdner (2 vols, 1861, 1863), I, pp. 233–4.
5. One of the points that does not seem to have been a particular problem was Archbishop Warham's concern over the validity of the six-year-old papal dispensation, which allowed for the fact that Katherine had had sexual intercourse with Arthur. D. Loades, *The Politics of Marriage* (Stroud, 1994), p.17.
6. N. Samman, 'The Henrician Court During Cardinal Wolsey's Ascendancy *c.* 1514–1529' (unpublished Ph.D., University of Wales, 1988), p. 175.

7. *Calendar of Letters, Dispatches and State Papers (CSP) Relating to Negotiations between England and Spain 1485–1558*, ed. G.A. Bergenroth, et al. (1862–1954) Supplement, p. 285. G. Mattingly, *Catherine of Aragon* (1971), pp. 110–12. W. Compton, *History of the Comptons of Compton Wynyates*, p. 15.

8. The Blounts of Kinlet were the descendants of Sir John Blount through his first marriage in 1347 to Isolda, the daughter and heir of Sir Thomas de Mountjoy. The Blounts, the Lords Mountjoy, were the descendants of his second marriage to Eleanor, the daughter of Lord Beauchamp of Somerset.

9. PRO, E36/215, f. 270. A. Somerset, *Ladies in Waiting*, p. 15.

10. Shropshire Record Office (SRO), 1878/3 29.

11. SRO 1878/3 27.

12. W.S. Childe-Pemberton, *Elizabeth Blount and Henry VIII*, p. 20.

13. BL, Cotton MS Titus A XIII, f. 187.

14. S.J. Gunn, *Charles Brandon, Duke of Suffolk, c. 1484–1545*, p. 6.

15. BL, Additional MSS 28585, f. 43.

16. The report came from the Imperial agent James Banisius and is not corroborated by any other source. David Loades is probably correct when he suggests that if there was a child it was 'almost certainly dead, and many weeks premature.' D. Loades, *The Politics of Marriage*, p. 24.

17. BL, Cott. MS Caligula D VI, f. 155.

18. In 1514 Charles Brandon had already contracted four marriages. He had put aside the first wife, Anne Browne, when she was pregnant with their daughter, so he could marry her aunt Margaret Mortimer, a wealthy heiress. He then had that marriage annulled in order to remarry Anne and, after her death, had made plans to marry his eight-year-old ward. Despite rumours of his interest in Margaret of Savoy, in 1515 he actually married the king's sister, Mary Tudor.

19. Or to be exact 'una grandissima ribald et infame sopre tutte', *Letters and Papers*, X, 450. E. Ives, *Anne Boleyn*, p. 34.

20. PRO, SP1/70, 61. SP1/10, 163.

21. For what little is known of Jane Poppingcourt's career in England see Samman, 'Henrician Court', p. 147. W. Richardson, *Mary Tudor, The White Queen*, p. 14.

22. PRO, E36/215 f. 449.

23. E. Hall, *Chronicle Containing the History of England*, ed. H. Ellis (1809), p. 703.

24. Ibid., p. 595.

25. Wolsey's two children by 'Mistress Lark' were a son, Thomas Winter, who received numerous clerical preferments and a

daughter, Dorothy, who secured a place in the wealthy convent at Shaftesbury Abbey. P. Gwyn, *The King's Cardinal* (1990), p. 351.

26. N. Samman, 'Henrician Court', p. 403.
27. G. Mattingly, *Catherine of Aragon*, p. 132.
28. H.S. Burke, *Historical Portrait of the Tudor Dynasty* (4 vols, 1879–83), I, p. 178. *Letters and Papers*, III, ii, Revels Accounts, p. 1559.
29. PRO, Durham 3, Portf. 177, p. 55.
30. W.C. Richardson, 'The Surveyor of the King's Prerogative', *English Historical Review*, (1941), p. 60.
31. Letters and Papers, III, ii, 2356. (18).
32. R. Warnicke, *The Rise and Fall of Anne Boleyn*, p. 49.
33. N. Samman, 'Henrician Court,' p. 186.
34. BL, Cott. Otho, CX, f. 234.
35. PRO, SP1/55 15.
36. PRO, SP1/55 14.
37. *Inventory of the Wardrobe of Henry Fitzroy, Duke of Richmond, 1531* [17], Historical Manuscript Commision, Longleat Miscellaneous Manuscripts (microfilm, reel 2) 97. The young Lord Tailbois would also receive other items of his half-brother's wardrobe in 1536. J.G. Nichols, *Inventories of the Wardrobe*, 1ff.
38. Alice Perrers was the infamous mistress of Edward III whose influence was matched only by her ambition.
39. E. Ives, *Anne Boleyn*, p. 20.
40. 14 & 15 Henry VIII. C.34.
41. BL, Add. MSS 46457, f. 56 ff.
42. *Letters and Papers*, IV, iii, 5750.

Chapter Two

1. S. Thurley, *The Royal Palaces of Tudor England*, p. 119.
2. BL, Cott. MS Tiberius E.VIII, f. 206. The earls who were chosen to accompany Fitzroy during this part of the ceremony were those who ranked first in the order of precedence. See H. Miller, *Henry VIII and the English Nobility*, p. 20.
3. BL, Egerton MS 2642, f. 7.
4. Arthur Plantagenet, Viscount Lisle, the bastard son of Edward IV, acquired his title in the reign of Henry VIII, through his marriage to Elizabeth, the daughter of Edward Grey, Viscount Lisle.
5. John Beaufort was the eldest son of four illegitimate children born to John of Gaunt and his mistress Katherine Swynford. As the product of an adulterous affair the children were not automatically

legitimated when their parents married in 1399. However, when Gaunt successfully petitioned the Pope for a dispensation their legitimacy was confirmed. C. Given-Wilson and A. Curteis, *The Royal Bastards of Medieval England*, pp. 147–53.

6. M. Jones and M. Underwood, *The King's Mother*, pp. 71–2.
7. In Matilda's defence, it must be said that Henry I created problems that any successor would be hard pressed to deal with. The celebrated peace of his reign belied tensions that were held in check through terror of the king. His personal government had been harsh and oppressive and it was inevitable that there would be a reaction on his death. For an account of Matilda's life see M. Chibnall, *The Empress Matilda*.
8. In his examination of Buckingham's rebellion against Richard III, Michael Hicks suggested that 'while it is easy to deduce . . . that the new unnamed king proclaimed at Bodmin was Henry Tudor, it need not have been. It could, for example, have been Buckingham', M. Hicks, *Richard III*, p. 158.
9. For a full account of the events which led to Buckingham's downfall see J.J. Scarisbrick, *Henry VIII*, p. 120–3.
10. Gilbert Tailbois was listed as a member of the king's chamber in the subsidy records of 1527 and was still at court in April 1529 when his mother complained he should 'go home and see good order kept in the county'. PRO, E179/69/2. PRO, SP1/53, f. 158.
11. Writing in 1973, Mortimer Levine proposed that 'the king's bitterness over the defeat of his French ambitions' was the inspiration for Richmond's elevation. M. Levine, *Tudor Dynastic Problems*, p. 54.
12. CSP Venetian, IV, 1053.
13. R. Wernham, *Before the Armada*, p. 111.
14. The marriage was supposed to take place when Mary was twelve years old in February 1528. Yet at eleven Mary was still considered 'so thin, spare and small as to make it impossible to be married for the next three years'. This suggests a degree of physical immaturity, which would have further delayed the prospect of children. It was not difficult for Isabella and her dowry of one million ducats to be a more tempting prospect.
15. *Letters and Papers*, IV, i, 1371.
16. PRO, SP1/35, pp. 185–92. That Richmond was termed 'Lord Henry Fitzroy' is evidence that the list was drawn up prior to 18 June 1525. Yet the contents can be identified as in use in his household at Sheriff Hutton.
17. J. Palsgrave, *The Comedy of Acolastus*, p. xxvii. His patron was, it seems, a distant relation.

Notes

18. *Chronicle and Political Papers of Edward VI*, ed. W.K. Jordan, p. 3.
19. BL, Harl. MS 304 125b. However, the register of the Order only records the elections of the Earl of Arundel and Lord Roos on St George's Day 1525. J. Anstis, *The Register of the Most Noble Order of the Garter* (2 vols, 1724), II, pp. 369–70.
20. C. Given-Wilson and A. Curteis, *Royal Bastards of Medieval England*, pp. 162–73.
21. 'Even if the king could canvass enough support for such a move, there was a strong argument that it was prejudicial to the rights of the king's lawful children. Not just those he had already, but those he might yet have – by his present wife or any subsequent wives. Therefore, it was beyond the competence of the king or the king and parliament to do so.' H. Nenner, *The Right to be King*, p. 39. The birth of Edward in 1537 justified this caution.
22. CSP Venetian, III, 1052.
23. While the Dukedom of Somerset had most recently been held by Henry VII's youngest son Edmund, who had died in childhood, it was almost certainly chosen for him because of the family connection.
24. The manors were: Englishcombe, Shepton Mallet, Midsomer Norton, Melton Falconbridge, Laverton, Farrington Gurney, Stoke under Hampton, Welton and West Harptree. G. Haslam, 'An Administrative Study of the Duchy of Cornwall 1500–1650' unpublished Ph.D thesis, Louisiana State University, 1970, pp. 123–5.
25. Sir John Arundel of Lanherne was also to be included, but cried off pleading lack of sufficient notice. It seems likely that Wolsey suggested his name, since Sir John's second son was in the Cardinal's service. Arundel was probably not included in the king's original design. H. Miller, *English Nobility* p. 22.
26. For a discussion of the other elevations see R. Warnicke, *Rise and Fall of Anne Boleyn*, p. 45. Normally, the next heir would have been the son of Henry's eldest sister, Margaret, the young James V of Scotland. However, the terms of her marriage to James IV, in which she had relinquished her hereditary rights, had in effect disqualified him. The same did not necessarily apply to her daughter from her second marriage, Margaret Douglas, who, conveniently, had also been born in England.
27. PRO, SP1/39, f. 17.
28. These included Chief Justice of the forest beyond the Trent and a commission as Lieutenant-General north of the Trent.
29. Prince Arthur's court at Ludlow, in the reign of Henry VII, had also

been primarily to oversee his own estates. Yet his interests as Prince of Wales had provided a natural link to the authority of the king.

30. For a complete history of the council see, R. Reid, *The King's Council in the North*.

31. Ibid., p. 103.

32. BL, Vespasian MS F III, f.18.b. Although calendared in *Letters and Papers*, IV (i), 2010 and 2011 as 4 March 1526, they cannot have been written in that year if Richmond was in the south. His skill with a pen also suggests a rather later date.

33. Not even Mary's parallel council at Ludlow could duplicate this experiment in bureaucratic government. Mary's status as a royal princess required that she was attended by persons of rank and her council included a countess, a marquess, a bishop and a lord among its members.

34. M. Jones and M. Underwood, *The King's Mother*, p. 83.

35. State Papers (SP) Henry VIII, IV, 135.

36. PRO, E101/424/18.

37. SP Henry VIII, IV, 135.

Chapter Three

1. SP Henry VIII, IV, 144.

2. Palsgrave was replaced on Richmond's council in April 1526 by William Bathorpe. R. Reid, *Council in the North*, p. 104.

3. I can find no evidence to support John Gough Nichols' suggestion that Richmond employed a whipping-boy, even in an honorary capacity. J.G. Nichols, *Literary Remains of King Edward the Sixth*, p. lxxiv.

4. PRO, SP1/46, p. 169.

5. *The Lisle Letters*, ed. M. St Clare Byrne, I, p. 182. PRO, E24/15/12, p.1 m.8.

6. PRO, SP1/40, p. 96.

7. BL, Cott. Appendix L, f. 68.

8. Their actual relationship was a little more distant. The Pope Giulio de Medici had a natural son, Giuliano de Medici, who was the great-uncle of Lorenzo, Duke of Urbino and Florence, who was Catherine's father.

9. Henry agreed to join the League of Cognac and give up his ancient titles in France in return for a pension and Francis' agreement to marry. An earlier demand that Francis should give him Boulogne was dropped. D. Loades, *Mary Tudor, A Life*, pp. 47–9.

Notes

10. SP Henry VIII, I, 127.
11. During the negotiations Wolsey asked that the duc d'Orléans should come to England and live among his future subjects so that they could grow to love him.
12. Getting wind of the proposal the Venetian ambassador reported that Henry VIII was to pay 500,000 ducats for the marriage. CSP Venetian, IV, 172.
13. In 1499 the King of France, Louis XII, had put aside his consort Jeanne, in order to marry the widow of his predecessor. D. Loades, *Politics of Marriage*, p. 3.
14. H. Miller, *Henry VIII and the English Nobility*, p. 217.
15. BL, Cott. Appendix L, F. 68.
16. Richmond's own links with the area were not immediately severed, since deputies, such as Sir Thomas Clifford, the Under-Warden and Under-Captain of Berwick-upon-Tweed continued to serve in his name.

Chapter Four

1. R. Warnicke, *Rise and Fall of Anne Boleyn*, p. 195.
2. For the best arguments of the canon law of Henry's divorce see J.J. Scarisbrick, *Henry VIII*, pp. 163–97.
3. G.E. de Parmiter, *The King's Great Matter*, p. 4.
4. PRO, Prob, 11/20.
5. A lack of evidence makes it difficult to reconstruct exactly how the board worked, although David Quinn sees some similarity with later procedures in Ireland where vice-regal authority was sometimes entrusted to a group of lords justices. D. Quinn, 'Henry Fitzroy, Duke of Richmond and his Connection with Ireland 1529–30', *Bulletin of the Institute of Historical Research*, 12 (1935) p. 175
6. CSP Spanish, III, ii, 632.
7. S. Thurley, *The Royal Palaces of Tudor England*, p. 189.
8. For a fuller discussion of the Duke of Norfolk's role in Richmond's lands and household affairs see chapter six.
9. E. Ives, *Anne Boleyn*, p. 259.
10. A second equally thorough inventory of Richmond's goods was taken at his death in July 1536. The procedure was also followed for the seizure of assets under attainder.
11. PRO, SP1/111, p. 221.
12. Angered by this intervention of her niece (who after all was not yet her queen) in so intimate a family matter, the duchess, rather

unwisely, made her feelings known. Anne responded in kind and the duchess was obliged to withdraw from the court.

13. Margaret, Countess of Salisbury, had been granted her title in her own right in 1513. Yet in her case the circumstances were rather different since she held it in descent from her maternal grandfather.
14. Estimates for the number of Anne's ladies vary between ten and thirty. E. Ives, *Anne Boleyn*, p. 199. If the 'lady Mary' listed was not Anne Boleyn's sister but her cousin Mary Howard, her betrothal to the Duke of Richmond might explain why she was given precedence over Lady Derby and the others. However, the view that the report was deliberately couched to suggest Henry's daughter was there would still be equally valid. D. Loades, *Mary Tudor*, p. 67.
15. E. Hall, *Chronicle*, p. 792.
16. Bibliothèque Nationale de France (BN), Fonds Dupuys 546.
17. BN, MS Français 15629.
18. After the death of his brother, Francis on 10 August 1536, Henri became the dauphin, and his brother Charles succeeded to his title of Orléans.
19. BN, Fonds Dupuys 547, f. 172.
20. Since the couple were related, Richmond, being a descendant of Elizabeth Woodville, whose sister Katherine, Duchess of Buckingham, was Mary's great-grandmother, the couple sought and obtained a papal dispensation for consanguinity.
21. In the same vein Anne also suggested that the Earl of Surrey might marry Mary Tudor.
22. R. Southall 'The Devonshire Manuscript Collection of Early Tudor Poetry 1532–41', *The Review of English Studies*, 15 (1964) p. 10.
23. CSP Spanish, V, 87.
24. SP Henry VIII, II, 108.

Chapter Five

1. These were 25 Henry VIII c.19, confirmation of the 1532 submission of the clergy, 25 Henry VIII c.20, suppression of annates, 25 Henry VIII c.28, Princess Dowager and 25 Henry VIII c.22 succession.
2. 25 Henry VIII c.22.
3. M. Levine, 'Henry VIII's Use of his Spiritual and Temporal Jurisdictions in his Great Causes of Matrimony, Legitimacy and Succession' *The Historical Journal*, 11 (1967), p. 6.

4. Several times Anne offered to intercede for Mary with her father in return for her acceptance of her legal position as queen. E. Ives, *Anne Boleyn*, pp. 247–9.
5. *Letters and Papers*, VIII, 909.
6. E. Ives, *Anne Boleyn*, p. 253.
7. John Uvedale served at various times as secretary to Norfolk, Anne Boleyn and Richmond. William Brereton was the son of Sir Randolph Brereton of Malpas, a close associate of Norfolk.
8. For an account of this progress see chapter six.
9. D. Loades, *Mary Tudor*, p. 93.
10. R. Warnicke, *Rise and Fall of Anne Boleyn*, pp. 191–233
11. CSP Spanish, V, 13. Henry's extreme reaction can really only be explained if the infant lost in 1534 had also been a son.
12. *Letters and Papers*, X, 494. In the event the meeting did not go ahead.
13. For more on Brereton's downfall and its impact on Richmond's position as a marcher lord see chapter six.
14. CSP Spanish, V, 55.
15. 34 Henry VIII c.40.
16. In fact it would take the 1536 Act of Succession (28 Henry VIII c.7) to confirm both Mary's and Elizabeth's bastard status in law. If he chose, Henry could still claim either of them had been born in good faith. Yet since everyone acted as if they were indeed illegitimate, this may well have been more of an oversight than actual policy.
17. CSP Spanish, V, ii, 70.
18. CSP Spanish, V, ii, 61.
19. The unfinished portrait of the Duchess of Richmond by Hans Holbein was perhaps commissioned to mark this momentous step. If the drawing was to commemorate their marriage in 1533, it seems strange that the work was interrupted.
20. S. Thurley, *Royal Palaces*, p. 36.
21. M. Tucker, *The Life of Thomas Howard 1443–1524*, p. 25.
22. 28 Henry VIII c. 7.
23. CSP Spanish, V, ii, 91.
24. Since Richmond had attended the previous sessions of parliament with such regularity it does seem worth noting that he was completely absent from business in 1536. This might be excused as no longer a necessary part of his education, although nor does it seem that he attended the Neville marriage celebrations held at Shoreditch on 3 July 1536, although the greater part of the court, including Norfolk, Suffolk, the Earl of Surrey and the king were present.
25. CSP Spanish, V, ii, 71.

26. For a detailed revision of the accounts of Edward's last illness see J. Loach, *Edward VI*, eds G. Bernard and P. Williams (1999), pp. 159–62.
27. I am grateful to S.J. Gunn for his advice on this point.

Chapter Six

1. Richmond was entitled to a pursuivant in his capacity as Earl of Nottingham. As a duke he was entitled to a herald. At his elevation in 1525 the Somerset Herald had sported Richmond's new coat-of-arms.
2. The lands had reverted to the crown after the recent death of the Duchess of Buckingham. That Ambrose had formerly been in the Duke of Buckingham's service may be a feature in the gift.
3. 22 Henry VIII c.17.
4. PRO, SP1/49, p. 135.
5. Rather sooner than he could have anticipated, Sir Giles Strangeways subsequently obtained the stewardship in Somerset when the lands reverted to the crown after Richmond's death in 1536.
6. R. Davies, *The Fawkes of York in the Sixteenth Century*, eds J.B. and J.G. Nichols (1850), p. 9.
7. S.J. Gunn, 'The Regime of Charles, Duke of Suffolk, in North Wales and the Reform of Welsh Government 1509–25', *Welsh History Review*, 12 (1985), p. 487.
8. R. Reid, *The King's Council in the North* p. 135.
9. In a covenant made at the time of her daughter Ursula Pole's marriage to Henry, Lord Stafford, Margaret agreed to pay a further 1,000 marks if she could 'get back certain lands from the King'. *Calendar of Manuscripts of George Alan Lowndes Esq*, p. 584.
10. PRO, SP1/50, p. 4.
11. PRO, SP1/69, p. 273.
12. George Lawson was evidently still enjoying his fee in May 1536, when he wrote to the Duke of Norfolk to protest at the possibility of again being made to relinquish it. *Letters and Papers*, X, 935.
13. Stephen Gardiner's biographer also sees his connections to Norfolk as a factor in deciding to invoke Richmond's assistance. G. Redworth, *In Defence of the Church Catholic*, p. 62.
14. It has been argued that 'it may even be that Brereton had seen a chance to fish in troubled waters and so initiated the enquiry himself in the name of the fifteen year old duke'. E. Ives, 'Letters and Accounts of William Brereton of Malpas', *The Record Society of Lancashire and Cheshire*, 116 (1976) p. 39.
15. Biddlecombe also had links with the duke's council, through his

association with Sir Giles Strangeways and was employed by the duke. As a former bailiff and mayor he already represented a respectable candidate, but this does not preclude that Richmond's influence was a factor.

Chapter Seven

1. R. Strong, *The English Renaissance Miniature*, p. 40.
2. A God's penny was a relief of a silver penny. A gressom was two years' rent. Both were customary charges on top of all normal payments in some areas of the north when a new lord took possession of his holdings. R. Reid, *Council in the North* (1921), pp. 135–6.
3. PRO, SP1/128 p. 92.
4. BL, Cott. Titus B I, f.383c. It is possible that the actual amount was supposed to be 1,000 marks. The valuation of the estates she was ultimately granted is listed as 'Clear total 744*l* 10s 9d ob, which exceeds 1,000 marks by 77*l* 17s 5d ob' (an ob was half a penny). *Letters and Papers*, XVI, 401.
5. He was free by October when he met with up with his father. *Letters and Papers*, XII, ii, 839.
6. PRO, SP1/111, p. 221.
7. This present danger 'made the military abilities of the House of Howard absolutely essential to Henry VIII. Consequently, even the slightest trace of doubt disappeared from the king's attitude towards them.' E. Casady, *Henry Howard, Earl of Surrey*, p. 70.
8. Far from being an innocent young girl, Catherine Howard had already had a string of past relationships, including the musician Henry Mannox, the gentleman pensioner Francis Dereham and a budding romance with Thomas Culpepper, a member of the King's privy chamber, when Henry first expressed his interest in her. In contrast, everything about Anne of Cleves' former life indicates she was indeed a virgin.
9. The account given by Edward Rogers is simply a report of what he had been told by Carew and should not be taken to suggest that he was an independent witness to the scene.
10. E. Cherbury, *Life and Reign of King Henry the Eighth*, p. 626.
11. PRO, SP1/227, f. 123
12. In particular, the evidence of Christopher Barker, Garter King of Arms, was both flawed and retrospective. The fact that Barker was knighted shortly after Surrey's execution seems to indicate his complicity. *Letters and Papers*, XXI, i, 1425.

13. For a fuller account of the details of the charges relating to Surrey's armorial bearings see E. Casady, *Henry Howard,* pp. 194–202.
14. The subsidy returns are not the most accurate guide to wealth, since it was a positive advantage to be assessed at less than you had, in order to pay less tax. However, Mary was not particularly in favour at this time and therefore this probably represents a reasonable assessment of her possessions. The baroness was Elizabeth, Lady Tailbois, the daughter and only surviving issue of Elizabeth Blount and Gilbert, Lord Tailbois.
15. PRO, Prob 11/37.
16. The date of Mary's death has often been taken as occurring in December 1557. However, a second grant to Thomas Gresham dated 19 January 1556 confirms that she was already dead.
17. L. Stone and H. Colvin, 'The Howard Tombs at Framlingham, Suffolk', *Archeological Journal*, 122 (1966), p. 161–8.
18. Neville Williams believed that he had correctly identified PRO SP14/55/n11 as an account of the Duchess of Richmond's funeral. N. Williams, *Thomas Howard 4th Duke of Norfolk* (1964), p. 30. However, this is probably the funeral of the second wife of the 4th duke, Margaret, the daughter of Thomas, Lord Audley, who was initially buried in Norwich at St John the Baptist Church.

Epilogue

1. T. Fuller, *The Church History of Britain*, III, p. 232.
2. J. Loach, *Edward VI*, pp. 8, 11, 153–8.
3. D. Loades, *Mary Tudor*, p. 146.
4. C. Ferguson, *Naked to Mine Enemies*, p. 343. Since Henry believed his marriage to Katherine to be unlawful he would probably have disputed the charge that Richmond was also born in adultery.
5. Sir William Paget was by this point a pivotal figure in Tudor government, one of two principal secretaries of state, an accomplished clerk and diplomat who helped lobby support among members of the privy council for Seymour's coup to raise himself up as Lord Protector after Henry died.

Bibliography

This is not intended to be a comprehensive bibliography of the period covered in this book. Rather it is a collection of those printed sources which best serve to illustrate the career of the Duke of Richmond and his immediate circle.

Place of publication is London unless otherwise stated.

Primary Printed Sources

Anstis, J. *The Register of the Most Noble Order of the Garter* (1724)

Banners, Standards and Badges from a Tudor Manuscript in the College of Arms in the De Walden Library, E. Thomas, Baron Howard de Walden (ed.) (1904)

Book of Martyrs, The Complete Version, Acts and Monuments of John Foxe, J. Pratt and G. Townsend (eds) (1870)

Calendar of Letters, Dispatches and State Papers Relating to Negotiations between England and Spain 1485–1558, G.A. Bergenroth et al. (ed.) (1862–1954)

Calendar of Manuscripts Belonging to the Borough of Plymouth County Devon (Historical Manuscripts Commission, 1883)

Calendar of Manuscripts of George Alan Lowndes (Historical Manuscripts Commission, 1884)

Calendar of Manuscripts of his Grace the Duke of Leinster (Historical Manuscripts Commission, 1884)

Calendar of Manuscripts of his Grace the Duke of Rutland (Historical Manuscripts Commission, 1905)

Calendar of Manuscripts of the . . . Marquess of Bath (Historical Manuscripts Commission, 1968)

Calendar of Municipal Records of Shrewsbury (Historical Manuscripts Commission, 1899)

Calendar of the Carew Manuscripts 1515–1574, J.S. Brewer and W. Bullen (eds) (1867–73)

Calendar of State Papers and Manuscripts Relating to English Affairs Preserved in the Archives of Venice, R. Brown et al. (eds) (1864–1954)

Calendar of the State Papers Domestic of the Reign of Edward VI, ed. C.S. Knighton (1992)

Calendar of the State Papers of Milan, A.B. Hinds (ed.) (1912)

Calendar of the State Papers Relating to Ireland of the Reigns of Henry VIII, Mary and Elizabeth 1509–1573, H.C. Hamilton et al. (eds) (1860–1912)

Calendar of the State Papers Relating to Scotland, J. Bain et al. (eds) (Edinburgh, 1896–1969)

Cavendish, G. *The Life and Death of Cardinal Wolsey*, R.S. Sylvester (ed.) (Early English Text Society, 1959)

Cherbury, E. *Lord Herbert, Life and Reign of King Henry the Eighth* (1602)

Chronicle and Political Papers of Edward VI, W.K. Jordan (ed.) (New York, 1966)

Collectanea Curiosa, J. Gutch (ed.) (1871)

Fuller, T. *The Church History of Britain* (1655), J.S. Brewer (ed.) (6 vols, Oxford, 1845)

Gardiner, S. *The Letters of Stephen Gardiner*, J. Muller (ed.) (Connecticut, 1970)

Giustinian, S. *Four Years at the Court of Henry VIII*, R. Brown (tr.) (1854)

Grafton, R. *Grafton's Chronicle or History of England 1189–1558* (1809)

Hall, E. *Chronicle Containing the History of England*, H. Ellis (ed.) (1809)

Inventories of the Wardrobe, Plate, Chapel Stuff, etc of Henry Fitzroy Duke of Richmond . . . Edited with a Memoir and Letters of the Duke of Richmond, J.G. Nichols (ed.) (Camden Miscellany, 3rd series, 1855)

Journals of the House of Lords (vol. 1, 1808)

Leland, J. *De Rebus Britannicis Collectanea*, L. Toulmin-Smith (ed.) (1784)

Letters and Papers, Foreign and Domestic, of the Reign of Henry VIII, J.S. Brewer et al. (eds) (1862–1910, 1920–1932)

Letters and Papers Illustrative of the Reigns of Richard III and Henry VII, J. Gairdner (ed.) (2 vols, 1861, 1863)

Letters of Royal and Illustrious Ladies, M.A.E. Green (ed.) (Wood) (1846)

Life and Letters of Thomas Cromwell, R. Merriman (ed.) (2 vols, Oxford, 1968)

Lincoln Wills 1271–1526, C.W. Foster (ed.) (Publications of the Lincoln Record Society, 1914)

Lisle Letters, The, M. St Clare Byrne (ed.) (6 vols, Chicago, 1981)

Bibliography

Literary Remains of King Edward the Sixth, J.G. Nichols (ed.) (Roxburgh Club, 1857)

Original Letters Illustrative of English History, H. Ellis (ed.) (3rd series, 1824–46)

Palsgrave, J. *The Comedy of Acolastus Translated from the Latin of Pullonius*, P.L. Carver (ed.) (Early English Text Society, London, 1937)

Privy Purse Expenses of King Henry VIII, The, N.H. Nicholas (ed.) (1829)

Privy Purse Expenses of the Princess Mary, The, F.E. Madden (ed.) (1831)

Report of the Deputy Keeper of the Public Records, 44 (1883)

Select Pleas in the Court of the Admiralty, R. Marsden (ed.) (2 vols, Seldon Society, 1894, 1897)

State Papers during the Reign of Henry VIII (1830–52)

Statutes of the Realm, A. Luders et al. (eds) (1810–28)

Stow, J. *A Survey of London* (1598), C.L. Kingsford (ed.) (1908)

Throckmorton, N. *The Legend of Sir Nicholas Throckmorton*, J.G. Nichols (ed.) (1874).

Turpyn, R. *The Chronicle of Calais in the Reigns of Henry VII and Henry VIII to the Year 1540*, J.G. Nichols (ed.) (Camden Society, 1864)

Valor Ecclesiasticus, J. Caley and J. Hunter (eds) (6 vols, 1810–34)

Visitations of Lincolnshire 1634 (Harleian Society Publication, 1898)

Visitations of Shropshire 1623 (Harleian Society Publication, 1889)

Visitations of Staffordshire 1614 (Harleian Society Publication, 1885)

Works of Henry Howard, Earl of Surrey and Sir Thomas Wyatt, the Elder, The, G.F. Nott (ed.) (2 vols, London 1815, 1816)

Wriothesley, C.A. *A Chronicle of England During the Reigns of the Tudors 1485–1559*, W.D. Hamilton (ed.) (Camden Society, second series, vols XI, XX, 1875, 1877)

York Civic Records Vol. III, A. Raine (ed.) (York Archaeological Society, 1942)

Secondary Sources

Ackroyd, P. *The Life of Sir Thomas More* (1999)

Alexander, J.J. and Hooper, W.R. *The History of Great Torrington in the County of Devon* (Surrey, 1948)

Bagwell, R. *Ireland under the Tudors* (3 vols, 1963)

Baldwin, D. *The Chapel Royal, Ancient and Modern* (1990)

Bapst, E. *Deux Gentilshommes Poètes de la Cour de Henri VIII* (Paris, 1891)

Barnwell, E. *Perrot Notes, Some Account of the Various Branches of the Perrot Family* (1867)

Baron, H. 'Mary [Howard] Fitzroy's Hand in the Devonshire Mss', *Review of English Studies*, 45 (1994).

Beckingsale, B.W. *Thomas Cromwell, Tudor Minister* (1978)

Bindoff, S. (ed.). *The History of Parliament, The House of Commons 1509–1558* (3 vols, 1982)

Blomfield, F. *An Essay Towards a Topographical History of the County of Norfolk*, C. Parkin (ed.) (11 vols, 1805–10)

Blunt, R. *Memoirs of Gerald Blunt* (London, 1911)

Bradner, L.B. *The Life and Poems of Richard Edwards* (Oxford, 1927)

Brenan, G. and Statham, E.P. *The House of Howard* (2 vols, 1907)

Brewer, J.S. *The Reign of Henry VIII from his Accession to the Death of Wolsey*, J. Gairdner (ed.) (2 vols, 1884)

Brooks, F.W. *The Council of the North* (1953)

Burke, S.H. *Historical Portrait of the Tudor Dynasty* (4 vols, 1879–83)

Carlton, C. *Royal Mistresses* (1991)

Casady, E. *Henry Howard, Earl of Surrey* (New York, 1938)

Chamberlain, J. (ed.). *Imitations of Original Drawings by Hans Holbein* (1792)

Chibnall, M. *The Empress Matilda* (1991)

Childe-Pemberton, W.S. *Elizabeth Blount and Henry VIII with Some Account of her Surroundings* (1913)

Chochrane, C. *Poole Bay and Purbeck 300 BC – AD 1660* (Dorchester, 1970)

Cockayne, G.E. *The Complete Peerage*, V. Gibbs et al. (eds) (13 vols, 1910–59)

Collections for a History of Staffordshire, William Salt Archaeological Society (ed.) (Kendal, 1880)

Colvin, N.M. *The History of the King's Works* (4 vols, 1962–83)

Compton, W. *History of the Comptons of Compton Wynates* (1930)

Cosgrave, A. (ed.). *A New History of Ireland: Medieval Ireland 1169–1534* (Oxford, 1987)

Craik, A. *Annals of our Ancestors* (Edinburgh, 1924)

Croke, A. *The Genealogical History of the Croke Family Originally Named Le Blount* (Oxford, 1823)

Davies, R. *The Fawkes of York in the 16th Century*, J.B. and J.G. Nichols (eds) (1850)

de Parmiter, G. *The King's Great Matter* (1967)

Derrett, D.J. 'Henry Fitzroy and Henry VIII's "Scruple of Conscience"', *Renaissance News*, 16 (1963)

Edwards, D. *The Edwardes Legacy* (Baltimore, 1992)

Ellis, S. *The Pale and the Far North* (Galway, 1988)

Bibliography

—— *Tudor Ireland 1470–1603* (1985)

Erickson, C. *Bloody Mary* (1978)

Ferguson, C. *Naked to Mine Enemies* (1958)

Fisher, H.A.L. *History of England from the Accession of Henry VII to the Death of Henry VIII, 1485–1547* (New York, 1928)

Fraser, A. *The Six Wives of Henry VIII* (1993)

Gillis, J.R. *For Better For Worse, British Marriages, 1600 to the Present* (Oxford, 1985)

Given-Wilson, C. and Curteis, A. *The Royal Bastards of Medieval England* (1984)

Grameme, J. *The Story of St James' Palace* (1929)

Gunn, S.J. *Charles Brandon, Duke of Suffolk c. 1485–1545* (Oxford, 1988)

—— and Lindley, P.G. (eds). *Cardinal Wolsey, Church, State and Art* (Cambridge, 1991)

—— 'The Regime of Charles, Duke of Suffolk in North Wales and the Reform of Welsh Government 1509–25', *Welsh History Review*, 12 (1985)

Guy, J. *Tudor England* (Oxford, 1990)

Gwyn, P. *The King's Cardinal* (1992)

Hackett, F. *Henry VIII* (1929)

Harriss, G.L. *Cardinal Beaufort* (Oxford, 1988)

Haslam, G. 'An Administrative Study of the Duchy of Cornwall 1500–1650' (unpublished Ph.D. thesis, Louisiana State University, 1970)

Head, M. 'The Life and Career of Thomas Howard: 3rd Duke of Norfolk 1473–1554' (unpublished Ph.D. thesis, Florida State University, 1978)

Hicks, M. *Richard III* (Tempus, Stroud, 2000)

Hoskins, A. 'Mary Boleyn Carey's Children – Offspring of King Henry VIII', *Genealogists Magazine*, 25, n.9 (1977)

Howard, H. *Indications of Memorials, Monuments, Paintings and Engravings of Persons of the Howard Family* (Corbey Castle, 1834)

Hume, M. *The Wives of Henry VIII* (1927)

Ives, E. *Anne Boleyn* (Oxford, 1986)

—— 'Faction at the Court of Henry VIII, the Fall of Anne Boleyn', *History*, 57 (1972)

—— (ed.). 'Letters and Accounts of William Brereton of Malpas', *The Record Society of Lancashire and Cheshire*, 116 (1976)

—— 'Court and County Palatinate in the Reign of Henry VIII, The Career of William Brereton of Malpas', *Transactions of the Historic Society of Lancashire and Cheshire*, 123 (1972)

Jones, M. and Underwood, M. *The King's Mother* (Cambridge, 1992)

Kelly, H. 'Kinship, Incest and the Dictates of Law', *The American Journal of Jurisprudence*, 14 (1969)

—— *The Matrimonial Trials of Henry VIII* (California, 1976)

Leach, T. *Lincolnshire Country Houses and their Families* (2 vols, Lincoln, 1990, 1991)

Lechnar, M. 'Henry VIII's Bastard: Henry Fitzroy, Duke of Richmond' (unpublished partial fufilment Ph.D. thesis, West Virginia University, 1977)

le Hamy, P. *Entrevue de François 1er avec Henry VIII à Boulogne sur Mer en 1532* (Paris, 1898)

Lehmberg, S. *The Reformation Parliament 1529–36* (Cambridge, 1970)

Levine, M. 'Henry VIII's Use of his Spiritual and Temporal Jurisdictions in his Great Causes of Matrimony, Legitimacy and Succession', *The Historical Journal*, 11 (1967)

—— *Tudor Dynastic Problems 1460–1571* (1973)

Loach, J. *Edward VI*, G. Bernard and P. Williams (eds) (1999)

—— *Parliament Under the Tudors* (Oxford, 1991)

Loades, D. *Mary Tudor, A Life* (Oxford, 1992)

—— *The Politics of Marriage – Henry VIII and his Queens* (Stroud, 1994)

MacCulloch, D. *Thomas Cranmer* (1996)

Martin, A.J. *The Church of St Michael, Framlingham* (Ipswich, 1985)

Mattingly, G. *Catherine of Aragon* (1963)

McLaren, A. *Reproductive Rituals* (1984)

Miller, H. *Henry VIII and the English Nobility* (Oxford, 1986)

Mordant, P. *The History and Antiquities of the County of Essex* (2 vols, 1763, 1768)

Neale, J.E. *Queen Elizabeth* (1934)

Nenner, H. *The Right to be King* (1995)

Newton, M. *South Kyme* (Lincoln, 1995)

Nichols, J.G. 'Additions to the Memoir of Henry Fitzroy, Duke of Richmond and Somerset', *Gentleman's Magazine* (August, 1855)

—— 'Mary Richmond, Female Biographies of English History, IV,' *Gentleman's Magazine* (May, 1845)

Noble, M. 'History of the Beautiful Elizabeth Blount', *Marshall's Genealogist*, II (1878)

Owen, H. and Blakeway, J. *A History of Shrewsbury* (2 vols, 1825)

Parshall, H. *The Parshall Family 870–1913* (1915)

Powell, E. and Wallis, K. *The House of Lords in the Middle Ages* (1968)

Quinn, D. 'Henry Fitzroy, Duke of Richmond and his Connection with Ireland 1529–30', *Bulletin of the Institute of Historical Research*, 12 (1935)

—— 'Henry VIII and Ireland 1509–34', *Irish Historical Studies*, 12 (1961)

Redworth, G. *In Defence of the Church Catholic* (Oxford, 1990)

Reid, R. *The King's Council in the North* (1921)

Robinson, J. *The Dukes of Norfolk* (West Sussex, 1995)

Robinson, W.R.B. 'Marcher Lords of Wales 1525–1531', *Bulletin of the Board of Celtic Studies*, 26 (1974–6)

Samman, N. 'The Henrician Court During Cardinal Wolsey's Ascendancy: c. 1514–1529' (unpublished Ph.D. thesis, University of Wales, 1988)

Sandeman, J. *The Spears of Honour and Gentlemen Pensioners* (Hants, 1912)

Scarisbrick, J.J. *Henry VIII* (1990)

Skeel, C. *The Council in the Marches of Wales* (1904)

Somerset, A. *Ladies in Waiting* (1984)

Southall, R. 'The Devonshire Manuscript Collection of Early Tudor Poetry 1532–41', *The Review of English Studies*, 15 (1964)

—— 'Mary Fitzroy and O Happy Dames in the Devonshire MSS', *Review of English Studies*, 45 (1994)

Starkey, D. (ed.). *Henry VIII: A European Court in England* (1991)

—— *The Reign of Henry VIII* (1985)

—— (ed.). *Rivals in Power* (1990)

Stone, L. and Colvin, H. 'The Howard Tombs at Framlingham, Suffolk', *Archeological Journal*, 122 (1966)

Stone, L. *The Road to Divorce: England 1530–1987* (Oxford, 1990)

Strickland, A. *Lives of the Queens of England* (8 vols, 1796–1874, 1940)

Strong, R. *The English Renaissance Miniature* (1983)

Thomas. H. *A History of Wales 1485–1660* (Cardiff, 1972)

Thomas, K. 'Age and Authority in Early Modern England', *Proceedings of the British Academy*, 62 (1976)

Thurley, S. *The Royal Palaces of Tudor England* (1993)

Tucker, M. *The Life of Thomas Howard 1443–1524* (1964)

Waldman, M. *The Lady Mary* (1972)

Warnicke, R. *The Rise and Fall of Anne Boleyn* (Cambridge, 1989)

Weir, A. *The Six Wives of Henry VIII* (1995)

Wernham, R. *Before the Armada, The Emergence of the English Nation 1485–1588* (New York, 1966)

Williams, N. *Thomas Howard 4th Duke of Norfolk* (1964)

Index

Aldridge, Robert, 138
Allen, John, Archbishop of Durham, 113
Almain, John, Count de Naussau, 89
Ambrose, usher, 76
Amy, Mistress, 212
Amyas, Robert, 131
Amyas, William, 68
Amyce, (perhaps Amyas) Roger, son-in-
    law of Sir George Lawson, 218
Andrews, Thomasyn, 197
Angus, Earl of see Douglas, Archibald
Anne of Cleves, Queen of England, 9, 109,
    170, 230, 231, 245
ap David Vaughan, Hugh, 206
ap Griffith Eyton, John, 210
ap Griffith Rhys, 206
Armstrong family, 82
Arnold, the brewer, 219
Arthur Plantagenet, Viscount Lisle,
    illegitimate son of Edward IV,
    51, 56, 135, 139–40, 151, 156,
    177, 179, 204, 216
Arthur, Prince of Wales, 3, 4, 12–13, 53,
    105, 106, 108, 137, 149
Arundel, Sir Thomas, 74
Ary, Alan, 191
Audley, Sir Thomas, 175, 205

Barlow, John, Dean of Westbury, 14
Beaufort, Cardinal Henry, 200
Beaufort, John, Duke of Somerset, 38,
    183
Beaufort, John, Earl of Somerset, 38–9,
    108
Beaufort, Margaret, Countess of
    Richmond, 38, 41, 53, 57, 61,
    63, 64, 124, 164, 171, 172,
    183–4, 196, 197, 201
Bellingham, James, 204
Berkley, Mary, ix
Bermingham, Patrick, 113
Biddlecombe, William, 212
Bindon, monks of, 204

Bingham, Robert, 199
Blanche, of Gaunt, 39
Blount, Albora, 33
Blount, Anne, 33
Blount, Edward, 16
Blount, Elizabeth
    background, 10–14, 26
    attributes, 1, 9, 11, 14–15, 18, 23
    Maid of Honour to Katherine of
        Aragon, 1–2, 9–10, 13, 15–16,
        16, 20, 24–5
    courtship, xi, 2, 17, 18–21, 23–4, 26–7
    marriage, 27, 28, 31–4
    subsequent relations with Henry VIII,
        28, 31, 34, 44, 108–11, 172,
        256–7
    relations with
        Anne Boleyn, 14
        Charles Brandon, Duke of Suffolk,
            14, 17
        Henry Fitzroy, Duke of Richmond,
            25–6, 27, 31, 44, 49, 72
        Jane (Jeanne) Poppingcourt, 19
        Lord Leonard Grey, 15, 18, 110,
            148
Blount, Sir George, 31, 33, 71, 156, 172,
    182
Blount, Henry, 31, 33, 71, 219
Blount, Sir Humphrey of Kinlet, 11, 12,
    15
Blount, Sir John of Balterley, 11
Blount, Sir John of Kinlet, 1–2, 11, 13, 14,
    16, 20, 31, 33, 51
Blount, Sir John of Soddingham, 11
Blount, John, son of Sir Humphrey, 12
Blount, Katherine (née Peshall), 1–2, 11,
    13
Blount, Mary, 12
Blount, Robert, 14
Blount, Rose, 172
Blount, Sir Thomas of Kinlet, 12, 16, 26,
    31
Blount, Sir Walter, 10–11

Blount, Walter, 1st Lord Mountjoy, 11
Blount, William, 4th Lord Mountjoy, 2,
    10, 16, 256
Blount, William, son of Sir Humphrey, 12
Blount, William, son of Sir John of Kinlet,
    33, 172
Boleyn, Anne, Queen of England
    attributes, 14, 94, 110, 132, 145, 158–9,
        226
    courtship, vii, 93–4, 107–8, 110,
        116–17, 126, 128–9, 132
    marriage, 136–41, 147, 151, 153, 155,
        157–61, 170, 187
    issue, viii, 9, 22, 24, 137, 140, 149, 151,
        152–3, 157–8, 160, 164, 177
    see also Elizabeth I, Queen
    downfall, 161–5, 250
    relations with
        Elizabeth Blount, 14
        Elizabeth Howard, Duchess of
            Norfolk, 117, 124
        Henry Fitzroy, 123, 126–7, 129,
            143–4, 146, 149, 152, 154,
            162–4, 205, 207, 212, 257
        Henry Percy, 6th Earl of
            Northumberland, 8
        Henry VIII, 110, 120, 123, 124, 144,
            155, 158, 222–3
        Mary, Duchess of Suffolk, daughter
            of Henry VII, 128
        Mary Howard, Duchess of
            Richmond, 123, 129, 138, 143,
            145, 222, 226, 241
        Mary Tudor, daughter of Henry
            VIII, 127, 146, 152, 159, 164,
            165–6
        Thomas Cromwell, 162–3
        Thomas Howard, Duke of Norfolk,
            94, 120, 123, 144, 155, 161, 162,
            222
        Thomas Wolsey, 115
Boleyn, Sir George, Lord Rochford, 138,
    139, 175, 193, 210
Boleyn, Mary, mistress of Henry VIII,
    x–xi, 17, 20, 22–3, 26, 31–2, 55,
    107–8
Boleyn, Sir Thomas, Lord Rochford, Earl
    of Wiltshire, 31, 55, 94
Boniface IX, Pope, 39
Bourbon, Charles, duc de, 19
Bourchier, Henry, Earl of Essex, 13
Boynton, Anne, 192

Boynton, Matthew, 79, 192, 204
Brabon, Henry, 248
Brandon, Charles, Duke of Suffolk, 14, 17,
    36, 38, 40, 42, 43, 54, 69, 74,
    115, 117, 125, 147, 172, 196, 218,
    255
Brandon, Eleanor, Lady Cumberland,
    55
Brandon, Frances, Duchess of Suffolk,
    253
Brandon, Henry (died in infancy), 54
Brandon, Henry, Earl of Lincoln, 54, 120,
    153
Brede, John, 188–9
Brereton, William, 156, 162–3, 207–8,
    210–11, 256
Bretton, John, 187–8
Brigman, Joan, 126
Broke, Ralph, 209
Bryan, Sir Francis, 24, 151
Bryan, Margaret, 30
Bulmer, Sir William, 99, 192
Burgh, Sir Thomas, 164
Burke, Hubert S., 27
Butler, Sir Piers, Earl of Ossory, 113, 146
Butts, Dr William, 95
Byland, Abbot of, 212

Campeggio, Lorenzo, Cardinal and papal
    envoy, 105–6
Capello, Carlo, 128
Carceres, Francesca de, lady-in-waiting to
    Katherine of Aragon, 7
Carew, Elizabeth, maid of honour, 17
Carew, Sir Garwen, 233, 234, 236
Carew, Sir Nicholas, 162
Carey, Catherine, x, 22
Carey, Henry, x–xi, 22
Carey, William, xi, 23
Carlisle, Bishop of *see* Kite, John
Caroz, Don Luis, Spanish ambassador, 7,
    19
Carver, P.L., 72
Casale, Sir Gregory, English ambassador
    in Spain, 83, 87
Cecil, Davy, steward of Collyweston, 64
Cecily, Duchess of York, mother of
    Richard III, 170
Chabot, Philippe de, 154
Chapuys, Eustace, Imperial ambassador
    in England, 117–18, 119, 123,
    124, 127–8, 142–3, 145, 146,

147, 154, 155, 163, 166, 167–8, 169, 174, 176, 177, 178

Charles, duc d'Angouleme, third son of Francis I, 129, 133–4, 136, 257

Charles II, King, 26, 31

Charles V, Emperor, xi, 3, 41, 44–7, 50, 52, 54, 79, 84–5, 87, 88–90, 92, 108, 109, 114, 118, 123, 132, 137, 138, 146, 157, 159, 172, 175, 228, 247, 251

Chichester, Elizabeth, 198

Christina, Duchess of Milan, 89, 90

Clarke, Richard, 209

Clement VII, Pope, 83, 92, 106, 108, 114, 132, 136–9, 149, 166, 229, 234, 250

Clerc, Agnes, 98

Clerke, John, 49

Clifford, Henry, Earl of Cumberland, 55, 102, 103, 180, 202–3

Clifford, Sir Thomas, 202–3, 216

Clinton, Bridget, daughter of Elizabeth Blount, 111, 253

Clinton, Edward, Lord Clinton, 110–11, 129, 171, 197, 246, 253

Clinton, Katherine, daughter of Elizabeth Blount, 111, 253

Clinton, Margaret, daughter of Elizabeth Blount, 111, 253

Clinton, Thomas, Lord Clinton, 110

Cocke, John, 218

Compton, William, gentleman of the privy chamber, 7–8, 189, 199–200

Conway, Sir Hugh, 4

Cooke, John, 205, 213

Cordell, William, 242

Cotton, Sir George, 75–7, 100, 120, 156, 178, 189, 193, 194, 215

Cotton, Richard, 100, 178, 194, 219

Courtney, Henry, Marquess of Exeter, 55, 69, 151, 153, 162, 174, 218

Courtney, Katherine, sister of Elizabeth of York, 55

Courtney, Sir William, 118, 183

Courtney, William, Earl of Devon, 55

Cox, Richard, 49, 76

Cranmer, Thomas, Archbishop of Canterbury, 137, 164, 192–3, 222

Croft, Anne, daughter of Sir Richard, 12–13, 14

Croft, Sir Richard, 12

Croke, Richard, 49, 72, 73–8, 92, 100, 125, 185, 194, 257

Cromwell, Thomas, secretary to Henry VIII, 18, 141, 146–7, 152, 154–5, 162–3, 175, 179, 201, 202, 203, 205, 206–11, 212, 217, 218, 219, 220, 221–2, 223–6, 227, 228, 230, 231

Crowland, Abbot of, 64

Crymer, Abbot of, 207

Curtis, Anne, ix

Dacre, Sir Christopher, 74

Dacre, Lord Thomas, 58, 60, 74

Dacre, Lord William, 69, 102, 103, 104

Darcy, Sir Thomas, 219

Darcy, Thomas, Lord Darcy, 74

Darnley, Lord Henry, 255

Darrell, Sir Edward, 14, 21, 26

de Bourbon, Nicholas, 257

de Heylwigen, Loys, 109

de la Pole, Edmund, 4

de la Pole, Elizabeth, 4

de la Pole, Richard, 4, 44, 55

de Meaux, Sir John, 195

de Medici, Catherine, viii, 83, 132, 138

de Montague, John, Earl of Salisbury, 200

de Venegas, Agnes, wife of William Blount, 4th Lord Mountjoy, 11

de Vere, Frances, wife of the Earl of Surrey, 130, 144–5, 244

de Vere, John, Earl of Oxford, 37, 123, 130

de Vere, John, Lord Bulbeck, 123

Delaryver, Thomas, 212

Derby, Thomas, 187

Devereux, Walter, Lord Ferrers, 118

Dingley, Joan see Dobson

Dobson, Joan, ix

Dom Luis of Portugal, xi, 228

Dorset, Marquess of see Grey, Thomas

Douglas, Archibald, Earl of Angus, 82, 168

Douglas, Margaret, niece of Henry VIII, 168–70, 223, 228, 230, 231, 242, 255

Drillard, Anthony, 207–8

Dudley, Ambrose, Earl of Warwick, 253

Dudley family, 206

Dudley, Guilford, 255

Dudley, John, Duke of Northumberland, 252–3, 255

Dudley, Sir John, Lord Ferrers, 196

Dudley, William, Bishop of Durham, 12

Durham, Bishop of *see* Dudley, William
Dymmock, Sir Robert, 28

Edmund, Duke of Somerset, 3
Edward III, King, 4, 38, 43, 238
Edward IV, King, 3, 4, 12, 43, 51, 53, 55
Edward V, King, 3, 252
Edward VI, King, son of Henry VIII, vii,
    ix, x, 30, 49, 51, 76, 176, 180,
    193, 194, 219, 224, 234, 240,
    241, 245–52, 254, 256, 257
Edward, Duke of Cornwall, 38
Edward, Earl of Warwick, 3, 4, 199, 201
Edwards, Richard, x
Eleanor, daughter of Philip of Burgundy,
    5, 84, 87, 89
Elizabeth I, Queen, daughter of Henry
    VIII, viii, x, 30, 78, 140–3, 144,
    150, 152, 157, 158, 159, 164–5,
    174, 228, 245, 249, 251, 255,
    256
Elizabeth of York, Queen, 3, 12, 94
Ellis, Hugh, 233, 237, 238
Elyot, Sir Thomas, 71
English ambassadors
    in France, 91
    in Spain, 45, 87, 89, 90
    see also Casale, Lee and Russell
Erasmus, Desiderius, 92
Essex, Earl of *see* Bourchier, Henry
Étampes, Duchess of, mistress of Francis
    I, 233
Eton, Nicholas, 81
Eure, Sir William, 102, 192
Eynns, Thomas, 193, 219

Fawkes, Henry, 191
Ferdinand I, King of Aragon, 5, 6, 7, 10,
    16, 19, 45
Ferguson, Charles, 250
Fernandez, Fray Diego, 19
Fiennes-Clinton see Clinton
Fisher, John, 73, 159
Fitzalan, Henry, Earl of Arundel, 37
Fitzgerald, Earl of Kildare, 112–13, 127,
    145–6, 147
Fitzpatrick, Barnaby, 76
Fitzroy, Henry, Duke of Richmond and
    Somerset, 233
    notices of, vii–ix, xi–xii
    birth, viii, 20, 22, 24–6, 27, 49
    infancy, 28–31, 49

arms, 47–8, 50, 62, 67, 69, 74
portraits, 214–15, 238
education, 30–1, 48–9, 67, 70–9, 117,
    118–20, 125, 132, 216
health, 52, 63, 95, 127, 133, 174–7
elevation to the peerage, viii, 36–9,
    43–4, 44–55
Order of the Garter, 50–1, 62, 125,
    130, 136, 151, 154, 162
prospects for legitimisation, viii, 34,
    38–9, 51, 108–10
creation as King of Ireland, viii, 85, 114
creation as Duke of Milan, 89–90
Cognac League, 79
Lord Lieutenant of Ireland, viii,
    112–17, 145–8, 216–17
Lord Admiral, 56, 205, 216
Marcher Lord, 205–10, 211–12, 216,
    217
attendance at Parliament, 116–17, 174
marriage, viii, 83–91, 105–6, 122–4,
    142–5, 155, 170, 220–3,
    239–40
    see also Howard, Mary, Duchess of
    Richmond
role in the succession, viii, 28–9, 34,
    38–9, 53–4, 55–6, 85, 92, 105,
    108, 111–12, 140–3, 150–1, 155,
    157, 160–8, 169, 170–6, 245,
    249–55
accorded adult status, 55, 64, 120, 150,
    181–7, 196–9, 204, 212
founder of Haltemprice Priory, 195
Summit at Calais, 127–31
travels in France, 130–9, 152
his council (Council of the North), 29,
    57, 58, 61, 65, 68–9, 72, 79, 95,
    97, 102–4, 118, 184, 187–8, 191,
    197, 208, 216
his estates, 38, 44, 53, 55–6, 60, 61,
    63–4, 96–7, 117, 129, 151–2,
    154–5, 182–3, 194–204,
    217–18, 229–30
his household, 242, 29–30, 48–9,
    55–6, 60, 62, 67, 78, 80, 81,
    96–101, 118–19, 121–2, 124–5,
    147, 156, 170, 172, 176, 178,
    192–5, 204, 212, 215–16,
    218–20
death and burial, viii, 177–9, 214, 223,
    243
relations with

Index

Anne Boleyn, 126–7, 143–4, 146, 149, 152, 154, 162–4

Elizabeth Blount, 25–6, 27, 31, 44, 172

Henry Howard, viii, 119–20, 125, 127, 128, 138–9, 145, 156, 225, 252

Henry VIII, vii, ix, xi–xii, 25–6, 26, 29, 34, 37, 39, 48, 49–50, 51, 53–5, 60, 61, 69, 74, 76, 76–7, 78–81, 85, 90, 95–6, 99, 100, 101, 111, 115–16, 117–18, 125–7, 132–3, 140–1, 142–3, 147, 149, 151–4, 157, 174, 177–80, 184–6, 189–91, 225, 257–8

James V, 79, 81–3

Katherine of Aragon, 26, 45, 69, 86

Thomas Cromwell, 146–7, 154–5, 162–3, 207–8, 219

Thomas Howard, 26, 56, 60, 69, 119–20, 122–3, 138–9, 144, 155–6, 162, 167–9, 171–2, 178–80, 181, 252

Thomas Wolsey, ix, 25–6, 29, 30, 36, 58, 59, 60–1, 62–3, 70, 75, 77, 78, 84, 98, 101, 104, 113–15, 119, 120, 124–5, 156, 181, 184–5, 256

William Brereton, 162–3, 256

Fitzwilliam, William, Earl of Southampton, 182, 216, 218

Folbury, George, 78, 118, 120

Foljambe, Sir Godfrey, 58

Forster, Giles, 175, 194

Fournes, Robert, 191

Foxe, John, 241

France
ambassadors of, 126, 175, 229, 232, 246
hostages, 26

Francis, dauphin, son of Francis I, 24, 47, 84, 87–9, 93, 129, 133–4, 136, 257

Francis I, King of France, 26, 44, 50, 83–6, 87, 89, 93, 127–34, 136, 137, 138–9, 214, 233, 234

Franklyn, William, Archdeacon of Durham, 60, 70

Fuller, Thomas, 245

Gacoigne, Elizabeth, wife of George, Lord Tailbois, 27, 33, 109

Gardiner, Stephen, Bishop of Winchester, 70, 205, 234, 248

Gascoigne, Sir William of Gawthorpe, 27

George, Duke of Clarence, 53

Giustinian, Sebastian, Venetian ambassador, 2, 21, 25, 41

Glasgow, Archbishop of, 74

Goodwyn, Thomas, Prior of St Lawrence, 25

Gostwyck, John, 215

Gourney, Matthew, 53

Gower, John, 1

Grenville, Antoine Perronet de, Cardinal, 86–7

Gresley, William, 172

Grey, Edward, Viscount Lisle, 51

Grey, Elizabeth, 51

Grey, Lady Jane, 76, 254, 255

Grey, Lord Leonard, 15, 18, 110, 148

Grey, Thomas, Marquess of Dorset, 16, 18, 37, 63, 69

Guilford, Sir Edward, Master of the Revels, 14

Gunn, S.J., 14

Hale, John, xi

Hall, Dr Edward, 62

Harrington, Ethelreda (Audrey), ix

Harrington, John, ix

Hartwell, George, 185

Hastings, Anne, sister of the Duke of Buckingham, 7–8, 21

Hastings, George, Lord Hastings, 7

Henri, duc d'Orléans, son of Francis I, 26, 83, 88, 91, 128, 129, 131, 132, 133–4, 136, 138, 256, 257

Henry I, King, 34, 41

Henry II, King, 37, 41, 114

Henry IV, King, 39, 200

Henry V, King, 53

Henry VI, King, 11

Henry VII, King, 2, 3, 4, 5, 10, 11, 12, 13, 19, 28, 38, 41, 53, 57, 61, 94, 170, 201, 246

Henry VIII, King, vii, 36, 79, 102, 103, 120, 123, 127, 155, 169, 181, 196, 205, 206, 212, 248, 257
as prince, 4, 52, 114
attributes, 2–3, 34, 157, 248, 255–6
health, 21–2, 40, 159–60
marriages see Katherine of Aragon, Anne Boleyn, Jane Seymour,

Anne of Cleves, Catherine Howard and Katherine Parr
infidelity, 7–10, 11, 18–20, 22–3, 26–7, 157–8
    see also Anne Hastings, Elizabeth Blount, Jane Poppingcourt, Mary Boleyn, Anne Boleyn and Jane Seymour
issue, ix–x, 6–7, 19, 24–5, 26–7, 39–40
    see also Henry, Mary I, Elizabeth I, Edward VI, Henry Fitzroy
chooses not to legitimise Richmond by subsequent marriage, 34, 108–10
role in Richmond's marriage, 53, 83–91, 105–6, 122–4, 143–4, 223
Ireland, 112–17, 145–8, 217
fall of Thomas Wolsey, 114, 119
relationship with Richmond, viii, 25–6, 28, 29, 34, 48, 49–50, 62, 69, 76–7, 78, 80, 95–6, 117–18, 125–7, 144, 149, 153, 157, 162, 163–4, 170, 176, 208, 214, 257, 257–8
his court, 1, 7–10, 12, 16, 20, 23–4, 105, 124, 142, 239
travels to France, 16–17, 127–33, 152
Hapsburg Alliance, xi, 3, 4–6, 16, 19, 41, 44–7, 47, 52, 54, 79, 84–5, 87–8, 88–90, 92, 107, 109, 114, 118, 132, 137, 139, 159, 172, 228, 247, 251
provision for the succession, vii, 2, 4, 38–9, 40–3, 44–7, 52, 53–6, 91, 92–3, 111–12, 140–1, 150–1, 153, 155, 157, 166–8, 172–6, 218, 234, 245–7, 248–52
use of Richmond's patronage, 60, 99, 100–1, 184–92, 204, 213
promotes and protects Richmond's rights and titles, 37–8, 48–52, 56, 60, 61, 198–204
dispersal of Richmond's land, goods and servants, 215–20
doubts about Richmond's marriage, 220–4, 225–30
downfall of the House of Howard, 234–9, 252
Henry, eldest son of Henry VIII (died in infancy), 8–9, 43, 153, 179

Heralds, 37, 50
Herbert, Sir Richard, 206
Higdon, Brian, Dean of York, 58, 195
Holland, Elizabeth (Bess), 225, 237, 240
Holland, Thomas, 219
Hollinshed, chronicler of England, 257
Hornebolte, Lucas, 214
Howard, Agnes, Dowager-Duchess of Norfolk, 231
Howard, Catherine, daughter of Henry, Earl of Surrey, 241
Howard, Catherine, Queen of England, 23, 230–1
Howard, Sir Charles, 231
Howard, Charles, 240
Howard, Dorothy, Lady Derby, 123
Howard, Elizabeth (née Stafford), Duchess of Norfolk, 117, 123–4, 129, 144, 212, 219, 222, 225–6, 235, 239, 241
Howard family, 211, 232, 235, 240–1, 243–4, 251
Howard, Henry, Earl of Surrey, son of 3rd Duke of Norfolk, 76, 162, 163, 241
    attributes, 119
    marriage, 130, 145
    in France, 133, 135, 136, 138–9
    downfall, 180, 235–8
    execution and burial, 238, 243–4, 252
    relations with Edward Seymour, 224–5, 232–3
    relations with Henry Fitzroy, Duke of Richmond, viii, 119, 127, 128, 156, 216, 257
    relations with Mary Howard, Duchess of Richmond, 232–9, 240, 242
Howard, Henry, son of Henry, Earl of Surrey, 244
Howard, Katherine, Countess of Derby, 123
Howard, Mary, Duchess of Richmond
    attributes, 144, 145, 220, 228, 239, 240–1
    marriage, 122–4, 139, 142–5, 155, 168
    widowhood, 178–9, 180, 215–16, 218, 220–1, 230, 231–2
    struggles to obtain her jointure, 220–3, 225–30
    prospects of remarriage, 226–8, 232–4, 239–40
    downfall of the Howards, 234–42

income, 229–30, 240–1
death and burial, 242–4
- relations with
    Anne Boleyn, 123–4, 129, 138, 143,
      145, 222, 226, 241
    Henry Howard, Earl of Surrey,
      233–9, 240, 242
      Henry VIII, 149, 232, 233
    Margaret Douglas, 169–70, 230,
      242
    Mary I, 241–2
    Thomas Howard, 3rd Duke of
      Norfolk, 169–70, 222
Howard, Thomas, 2nd Duke of Norfolk,
  26, 27, 42, 237
Howard, Thomas, 3rd Duke of Norfolk,
  117, 225–6, 235, 239, 241
  children *see* Henry Howard, Earl of
    Surrey, Mary Howard, Duchess
    of Richmond, Katherine,
    Countess of Derby, and
    Thomas, Viscount Bindon
  his wife, Elizabeth (née Stafford),
    Duchess of Norfolk *see*
    Howard, Elizabeth
  as Earl of Surrey, 26, 57, 112, 119
  as Duke of Norfolk, 18, 42–3, 43, 74,
    181–2, 184, 203, 208–9
  Lord Admiral, 56, 118, 156, 216
  Government of the North, 56, 104,
    119–20, 223
  in France, 138–40
  death, 242, 243
  relations with
    Anne Boleyn, 94, 120, 123, 144,
      155, 161, 162, 222
    Catherine Howard, Queen, 230–1
    Edward Seymour, 168, 232, 234,
      253
    Henry Fitzroy, Duke of Richmond,
      26, 36, 38, 50, 56, 60, 63, 69,
      117, 122–3, 124, 125, 143–5,
      145–6, 147, 151, 155–6, 162,
      167–72, 178–80, 193, 207,
      208–9, 217, 252
    Margaret Douglas, 168–70
    Mary Tudor, daughter of Henry
      VIII, 165–7
    Thomas Cromwell, 147, 179,
      223–4, 230, 231
    Thomas, Viscount Bindon, 239
    Thomas Wolsey, 60, 114–15, 156

Howard, Thomas, 4th Duke of Norfolk,
  232, 240, 241
Howard, Lord Thomas, half brother of the
  3rd Duke of Norfolk, 169–70,
  223
Howard, Thomas, Viscout Bindon, son of
  the 3rd Duke of Norfolk, 232,
  239
Huntingdon, John, 239
Husse, Sir John, 64, 151, 156, 177

Incent, John, 200
Isabella, Infanta of Portugal, 46
Isabella, Queen of Castille, 5, 19, 41
Isabella, Queen of Denmark, 87, 88
Ives, Eric, 94

James IV, King of Scotland, 3, 237
James V, King of Scotland, 47, 79, 81–3,
  83, 85, 154, 157, 160, 162, 172,
  214, 247
Jekyll, Sir William, 61, 63
Jenny, John, 193, 212
Jenny, Mistress, 212
John of Gaunt, son of Edward III, 38–9,
  59
John, King of England, 114
Johns, Hugh, 101, 121–2, 192, 193, 219
Johns, Robert, 192
Juan, Prince, son of Ferdinand I, 143
Juana of Castille, daughter of Ferdinand I,
  6, 47

Katherine of Aragon, Queen of England
  attributes, 1, 5–6, 15, 34, 141, 171, 254
  courtship, 5
  marriage to Henry VIII, vii, ix, 5–9, 15,
    16, 18–22, 25, 26, 91–2, 158,
    170
  marriage to Arthur, Prince of Wales, 4,
    5, 12, 105, 106, 108
  issue, ix, 6–7, 8–9, 17, 19–20, 21, 22,
    24, 34, 40, 47, 107, 153, 179
    see also Henry, eldest son of Henry
    VIII, and Mary, daughter of
    Henry VIII
  her household, 1, 7, 9–10, 12, 15–16,
    19
  death, 159, 166, 250
  relations with
    Henry Fitzroy, Duke of Richmond,
      26, 45, 69, 86

Sir Edward Darrell, 14, 21
William Blount, Lord Mountjoy, 11, 16
Kite, John, Bishop of Carlisle, 57

la Baume, Etiennette, 9
Lacon, Richard, 33
Lacon, Sir Thomas, 33
Latimer, John, Lord Latimer, 60
Lawson, Sir George, 58, 96, 118, 184, 191, 204
Laybourne, Sir Jason, 192, 202–3
Lee, Dr Edward, Archbishop of York, English ambassador in Spain, 84, 85, 87, 89
Lee, Roland, Bishop of Coventry and Lichfield, 206–7, 209
Leland, John, 66
Leland, Thomas, 71
Leo X, Pope, 13, 29
Lisle, Sir William, 82, 97
Lloyd, Randall, 198
Longsword, William, Earl of Salisbury, 37
Longueville, duc de, 19
Louis XI, King of France, 13
Louis XII, King of France, 4, 6, 19, 42
Lowther, Sir John, 202
Lucy, Elizabeth, 51
Lumley, Lord John, 202

Magnus, Sir Thomas, 60, 80, 81, 82, 95–6, 97, 98, 99–100, 101, 102, 104, 119, 190, 200
Manners, Sir Thomas, Lord Roos, Earl of Rutland, 50, 55, 231
Margaret, daughter of Henry VII, queen of James IV of Scotland, 2nd husband: Archibald Douglas, 3, 19, 81, 82, 168
Margaret of Savoy and Austria, Archduchess, Regent of the Netherlands, 9, 41, 90, 117, 143
Markham, Robert, 188
Mary, daughter of Henry VIII
    as princess, 21, 27, 29, 30, 34, 39, 40, 41, 45–7, 52–4, 55, 69, 70, 85, 87, 88, 91, 92–3, 120, 150, 151
    at Ludlow, 54, 57, 67, 69, 71, 79, 96, 101, 103
    as Lady Mary, 55, 91, 111, 115, 141–2, 144, 150, 151, 157, 160, 161, 164, 165–7, 168, 169, 170–1, 174, 219, 248, 251, 253–5

as queen, x, 241
    marriage negotiations, xi, 24, 46–7, 52–3, 83–8, 91, 105–6, 228, 257
    relations with
        Anne Boleyn, 127, 146, 152, 159, 164, 165–6
        Henry Fitzroy, 69, 85, 105, 114, 142, 154, 170–1, 176, 215, 245, 256
        Henry VIII, viii, 126, 141–2, 146, 247, 249
        Mary Howard, Duchess of Richmond, 241–2
        Thomas Howard, 3rd Duke of Norfolk, 165–7, 171, 241
Mary, Duchess of Suffolk, daughter of Henry VII, 3, 15, 19, 24, 42, 54, 69, 70, 72, 73, 110, 117, 128, 172
Mary of Guise, Queen of Scotland, 239
Mary of Hungary, 250
Mary, Infanta of Portugal, 84, 86, 87, 89–90, 257
Matilda, daughter of Henry I, 41
Mattingly, Garrett, 7, 26
Medici, Catherine de *see* de Medici, Catherine
Mendoza, Inigo de, Imperial Ambassador in England, 85, 86, 88, 90–1
Metcalf, Robert, 194
Montmorency, Anne de, 135
More, Sir Thomas, 6, 37, 70, 71, 72, 73, 159
Morice, James, 184, 192–3, 196
Morice, Philip, 192
Mountjoy, Lords *see* Blount, Walter; Blount, William

Neville, Catherine, Countess of Westmorland, 212
Neville, Henry, Lord Neville, 69, 96
Neville, Sir John, Sheriff of Yorkshire, 101
Neville, Ralph, Earl of Westmorland, 69, 96, 97, 102
Nichols, John Gough, viii
Norris, Henry, 175, 210, 216

Orio, Lorenzo, 49, 51
Orrell, William, 217

Page, Sir Richard, 58, 73, 191, 211
Paget, Sir William, 253

Index

Palsgrave, John, 30–1, 48, 62, 67, 70–4, 78, 132
Parker, Arabella, 27
Parker, Margery, 27
Parr, Katherine, Queen, 63, 218, 232, 234
Parr, Maud, Lady Parr, 61, 63
Parr, William, 71, 75, 201–3
Parr, Sir William, 61, 71, 73, 75, 100, 101, 162, 189, 192
Partridge, Anne, 67, 70, 76, 126, 192
Partridge, Henry, 192, 193
Percy, Henry, 3rd Earl of Northumberland, 27, 59
Percy, Henry, 5th Earl of Northumberland, 37, 58, 69, 184
Percy, Henry, 6th Earl of Northumberland, 8, 102
Perrers, Alice, 31
Perrot, Sir John, ix–x
Perrot, Sir Thomas, ix
Peshall, Katherine see Blount
Peterborough, Abbot of, 64
Pole, Henry, Lord Montague, 201
Pole, Margaret, Countess of Salisbury, 30, 108, 120, 142, 183, 194, 199–201
Pole, Reginald, 108
Poppingcourt, Jane (Jeanne), 19–20
Poynings, Jane, 110
Poynings, Sir Edward, 110
Prior, Simon, 98

Radcliffe, Thomas, Earl of Sussex, 148
Ramsey, Abbot of, 62
Ratcliffe, Elizabeth, sister of the Duke of Buckingham, 7
Rawson, John, 113
Redman, William, 202
Renée of Anjou, daughter of Louis XII, 93
Richard II, King, 39, 52
Richard III, Duke of York, King, 3, 42, 43, 57, 170, 251
Richard, Duke of York, son of Edward IV, 252
Richmond see Fitzroy, Henry
Robert, Earl of Sussex, 167–8, 180
Roos, Lord see Manners, Sir Thomas
Rudd, Nicholas, 103
Russell, John, English ambassador in Spain, 83, 87
Ruthin, Steward of, 211, 217

Rutland, Earl of see Manners, Sir Thomas
Rutland, Eleanor, Countess of, 245

St Clare Byrene, Muriel, 80
St John's, Prior of, 95, 97
St Mary's, Abbot of, 96, 97, 101
Salisbury, Countess of see Pole
Salisbury, Mayor and Alderman of, 152
Salisbury, Robert Abbot of Valle Crucis, 207
Saunders, William, 70
Seymour, Sir Edward, 62, 161–2, 168, 189–90, 194, 216, 219, 223, 224, 227, 232, 251, 253, 254, 255
Seymour family, 164, 180, 224, 227–8, 232, 233, 236, 251
Seymour, Jane, Queen of England
    issue, 9, 24, 165, 166, 167, 173, 175, 177, 218
    see also Edward VI
    marriage, vii, 40, 164, 168, 250
    courtship, 23, 94, 158, 161
    death, 224, 227
Seymour, Sir Thomas, 227–8, 232–3, 255
Sforza, Francesco, Duke of Milan, 89, 90
Shelton, Lady Anne, 150
Shrewsbury, bailiffs and council of, 209
Shrewsbury, Earl of see Talbot, George
Sidney, John, 198
Simnel, Lambert, 3
Skeffington, Sir William, 115–16, 145, 148, 192, 193
Skelton, Ambrose, 185
Smeaton, Mark, 210
Snappe, John, 157
Somers, Will, 159
Somerset, Henry, Earl of Worcester, 217
Southwell, Sir Robert, 237
Spain, ambassadors of, 19, 85, 90–1, 229, 246, 251
    see also Caroz, Don Luis; Mendoz, Inigo de
Spinelly, Leonard, 13
Stackhouse, John, 185
Stafford, Edward, Duke of Buckingham, 4, 7, 27, 42, 43, 123, 144, 237
Stafford, Henry, 172
Stanley, Edward, Earl of Derby, 123–4
Stanley family, Earls of Derby, 14
Stanley, Isabel, daughter of Sir John of Elford, 14

Starkey, David, 223
Stephen, King, Count of Boulogne, 41
Stevinson, William, 72
Stoner, Mrs, mother of the maids, 11
Stourton, Ursula, 111
Stourton, William, Lord, 111
Strangeways, Sir Giles, 189–90
Stukely, Thomas, ix
Sutton family, Lords Dudley, 14
Sutton, John, Lord Dudley, 14
Swallow, William, 185
Swynford, Katherine, 38–9

Tailbois, Elizabeth, daughter of Elizabeth
    Blount, 27, 29, 108, 253
Tailbois, George, Lord, 27–8, 32–4, 156
Tailbois, George, Lord , son of Elizabeth
    Blount, 29, 31, 108, 111, 122,
    182, 215
Tailbois, Gilbert, Lord, 27–8, 32–4, 44,
    108
Tailbois, Robert, Lord, 27
Tailbois, Robert, Lord, son of Elizabeth
    Blount, 29, 108
Talbot, Constance, 33
Talbot, George, Earl of Shrewsbury, 14,
    16, 33, 124, 183
Talbot, Sir John of Grafton, 33
Talbot, Margaret, 33
Tarne, Robert, 201–2
Tate, Robert, 133
Tempest, Sir Thomas, 99
Throckmorton, Nicholas, 192, 193
Travers, John, 207
Tunstall, Cuthbert, Bishop of Durham,
    104
Tutbury, Prior of, 131
Tyndale, William, 112

Uvedale, John, 156, 187–8

Vaux, Edward, 186
Venice, ambassadors of, 21, 41, 45, 54,
    126, 129, 131, 133, 139, 175

see also Capello, Carlo; Giustinian,
    Sebastian
Villiers, Barbara, 31

Wallop, Sir John, 135
Warbeck, Perkin, 3
Warham, William, Archbishop of
    Canterbury, 137
Warnicke, Retha, 210
Wentworth, Lord Thomas, 240
Westbury, Dean of see Barlow, John
Westmorland, Earl and Countess of see
    Neville, Catherine; Neville,
    Ralph
Weston, Francis, 211
William I, King, 52
Williams, Sir John, 240
Wilson, Nicholas, 185
Wingfield, Sir Richard, 48, 72, 73
Wingfield, Robert, 217
Wolsey, Thomas, Cardinal, Henry VIII's
    chief minister, 8, 22, 24, 28, 42,
    43, 57–8, 59, 68, 69, 73–4, 78,
    79, 81, 84, 85, 87, 89–90, 91,
    93, 97, 99, 100, 101, 102–4, 105,
    124–5, 146, 188, 191, 196, 200
  downfall, 103–4, 119, 125, 156, 256
  relations with
    Elizabeth Blount, 24–6, 33
    Henry Fitzroy, Duke of Richmond,
      ix, 25–6, 29, 30, 36, 47, 49, 57,
      58, 59, 60–1, 62–3, 69, 70, 75,
      77, 80, 81, 84–6, 88–91, 95, 98,
      105, 113–15, 156, 181, 184–5,
      189, 194, 208, 220, 257
Wood, William, 219–20
Woodville, Elizabeth, 43
Worcester, Earl of see Somerset, Henry
Wriothesley, Charles, 164, 175
Wyatt, Sir Thomas, 211

York, Council of, 191